Poland was a problematic issue for the Big Powers throughout the Second World War. For Britain, Poland was a major stumbling block in British–Soviet relations, as Polish–Soviet territorial disputes clashed with the needs of the British–Soviet–United States alliance. As the Polish government-in-exile attempted to obtain a guarantee of British support, and many thousands of Polish troops fought for the British cause, the perception grew that the Churchill government had a debt to pay. Ultimately, however, it was a debt which Britain could not discharge because of its dependence on Soviet participation in the war.

In this book Anita Prażmowska looks at British policies from the point of view of wartime strategy, relating this to Polish government expectations and policies. She describes a tragic situation where Polish soldiers were trapped between the grandiose and unrealistic plans of their government and the harsh realities of a war which they fought with no prospect of a satisfactory outcome for them or their country.

GW00497924

BRITAIN AND POLAND, 1939–1943

Cambridge Russian, Soviet and Post-Soviet Studies

Series list continues on page 234

BRITAIN AND POLAND, 1939–1943

The betrayed ally

ANITA J. PRAŻMOWSKA

CAMBRIDGE
UNIVERSITY PRESS

Published by the Press Syndicate of the University of Cambridge
The Pitt Building, Trumpington Street, Cambridge CB2 1RP
40 West 20th Street, New York, NY 10011–4211, USA
10 Stamford Road, Oakleigh, Melbourne 3166, Australia

First published 1995

A catalogue record for this book is available from the British Library

Library of Congress cataloguing in publication data

Prażmowska, Anita.
Britain and Poland, 1939–1943: the betrayed ally / Anita J. Prażmowska.
    p.   cm. – (Cambridge Russian, Soviet and post-Soviet studies; 97)
Includes bibliographical references.
ISBN 0 521 40309 X
1. World War, 1939–1945 – Diplomatic history.
2. Great Britain – Foreign relations – Poland.
3. Poland – Foreign relations – Great Britain.
I. Title. II. Series.
D750.B7 1995
940.53'2 – dc20   94–26412   CIP

ISBN 0 521 40309 X hardback
ISBN 0 521 48385 9 paperback

Transferred to digital printing 2003

CE

Contents

Preface

I would not wish to deny that I have come to this subject because of its deeply emotive nature. Most current analysis of contemporary Polish history seems inevitably to founder on the question of why it was that Poland neither obtained recognition for her suffering and sacrifices during the Second World War nor secured the return of her territories after the war. Thus the search for those who are in some way responsible for this disaster is a common theme in political and historical debates. This work has been my attempt to face some of the most puzzling and painful events in recent Polish history. I do not wish to seek those responsible for failures.

In this enquiry into the nature of Polish–British relations during the years 1939–1943, I did not find within the two governments' war aims areas of common concern going beyond their obvious wish to see Germany defeated. During the inter-war period, Polish territorial and political objectives had been different from those of the British government. While I do not claim that major issues separated the two from the first day of the war, I have found that little united the two Allies. The Polish government-in-exile set out for itself a programme of establishing for Poland a right at the end of the war to sit at the negotiating table as one of the key wartime Allies. The means of achieving this was to make a vital and credible military contribution to the joint war effort. It was inevitable that this programme would not be taken seriously by the British government. Britain's continental policy developed hesitantly during the course of 1939 and the first half of 1940. The need to secure imperial support and to guarantee communication links was a powerful distraction from purely Central European preoccupations. In addition to that the need to take into account the foreign policy objectives of the Roosevelt administration and to deal with the consequences of Japanese aggression became the top priorities by 1941.

The German attack on the Soviet Union and the consequent drawing in of the Soviet Union into allied political negotiations was to confirm the incompatibility of Polish–British war aims. Henceforth the Poles would have to fight for British attention in the face of the increasingly important Soviet factor in British political and military considerations. The Polish government, in spite of offering increased numbers of men for co-operation with the British forces, became a potential source of embarrassment and a constraint on Churchill's dealings with the Soviet Union. By the beginning of 1943 the British need for Soviet co-operation was too important for the Poles to be able to compete with it. To Stalin, the Polish case became no more and no less than a test of British goodwill. Churchill understood this. While he strove to maintain Soviet co-operation it was inevitable that he should view the Polish issue as a source of possible embarrassment.

While writing this book I have had to tackle assumptions which form part of my heritage. I hope that I have been successful in this and that I have by this process challenged some of those preconceptions, or at least signalled the need to challenge them.

My work has been assisted throughout by grants from the British Academy. I have been fortunate in being granted access to most of the archives containing papers relating to the period. I am therefore grateful to the Public Records Office and the University of Birmingham where I consulted the Neville Chamberlain papers. The Polish Institute and Sikorski Museum in London has been particularly generous with their help. There I was guided and generously advised by Andrzej Suchcitz and Wacław Milewski. The Piłsudski Institute in London and the Instytut im. Ossolińskich in Wrocław allowed me to examine the General Sosnkowski archives in both institutions. The Archiwum Akt Nowych and the archives of the Archiwum Ruchu Ludowego, Warsaw made available to me the papers of Professor Kot. The Liddel Hart Centre for Military Archives at King's College London allowed me to consult the Alanbrooke papers. At the House of Lords I was allowed to look at the archives of Lord Beaverbrook. I am grateful to the librarians and archivists in all these institutions for their assistance which was always generously given. Sir Edward Cazalet was particularly helpful in arranging for me to see the personal and private papers of Victor Cazalet.

Friends and colleagues have offered their support and advice. Professor Gabriel Gorodetsky explained the context of Soviet–British co-operation in Iran to me. I remain grateful to him for allowing me to see his notes on Cripps' personal papers, which were not available to me. Dr Daniel Silverfarb generously let me read chapters of his unpublished book. His work on British–Iraq relations clarified numerous points and enabled me to explain the British need for Polish units there.

I am particularly indebted to Professor Paul Preston for his critical comments. Dr Jan Toporowski gave me his assistance, support and invaluable advice. Any formal thanks which I might offer here can never fully express my gratitude. This book is dedicated to my daughter Miriam so that she may one day come to see that things that happened 'in the olden days' can be interesting and challenging.

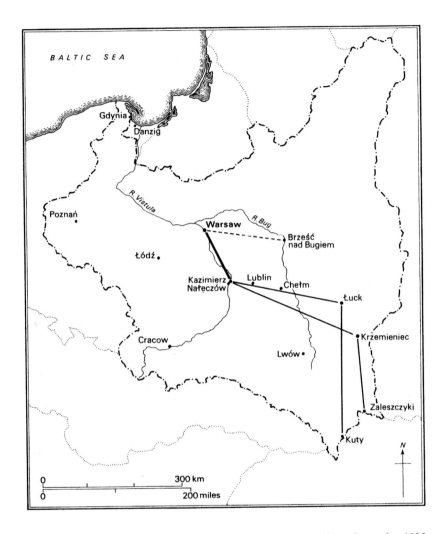

BALTIC SEA

Gdynia
Danzig
Poznań
R. Vistula
Warsaw
R. Bug
Brześć nad Bugiem
Łódź
Kazimierz Nałęczów
Lublin
Chełm
Łuck
Cracow
Lwów
Krzemieniec
Zaleszczyki
Kuty

N

0   300 km
0   200 miles

The escape route of the Polish Ministry for Foreign Affairs, September 1939

------- line represents the route taken by the High Command

——— line represents the route taken by the Ministry for Foreign Affairs and the Diplomatic Corps which accompanied it

1 The formation of the Polish government-in-exile: ideology and war plans

When the German army and air force attacked in the early hours of 1 September 1939 it was difficult to predict how long the Poles would be able to hold out. Initially, the Polish political and military leaders were convinced that, if in due course they obtained British and French assistance, they would be able to create a credible Eastern front. But by 5 September they were more preoccupied with leaving Poland and transforming themselves into a leadership-in-exile. The immediate fate of Poland, and the Polish people facing the onslaught of the German troops, became a matter of secondary importance.

During the course of their joint military talks in May 1939 neither British nor French military leaders had credited the Polish army with an ability to withstand a full-scale German attack. They were, of course, thinking of the Polish army's organization, its strategic thinking and degree of preparedness, and the supplies available to it. They did not doubt the Polish leadership's commitment to fighting, its bravery and most of all its political unity and organizational skills. These turned out to be as much a source of Polish military weakness as was the general Polish unreadiness to face the German attack. In the years to come these problems of the government-in-exile's political disunity and organizational ineptitude were to remain unresolved.

The Polish–German war was not concluded by a negotiated armistice. This fact itself moulded the mentality of the Poles who subsequently went into exile. The refusal of the then military, political and social leadership to concede that indeed the Polish army had been soundly defeated shaped the ideology of the exile government. The delusion that what had happened in September 1939 had been a tactical retreat, at best a manoeuvre, the long-term aim of which was to regroup and return to the battlefield once the British and French started the inevitable major offensive against Germany, firmly took root and was cherished and cultivated during the coming years of humiliation and suffering. This conviction that the Polish military leadership had nothing to be ashamed of stood in the way of a major reappraisal of the inflated and grandiose visions of Poland's role in European politics which had been encouraged by the Polish military ('Sanacja') regime of the 1930s. It also meant that they did not have to face the stark reality, which became more brutal as the war wore on, that they would have at best a limited influence, at worst none at all, on wartime politics.

These were ideas with which General Władysław Sikorski, the leader of the Polish exile government from October 1939 until his death in 1943, had to contend. To some extent he shared them with his Polish rivals in exile. At times he came to doubt the validity of these nationalist preconceptions. In any case he was constantly forced to weave a precarious line between the expectations of the Polish military and political leadership in exile, on the one hand, and the pressures of the Allies to fall in line with their military plans, on the other hand.

The German attack on Poland caused total disarray. Full-scale mobilization had been delayed in the closing days of August at the request of the British and the French. Far more devastating was the disorder which prevailed in the whole army even before the German attack. Belatedly it was realized that supply routes could easily be cut off by German aerial action and that troop movements and continuing mobilization, so carefully worked out in theory, were impossible unless the railway system continued to work, which it did not. The departure of the military command to new headquarters compounded the chaos because communication systems linking the central authorities and individual units, and between various units which were supposed to co-ordinate their actions, failed. Government politicians abdicated responsibility for civilian matters and either tried to join the military headquarters or fled Warsaw on the assumption that the preservation of the organs of government was more important than any responsibility for the fate of the civilian population. Nevertheless, the members of the Sanacja government refused to accept that they were in some way responsible for the extent of the military defeat.

On 1 September German infantry action against Polish troops started from three directions. In the north-west the 4th Army aimed at cutting through the Danzig Corridor. The 3rd Army moved from East Prussia with the aim of joining with the 4th Army and then moving down against Warsaw. In the south-west the 8th and 10th Armies moved into the industrial triangle of Łódź and Cracow. From the south came an attack by the 2nd Mountain Division from Slovakia. By 3

September the Polish army Pomorze was dispersed by the 4th Army and tried to regroup and move south to defend Warsaw. This had been necessitated by the success of the 3rd Army from East Prussia which had routed the Polish army Modlin and was poised to march on the capital. In the south the defeat of the Polish units proceeded no less relentlessly. By 5 September German control over the region had been virtually assured by the 8th Army success against the Polish army Lódź and furthermore by the German 10th Army separating the Army Lódź from the as yet not fully mobilized Army Prusy. The German 14th Army completed the dispersal of the Polish forces by cutting off the Polish army Cracow from the other two main southern armies. The Poles tried to regroup by ordering their remaining units to cross the two major rivers which flow from the south to the north, the Vistula and the Dunajec, which they hoped would form a defensive line. Thus by 6 September an attempt was made to transform the now retreating Army Cracow and Army Karpaty into an Army Małopolska which would operate from beyond the Dunajec River. In Central Poland Armies Poznań, Modlin and Lódź were to regroup beyond the Vistula to form a new Army Lublin. These were extremely ambitious plans which depended on the orderly transportation on a large scale of troops to new operational areas. Such transport facilities were simply not available. Polish plans for a counter-offensive were therefore unsuccessful even before they were attempted.

The reality was that by the end of the first week of fighting the Polish High Command had lost control and contact with most units. Plans for counter-offensive actions tended to be overtaken by German successes. The Commander-in-Chief Marshal Rydz-Śmigły was an unimaginative leader, timorous and unwilling to take risks. Several opportunities had been lost by him for counter-offensive action, most notably one for the Army Poznań to strike south in defence of Warsaw. When this action was finally authorized on 9 September, Army Pomorze, whose escape towards Warsaw this operation was to facilitate, had been to all purposes destroyed. On 7 September, fearing the fall of Warsaw, Rydz-Śmigły authorized the removal of the High Command east to Brześć. Since no provisions had been made for radio links with units and army commanders, this dispersed the still fighting Polish units as effectively as the relentless German action had done.

The most successful Polish action was the Bzura counter-offensive, the aim of which was to defend Warsaw. Led by General Kutrzeba it appeared briefly to halt the German advance between 9 and 18 September. Warsaw surrendered on 26 September, by which time all fighting in other parts of Poland had ceased and the High Command and government had departed for Romania. One of the last initiatives of the High Command had been to try to build a defensive redoubt in the south-east on the border with Romania. The idea was to gather there troops which would be ready to strike out as soon as the much anticipated French and British offensive took place. A Soviet initiative was neither anticipated nor even considered. Therefore the entry of Soviet troops into Poland on 17 September hastened the flight of the High Command towards the border crossing with Romania. Rydz-Śmigły and a high percentage of the officer corps left Poland without having acknowledged defeat. Armistice was neither signed nor sought by them.

The bulk of the officer caste viewed the September defeat as a temporary setback. It would seem that early in the campaign, without acknowledging the enormity of the looming fiasco, they switched their attention from the present war to the future one. The need to conserve troops went hand in hand with badly executed plans for the continuation of the fight against the invader. Naval units were instructed to seek to leave the Baltic as soon as the war started. Accepting the superiority of the German air force, similar plans were developed in relation to the Polish air force. Orders were given to pilots to flee with their aeroplanes. Equally intriguing was the flight of the military leadership towards the Romanian border. While on the one hand there were sound reasons for moving east beyond the Vistula, the progressive movement of the government to the south-east seems to suggest that the idea of departing from Poland in the face of defeat was always an option. The Polish High Command set an example by claiming that the alternative to accepting defeat was to save itself in order to lead the troops in the next war. Thus while sparing itself the humiliation of having to concede that policies and military doctrines of the inter-war period had been at fault, a claim was being made to continuing leadership of the nation.

The members of the regime (which was made up of serving and retired officers) also added to the chaos by confusing their political with their military functions. During the September campaign they abandoned political responsibilities in order to take up military commands. This seems to have been most apparent in the case of Colonel Józef Beck, who felt that his role as Minister for Foreign Affairs had come to an end and considered that he should be in the army headquarters where he spent a few days, unavailable to foreign diplomats.

The most important decision, which effectively spelled the end of the government's role in relation to all non-military matters, was made on 4 September. The German 3rd Army was breaking through from East Prussia towards Warsaw and was considered likely to cross the Vistula near Modlin. The German Army Group south was moving east towards the Vistula and was likely to capture the town of Sandomierz. This meant that the Vistula would be crossed in two places north and south of Warsaw. The only natural obstacle to the German move into eastern Poland was thus likely to be penetrated by the end of the day. In view of this the Council of Ministers decided to evacuate all governmental bodies to the south-east. The Ministry for Foreign Affairs and the diplomatic corps were instructed to proceed immediately to the two towns of Nałęczów and Kazimierz, both near Lublin.[1] Few provisions were made for the maintenance of communication lines between various ministries and the army. Civil servants were informed that unless they obeyed the order to evacuate immediately they would be treated as having left their posts and thus forfeit all entitlements.[2] As the destruction of secret papers proceeded, Beck handed all ministerial matters to his deputy minister Jan Szembek while he himself departed for Brześć to join the military leaders in his capacity as Colonel of the Cavalry. Only under extreme pressure did he finally return to join the disgruntled diplomatic corps on 11 September.

Once various ministries left Warsaw it proved impossible to resume responsibility over civilian matters. Lack of contact with the government and the collapse of all communication lines combined with the relentless progress of the German army meant that most were reduced to shedding their archives and personnel as they proceeded in disarray towards the south-east. On the morning of 5 September as the Ministry for Foreign Affairs and the diplomatic corps left Warsaw it was announced that, although they had been instructed to go to Nałęczów and Kazimierz, they would have to move on within the next few days. On 7 September they proceeded to Łuck and Krzemieniec, this time beyond Lublin. On 14 September they moved further, crossed the River Dniestr and arrived in Kuty. While this evacuation was badly co-ordinated, there is no doubt that the Polish leadership was heading towards the Romanian border. The German air force was constantly harassing them, but anxiety about being cut off from the escape route was a strong motive for continuing to move in the direction of the south-east. The Soviet army's entry into Polish territory on 17 September precipitated a stampede towards the bridges over the River Czeremosz that formed the frontier with Romania.

The evacuation of the Ministry and the accompanying diplomatic corps was made extremely difficult by the fact that most evacuees had decided to take their families with them. A semblance of normality was retained by lorries from the Ministry of Finance accompanying them and paying out cash as deemed necessary. The diplomatic corps was left with virtually no contact with the outside world. The British and French Ambassadors and military missions were unable to assure the Poles of any aid. Nor were they able to obtain information either about the military situation or the government's plans. Through being constantly on the move they were not able to maintain radio links with their capitals and therefore were as badly informed about the Allies' decisions as was the Polish government. Nevertheless diplomatic life had to continue. At one point the Spanish Ambassador noted that nine counsellors of various nationalities who had been accommodated together in one dormitory had to guard their diplomatic ciphers against each other's prying eyes: fear of German bombing was only outweighed by their anxiety lest they compromise their states' secrets.

The departure of the civilian authorities from Warsaw had a demoralizing effect on the population. It was generally noted by foreign diplomats that the flight of the ministries was accompanied by the equally determined departure for other countries of the intellectual, political and military leadership. This relentless and desperate stampede to the south-east to secure an escape route through Romania raises questions as to what was the reason for so consistent a determination not to stay in occupied Poland. A basic instinct to get out of the battlezone was the obvious reason. In other words the political and military leaders had no compunction about leaving and no feeling of responsibility for the military defeat which they were witnessing.

A more charitable interpretation, and one that those leaders would have wanted to pass on to future generations, was that they sought to save themselves and the army in order to fight another war. Drexel Biddle, the American Ambassador to Poland and Beck's confidant, recorded as early as March that he had been made aware of Polish government plans to avoid throwing all troops into battle against the German invaders. The idea was to conserve the Polish forces until the onset of autumn rains made Poland impassable and until the western Allies were able to launch their offensive.[3] To put it more precisely, the Polish High Command had developed a strategy for the defence of Poland on the assumption that the conservation of military resources for joint military action in the future with the western Allies was more important than the defence of western and central Poland. Nevertheless, the swiftness with which the military and political leadership was willing to abandon most of Polish territory to the German invaders was startling. Beck's secretary notes that on the evening of 3 September his chief was already musing about pulling the bulk of Polish military units to a south-eastern triangle around the town of Lvov. This defensive position would be held until the anticipated major western campaign against Germany was started.[4]

Biddle's intimacy with Beck made it possible for him to have relatively easy access to information during the course of the evacuation, but even he must have wished that he could have been spared some confessions. On 14 September Beck told the American Ambassador 'that he had participated personally in two wars: the Great war and the Polish–Soviet war. During the third war (the present one) he had been forced to stand on the sidelines. He nevertheless hoped that he would take an active part in the fourth war and perhaps end his life on the battlefield, as his forebears had'.[5] Military ambition therefore seemingly made it necessary for him to make sure that he did not inadvertently perish in the present war. Biddle concluded that Beck was very depressed.

The Polish government had good reasons to presume that the Romanians would facilitate their departure from Poland and either would accommodate them on their territory until the western Allies gathered their forces together, or would facilitate their progress to France. The newly appointed Romanian Ambassador Gheorghe Grigorcea, who had only presented his credentials on 2 September, encouraged the Poles throughout the evacuation to consider his country as well disposed towards their predicament. On 9 September Grigorcea assured deputy minister Szembek that although Romania was going to declare her neutrality, war supplies could be transported to Poland through Romanian territory and furthermore that oil could be purchased from private Romanian oil companies.[6] On 16 September when the decision to evacuate to Romania was a foregone conclusion, Grigorcea suggested that his government was willing to purchase Polish anti-aircraft guns.[7]

The Poles were thus lulled into a feeling of security which was brutally shattered once they arrived on Romanian territory. It would appear that the decision to intern the Polish government had been made before they had crossed into Romania. On arriving in the Romanian border town of Czernowiec, the President and other dignitaries were separated and henceforth contact between them was broken. The Polish Ambassador in Bucharest, Roger Raczyński, the brother of the Ambassador in London Edward Raczyński, was able with difficulty to communicate with them and to convey their instructions to Paris where a battle for the leadership of the future exile government was already taking place.

Romanian support for the Polish cause had not been at all clear cut, even if the Polish leadership had presumed that it could depend on such support. Unknown to Beck, the Romanian government had been desperately attempting not to get drawn directly into the conflict since the outbreak of German–Polish hostilities. This position was made particularly difficult by German pressure on the Romanians to declare neutrality and to stop assisting the Poles. Furthermore, a number of the Romanian King's key advisors held conflicting views on the subject. The Prime Minister favoured disassociation from the German war effort, while the Minister of the Royal Palace and the army wished to see Romania embark on a pro-German policy.[8] As the defeat of Poland appeared more likely, other events made it difficult for King Carol to keep his options open. German pressure increased, Hungary stationed troops on the border with Romania and finally Romania's dreaded neighbour, the Soviet Union, entered directly into the conflict. It was the Soviet entry into Poland which tipped the balance.[9] Henceforth the Romanians would try to placate Germany by continuing the supply of oil and by hampering Polish efforts to get their government and soldiers to France, while at the same time trying to retain French and British goodwill. On 15 September attempts to strengthen their own security led Romania to request the Germans to let them have Polish war materials, and with them presumably the anti-aircraft guns which the Romanian government tried to purchase from the Poles a day later.[10] Unofficially, Romania remained the Poles' good friend, officially her policy became increasingly bound by German pressures.

When leaving Poland the government believed it would be free to proceed to France, from where it would be able to mobilize and direct the fight against the occupying powers. Of equal importance was the need to mobilize international support for Poland. Thus the task of the future exile government was clearly marked out even before it had been established. While moving towards the Romanian border during the September campaign the government had steadfastly refused to consider broadening its political base to include previous opponents or other parties. In fact no effort was made either to bring new people into the government or to open up talks. Once interned in Romania it became apparent that a transfer of power from the President had to proceed swiftly in order to ensure that opponents of the government were not able to exploit the temporary power vacuum. It was known that opposition figures too were converging on Paris. Among those who were leaving Poland together with the government and army were men who had been critical of the government's policies.[11] Haste and the need to prevent opponents from capturing key positions within the exile government dictated President Ignacy Mościcki's choice.

In the first place it was considered that the ambassadors should, where possible, remain where they were. This in particular applied to the Polish Ambassadors in Paris and in London, Juliusz Łukasiewicz and Edward Raczyński respectively. They were considered too important to be moved from those tasks to governmental ones. Łukasiewicz in particular was strongly associated with Beck's foreign policy. His appointment to Paris in 1936 coincided with the initiation of Beck's policy of putting Polish–French relations on a so-called new footing, that of equality.[12] Handsome and arrogant, he was known to be Beck's personal friend, and was one of the key ideologists of the Sanacja government. His role in the transfer of power from the government now in Romania to a new one in Paris was to ensure continuity. Circumstances made it difficult to decide who would actually head the new government. Ironically the fear that new appointees would not relinquish their posts in the event of the existing titular holder of the post getting out of Romania, seems to have been as much a consideration as a determination to prevent the opposition from capturing the initiative.[13] Fear of French interference only compounded Łukasiewicz's determination to act as custodian of the pre-war government's rights. Initially he tried to keep key decisions within a very narrow circle of Polish government loyalists who had made their way to Paris, in effect the heads of the military and financial missions to France and himself.[14]

The main reason why these intrigues failed was because the first attempt to form a government-in-exile was vehemently opposed by the French government. President Mościcki resigned and appointed General Wieniawa-Długoszowski, the then Ambassador to Rome, to succeed him as President of the new Polish government in Paris.[15] Wieniawa-Długoszowski was another of Beck's cronies. His diplomatic skills were negligible, and he was known to have struck up a close friendship with Ciano, Mussolini's son-in-law, with whom he apparently shared a love of soldiering and horseriding. French opposition to the appointment of a man who would have guaranteed the survival of the pre-war government in a new guise was implacable.

Indirectly the French authorities let it be known that they would accept one of three alternatives, August Zaleski, Cardinal Hlond, whose elevation to a temporal position was in any case opposed by the Vatican, or Władysław Raczkiewicz.[16] The latter was an eminent lawyer, one time Minister of the Interior and speaker of parliament in the last government. As a result of complex intrigues Raczkiewicz emerged as the President forming the first government-in-exile on 3 October. Control over new appointments eluded the old guard and, under French pressure, a government of national unity was formed.

The successful and swift transfer of power created an impression of consensus but this was confined only to the basic principle of the need to continue the fight for the liberation of Poland and masked major differences within the government and Polish society as a whole. The government-in-exile went some way towards conciliating the opposition. But since the arrival of individuals in France was a haphazard and uncoordinated process, most representatives of various pre-war parties were not genuine leaders, merely prominent personalities. This immediately created a possibility of conflict between those in Poland and individuals in exile who would inevitably aspire to some sort of leadership role. Nevertheless, a real attempt was made to take into account all shades of political opinion by appointing to ministerial posts men from as varied movements as the extreme right National Democratic Party (Narodowa Demokracja, ND), the Socialist Party (Polska Partia Socjalistyczna, PPS) and the Peasant Party (Stronnictwo Ludowe, SL).

The appointment of Raczkiewicz as President and of General Władysław Sikorski to share power with him as Prime Minister was a virtual guarantee that the Polish government-in-exile would become a hive of intrigue and a permanent battleground between various coteries and factions. The supporters of the old regime, represented by Łukasiewicz, had fought to retain control over the Presidency. They appeared to have won, but the man who assumed the post was a weak and indecisive individual. Influence still eluded Łukasiewicz. The French appointed General Władysław Sikorski, the most senior ranking military man in France, as leader of the Polish military units which were in the process of being formed in France. As a result of further French support, and due to strong pressure of leaders of the opposition, Sikorski became Prime Minister, in addition to which he held the portfolios of Justice and of Military Matters. In due course he also assumed the post of Supreme Commander and Inspector General of the Armed Forces.

Even though his pro-French credentials were impeccable, it would assume a great degree of clarity and foresight on the part of the French government to presume that the French had, early during the September campaign, identified Sikorski as the man whom they would have wanted to head any Polish authority to be formed in exile. A more haphazard course of events seems to explain the appointment of Sikorski to head the first Polish government-in-exile. Sikorski had opposed Piłsudski's coup in 1926. Throughout the period which followed he remained in the army but was denied any command responsibilities. This allowed him to spend extended periods in France where he studied French military strategy and was notable in his support for the idea of Franco-Polish co-operation with the Soviet Union. He and his ideas were well known to the French High Command.[17] On 1 September Sikorski found himself without a command and was in the humiliating position of having to follow the government on its peregrinations towards the Romanian border in the hope of obtaining one. On 18 September the French Ambassador to Poland, Léon Noël, met Sikorski and advised him not to go with the government to Romania but to proceed directly to Paris.[18] It would appear that at this stage the French authorities had no clear plans for the creation of a representative exile Polish government in France. Sikorski's pro-French credentials and his well-publicized differences with the Piłsudski coterie simply made him a useful person to have in Paris in the event of such ideas crystallizing. Sikorski's opponents were to read more into this situation. In future months in the fevered atmosphere of the rapidly growing Polish community in Paris rumours about French unwillingness to allow those who had been associated with the Sanacja government to enter France prevailed. In some cases this is indeed what happened. In others France's anxiety about her own economic and military situation influenced her attitude towards the exiles.

The Poles who found themselves in exile were generally convinced that the spiritual and political leadership of the nation had been entrusted to them and that they therefore had to lead the fight for Poland. While these sentiments are easy to understand they were heavily tainted by a conviction, verging on parasitic arrogance, that it was now the western Allies' turn to show what they could do. The Allies owed a debt to Poland which should be discharged to those who had subjected themselves to exile in order to continue the struggle from afar. The atmosphere prevailing within the Polish groups in France was not conducive to realism.

By the end of September Sikorski had managed to outwit Łukasie-wicz by combining with members of opposition parties. In due course he was able to think of purging the Polish legations abroad of Pił-sudski'ites.[19] The embassy in Ankara proved to be the only exception: the Turks threatened not to accept a new nominee, which forced Sikorski to retain an arch-Piłsudski'ite, Michał Sokolnicki. Łukasie-wicz was forced to resign at the beginning of October. But this did not precipitate within the Polish ranks a mood of unity and support for the Prime Minister.

From the moment of his appointment Sikorski's relations with the President were difficult. The precise nature of the President's authority was never worked out. Raczkiewicz believed himself to be the real leader of the government in accordance with the constitution of 1935. Sikorski cast doubts upon the legality of that constitution and insisted that the President should resign those powers. Since neither was willing to accept the dilution of powers, however imprecise, which they believed to be legitimately theirs, constitutional ambiguities increased the potential for intrigues. The Presidency came to be associated with the old regime and indeed Raczkiewicz frequently tried to limit Sikorski's authority in contentious matters relating to foreign relations. On the other hand Sikorski had no clear power base. The Polish army and the officer corps in France were dominated by the supporters of the pre-war regime. The very instrument through which the government-in-exile planned to assert Poland's power became the mainstay of opposition to Sikorski.

From the beginning, the Sikorski government hoped that the large Polish community in France could be used to build an exile army. The continuous flow of refugees was to provide further personnel. Volunteers would be sought among the Polish community in Canada and the United States. As it turned out the first two (the Polish community in France and the refugees) provided the bulk of men for the Polish army in France. The supposition that a patriotic call to arms would obliterate all differences was not to be realized either. The character of the army was decided by its social composition and the origins of those who joined up.[20] The varied social background of the men meant that not only did they differ in their political ideas and experiences, but the latter also gave rise to differing expectations. As will be shown in subsequent chapters the army became involved in exile politics. The officer corps was fraught with intrigues and dissent and throughout the war, albeit at different times, various groups within it harboured military and political aspirations which were at variance with the government's objectives.

In October 1939 when the Polish embassy authorized the registration of all Poles in France and Belgium 103,000 men were recorded as fit for military service.[21] These were predominantly employed in mining and large industries. They had formed part of the great migration of labour into France in the 1920s which had mainly originated from villages. In France the majority occupied blue-collar jobs. Politically they had gained their experiences in France and thus were mainly associated with the French left, in particular the French Communist Party and the Communist trade unions. In the Polish army, which some of them joined, they were not influential as few among this group had relevant or recent military experience. Those who did represented the several hundred Poles who had fought on the Republican side in Spain, most of whom ended up in France.

Refugees from Poland were considered to be better military material. Those who were not military men had some recent training as approximately 90 per cent of the recent refugees had been called up during the September campaign.[22] They continued to arrive in France travelling through Romania and Hungary, then proceeding to Greece and Yugoslavia. The Baltic states too turned a blind eye to westward movements of Polish men. In most cases the transit routes operated with the tacit support of the neutral governments despite strong German pressure to block these routes. By the end of 1939 the political situation in all neighbouring states became sufficiently difficult to deter movements of Poles to the west, but at the same time numbers of those willing to flee stabilized. It has been calculated that approximately 34,000 people arrived in France following one of the above routes.

In these circumstances the Polish army-in-exile inevitably consisted of a high proportion of supporters of the pre-war government concentrated, because of their military experience, in the officer corps. Indeed, they were indispensable in the process of forming an army in France. As a social group they were committed to the Sanacja government and opposed to any social and political changes which might form part of a programme for post-war Poland. They also opposed Sikorski and his political Allies. Far from being embarrassed by the failures of the September campaign and contrite about the army's political interference in the internal affairs of inter-war Poland they were determined to maintain what they considered to be the achievements of that period. Neither democracy nor social and economic reforms would be the key objectives of their war effort. Instead they sought restoration of the great days of Piłsudski's rule, when they felt Poland was ruled successfully by strong men.

The numerical expansion of the army in France was limited by the availability of manpower. Very soon it was realized that, unless communities in exile could be fully exploited, grandiose plans for a great Polish army-in-exile were going to be thwarted. Attempts to induce Poles in Canada to volunteer for the Polish army in France were not successful, while negotiations with the United States government to permit recruitment there were fraught with difficulties. This explains one of Sikorski's early comments on the possibility of changing the course of Polish–Soviet relations. Sikorski believed that the Soviet Union would ultimately become Germany's victim. For the time being he was mainly concerned to get Poles out of the Soviet Union in order to continue building up the Polish army-in-exile. On 20 December 1939 he was reported as expressing regret that Polish–Soviet relations were so bad. His initial plans for resuming diplomatic contacts were justified by the need to care for the Poles now incorporated in the Soviet Union.[23] But at this stage nothing could be done.

The plans of the Polish government-in-exile were viewed sympathetically by the French. There existed a historic tradition of Polish formations in France, most recently during the First World War. Decisions to raise Polish units in France had been made even before the fall of Poland. On 9 September the two sides signed an agreement for the creation of a Polish division in France. This was followed by a further agreement signed on 21 September. During the next few months clearer plans for the Polish army in France were developed. The key element of these agreements was a statement that the Polish army was subordinate to the Polish government-in-exile. For operational purposes it was nevertheless to come under the command of the French military leadership.

The Poles confidently estimated that they could recruit up to 180,000 men by the middle of 1940.[24] This was an extremely unrealistic estimate based more on political aspirations than on a realistic assessment of possibilities. At the time of the German attack on France the Polish army consisted of 83,000 men. Coetquidan in Brittany was the first and main area of concentration of Polish units. In due course another one was established in Parthenay. All Polish camps were established in the northern departments. But they were so dispersed that it was impossible to maintain unity and to co-ordinate training.[25]

The biggest problem was the inconsistent and ambivalent attitude of the French authorities towards the Polish army. While they appeared to have facilitated the process of recruiting and equipping the Poles, the policy that was implemented was quite different. The Poles felt that there was a certain amount of racial hostility towards the foreigners flooding into France. This was exacerbated by very real conflicts between the military and civilian authorities on the subject of the desirability of allowing the Polish government to conscript into their army men who were working in French industry. Since the largest numbers of Poles in France were employed in mining, there were calls for them to be treated as reserved labour.[26] At the same time a grudging attitude towards the question of equipping the Poles surfaced.

In the background to this lay the French High Command's conviction that the Poles had no one but themselves to blame for the German defeat of their army. This prejudice meant that there was a limited willingness to learn from the military experiences of that war and led to an extremely patronizing attitude towards the plans developed by the Poles in France.[27] There were also very real differences between the Poles and the French in their plans for the use of the Polish army in France. To the French High Command it was a straightforward case of increasing the numbers of fighting men while maintaining a friendly allied authority which in the future could become a pro-French government in Poland. Nothing so modest or simple constrained Polish military and political planners in France. The Polish military contribution to the allied war effort was to serve a multiplicity of political purposes both in the international arena and in the forthcoming battle for political power in liberated Poland.

The Polish High Command based plans, developed without reference to the French and British planners, on the assumption that the war against Germany was going to be a short one. In this respect they were unwilling to accept French and British estimates that the struggle to defeat Germany was going to be long and drawn out. The liberation of Polish territories would take place as a result of a concerted allied effort, and this, according to the Poles, would enable the army to enter Polish territory victorious and as part of the great co-ordinated effort. A natural consequence of this planned action was an assumption that the post-war Polish state would be the dominant power in Central and South-eastern Europe. Polish aspirations to fill the power vacuum in that region after the defeat of Germany were mapped out by diplomatic and military preparations which were aimed at placing Poland in a commanding position in the region. Thus while it was presumed that the main thrust of military action against Germany would take place through the Baltic Sea and from the west, the advantages offered by the Balkan front were considered to be very big.[28] Among the reasons for maintaining diplomatic relations with Italy was the hope that the Poles would obtain Italian acquiescence in these plans.

In order that Poland be accorded the full status of a fighting ally, the Polish military contribution had to be of some consequence, reasoned the Polish leaders. Conversely, the Polish contribution to the allied effort had be rewarded by an admission to the intimate circle of joint consultative bodies. Thus, during his first wartime visit to London in November 1939, Sikorski told General Ironside, the Chief of the Imperial General Staff, that it was in the interests of Poland and the Allies to create a strong and numerous Polish army. Furthermore, Poland needed to be represented on the Supreme War Council and any other body created to discuss war aims.[29]

This idea was greeted with little enthusiasm by the British and French political and military leaders alike. They knew that the process of extending the membership of key committees to small participating Allies would only result in tying the hands of the major Allies. It was conceded that Polish representatives would be invited to attend the meetings when matters relating to the use of the Polish troops would be discussed. The British and French were right in their suspicion that the Polish request for representation was really an attempt to obtain disproportionate influence over matters relating to the course of the war and to post-war planning. This was precisely why the Polish request met with an outright refusal in 1939 and subsequently whenever it was made.

In January 1940, a Polish government memorandum reviewing the state of political–military issues raised by the creation of the Polish army reveals Sikorski's ambitions in this respect:

> Of particular importance to us is the question of our participation in the Supreme War Council and the Executive War Council. Our absence (from these) relegates us to the background and threatens our most vital interests. Generally, the army and strategy are aspects of politics; at this moment the outcome of our cause will depend primarily on our political work.[30]

One of the most difficult and divisive subjects to be tackled by the Polish government in France was that of the future political reforms in Poland. During the first meetings of the Council of Ministers a lot of time was spent criticizing the pre-war government without formulating a clear plan for post-war political and economic changes. It soon became apparent that these had to be confined to general commitments to democracy, the right to work and respect for minorities. The unwillingness to go beyond generalities was justified by statements that the nation would make its own decisions after the war, but the need to maintain unity in the exile government most probably accounts for this apparent reluctance to address more fundamental issues.[31]

Within the first months of its existence the Polish government expressed views and adopted policies which showed the extent to which it overestimated its importance in the allied coalition. The phrase that Poland was France's and Britain's wartime ally was repeated too frequently by the Polish leadership for them to note the specious nature of this claim. More worrying and potentially dangerous to allied co-operation was the basing of plans for the establishment of post-war Polish frontiers, and for securing for Poland a dominant role in Central Europe, on French and British military and political assistance.[32] From the beginning, diplomatic exchanges between Polish politicians in the government-in-exile and their French and British counterparts were aimed at eliciting statements of support for the Polish politicians' programme. During his visit to London on 11–12 October 1939 the Polish Minister for Foreign Affairs, August Zaleski, sought to obtain an official statement of support for Poland's war aims.[33] In November Sikorski sought the same when he came to London. Both were unsuccessful, mainly because the British government was unwilling to define war aims at this early stage, but not least of all because Polish territorial claims were clearly going to go beyond that which Britain would be prepared to approve.[34] By the end of November 1939 the Poles officially defined them as the elimination of the German presence in East Prussia and the establishment of regional pacts.

The destruction of Soviet power and the return to Poland of territories which had been captured by the Soviet Union in September 1939 formed a central plank of the exile government's programme. But both Zaleski and Sikorski quickly realized that open calls for war against the Soviet Union elicited ambivalent responses. Both tried to persuade the British during their respective visits to London that they did not seek to prejudge the situation. As Zaleski put it, 'It might well be that as the war developed Soviet policy might evolve in an unexpected direction and he therefore himself would be in favour of adopting what he described as a cautious policy towards the Soviet'.[35] Nevertheless, it was hoped that in due course support would be given to Poland in any future confrontation with the Soviet Union. Reporting on his visit to London in November 1939, Sikorski reassured his government that both France and Britain were likely to come round to Poland's view of the Soviet Union:

> Our Allies nevertheless will have to understand eventually the
> danger which threatens the West from the East. They will have to
> counteract politically and eventually also militarily – when the time
> comes – the continuing westward march of the Red Army.[36]

Thus on an official level the Poles decided not to seek an outright
declaration of support for Polish objectives in relation to the Soviet
Union. Instead they decided to wage a propaganda campaign aimed at
discrediting the Soviet Union, drawing attention to the need to restore
to Poland territories captured by the Soviet army, and generally establishing a reputation as experts on Soviet matters.[37]

The onset of the Finnish–Soviet conflict appeared to offer the Poles
an opportunity to use military co-operation as an entrée into the
political forum of debate. But the aims of the Finns aroused the British
and French governments' anxieties about getting involved in military
action which might draw them into a war with the Soviet Union on
top of the one which they were supposed to be fighting with Germany.
The result was that support for the Finns was lost in indecision. The
Poles saw this as an opportunity which the British and French had
failed to exploit.

From a strictly legal point of view it was not clear whether the Polish
government-in-exile, representing Polish interests, and the Soviet
Union were at war, or merely had no diplomatic relations. This nuance
of legal interpretation seemed irrelevant for the Soviet Union was
clearly Poland's enemy. The Soviet attack on Finland on 30 November
1939 was nevertheless a matter of direct concern to the Poles. Britain
and France were not at war with the Soviet Union notwithstanding
the latter's attack on their ally, Poland. Poland's initial response to the
Soviet attack on Finland was muted, as was that of the French and
British governments. It was only with time that ideas crystallized, even
if the situation did not necessarily become clearer. At the beginning of
January 1940 the French government directed an enquiry to the Poles
to ascertain whether they would be willing to participate militarily in
sending an expeditionary force to assist the Finns.[38] By 24 January
Sikorski had formulated his ideas on the subject. The Soviet–Finnish
conflict offered an opportunity to draw the British and French, who so
far appeared ambivalent on the subject of the Soviet Union, into war
with Poland's other enemy. By 21 February the Poles had warmed to
the project. By then they had considered what they thought were the
extensive political advantages, rather than just the localized military
benefits, of aiding the Finns. As the Polish Chiefs of Staff *aide-mémoire*
on the subject stated:

Polish participation in aiding Finland has a dual political meaning:
1. Polish units on Finnish territory will offer vital proof that Poland exists and is fighting as part of the allied front.
2. The very fact of Poland taking part in allied action will permit us to place unequivocally the issue of Poland's relations with the other two Allies externally and internally.[39]

Polish enthusiasm was misplaced. Not only were the Finns still unclear as to whether they wanted help from the Poles, since this would exacerbate Finland's relations with the Germans and might be interpreted by the latter as provocative, but the British and French governments also procrastinated.[40] Within those governments there were disagreements, and the possibility that such action might lead to a direct conflict with the Soviet Union continued to be voiced. Hopes that German–Soviet co-operation might break down were seriously entertained within military and political circles. In Britain assistance for Finland was linked with a matter which came to be seen as more important, namely the question of how to draw Norway and Sweden out of their neutrality and into declaring support for the allied cause. Supplies of Swedish iron ore, transported to Germany via the Norwegian port of Narvik, were considered crucial for the German war economy.

In February the Poles launched a full-scale political campaign to gain credit from their willingness to place troops at the British and French disposal in Finland. This was swiftly followed by a renewed attempt to coax the British into accepting a Polish representative on the Supreme War Council. According to Sikorski, Poland's exclusion from the body was symptomatic of the absence of political preparation for the end of the war. He both pleaded and threatened that the Polish nation would fight but, 'it must have an opportunity to discuss, in the company of its allies, matters which relate to it [the war]. Otherwise it [the Polish nation] will be ready to believe enemy propaganda, which claims that the rebuilding of Poland is not one of the main war aims'.[41]

Anticipating action in Finland, Sikorski agreed with the French authorities to form the Independent Highland Brigade consisting of approximately 5,000 men. On 12 March, after a period of intensive training, this unit joined French ones which were to be landed in Narvik. The northern port in Norway was chosen as much to force the neutral states of Norway and Sweden on to the allied side as to secure a territorial route to Finland. On 13 March the Finnish and Soviet governments ended their hostilities. The Polish Brigade was nevertheless sent into Norway, but with a different mission, namely to counter the German invasion of that country. Between 23 April and 14 June 1940 the Brigade took part in allied action in the region of Narvik.

The Norwegian campaign gave the Poles an opportunity to participate directly in the only campaign of the so-called 'phoney war'. Polish naval units and soldiers fought jointly with the British and French naval and land units. The military performance of the Poles was ranked highly and their prowess during the fighting around Narvik was visible. But the political benefits of co-operation were not secured. The Polish hopes that the Scandinavian campaign might draw the Allies into direct conflict with the Soviet Union were not realized. Equally unfulfilled were hopes that joint military action might in some way be translated into political co-operation. Prior to the fall of France, the Polish government-in-exile was offered two opportunities to participate in the deliberations of the Supreme War Council – on 23 and 27 April 1940 – on both occasions because of the allied use of Polish units in the Norwegian campaign. The Polish delegates, Sikorski and his Minister for Foreign Affairs, Zaleski, during the first meeting and Edward Raczyński, the Polish Ambassador to London on the second occasion, were allowed to attend only the later part of the deliberations. Significantly, they were not present when the political and military implications of the campaign were discussed and were merely allowed to make a statement at the end when no further discussions were taking place. On 23 April, Sikorski presented a report on the state of the Polish army.[42] The British and French responses were polite but conspicuously non-committal. On the second occasion, Raczyński was allowed merely to hear a statement on the progress of the campaign.[43] This consisted of sentimental and bland expressions of sympathy and appreciation for Polish heroism.

The Polish delegates were not to know that their performances at the two council meetings were no more than set pieces. They were not aware of the complexity of the debates, on a variety of issues related to the campaign, which had preceded their entry to the meetings. They therefore did not know that their attendance at both meetings had been devoid of political significance. Their initial conviction was that they had made a great impression on their allies and had secured all that they had set out to obtain. On his return, at a meeting of the Polish Council of Ministers in Angers, Zaleski boasted that Sikorski's behaviour, as leader of fighting partners, signalled that he was of equal stature to the Allies, unlike the Norwegian delegation, who were mere supplicants for allied assistance.[44] This euphoria was short lived. Doubts and anxieties about the Polish government not being accorded its full standing remained a constant theme of discussions within the military and political councils of the exile government.[45]

The Polish government keenly watched to see which joint allied organizations could become the forum for debate of matters relating to joint war strategy and post-war reconstruction. They focused on the Executive War Council as another committee on which they should be represented. As a result of continued pressure a Polish delegate was allowed to attend a meeting on 30 March, only to be told by General Lelong of the French General Staff that, since the Polish army still had not reached operational strength, its participation in the Executive's meetings would be unnecessary. A British compromise suggestion that the Polish delegate be invited to meetings dealing with Polish topics was accepted.[46] Colonel Leon Mitkiewicz, who had been appointed by Sikorski to the Executive War Council, soon realized that he was not informed of the meetings of the Executive War Council and felt that when he did attend, he was treated with disdain.[47]

During the last months of peace the Polish government had been negotiating a joint loan with the French and the British. Minister Beck had found both governments extremely unwilling to shoulder the burden of Polish rearmament and preparation for war. As a result he broke off talks at a time when the British were prepared to offer credits to the value of £5 million and the French 600 million francs. As the war broke out both governments renewed their offers which were this time accepted.[48] These became the first funds which were available to the exile government. In addition gold deposits from the Polish national bank were successfully taken out of Poland. They were kept intact in order to provide the first post-war government with funds for the first recovery programmes.[49] The government's running costs were covered from the credits available and subsequent ones obtained from allied governments.

The Polish army in France was equipped and maintained by the French government. But the signal feature of the first war budgets was the amount of money devoted to maintaining inflated and increasingly complex ministerial offices. Military costs, excluding the feeding and equipping of the troops, exceeded half of the whole governmental budget. Clearly the civilian and military organizations established in exile were not aimed at merely providing back-up for the limited diplomatic and military organizational matters with which the government had to deal. In fact what evolved was a skeleton but nevertheless comprehensive government apparatus with an equally comprehensive plan for the continuing development of the army. This immediately raised questions of further recruitment and of the relationship between the government-in-exile and the underground movements which were evolving in Poland.

In all plans for the future of the Polish armed forces and their role in the forthcoming battle against Poland's enemies the Polish leadership was inhibited by uncertainty as to whether the Allies would take action against the Soviet Union. While this remained a quandary which the leadership was not able to resolve, other anxieties came to haunt all discussions relating to the use of the Polish army. A consequence of the assumption that the Polish government-in-exile could only secure for itself a position of equality within the community of the allied powers by making a direct contribution to the joint military effort was the real threat that the Polish contribution would exhaust and deplete its troops before the liberation of Poland. In such an event, there were doubts as to whether the Allies could be relied upon to complete the task and restore Poland in pre-September 1939 borders, which the Polish exiles hoped to enlarge by the addition of at least East Prussia. This further underlined the need to continue expanding the Polish military effort while simultaneously proceeding with the task of capturing and holding areas which would either become Polish spheres of influence or would be incorporated outright into Poland.

These and other problems were faced in a memorandum entitled 'Aims of the Polish army' dated 28 February 1940.[50] In it a clear statement was made that the choice of operational areas would be to a large extent determined by the above considerations, relating to the need to continue recruitment into the army and to building up a pro-Polish orientation in the areas surrounding Poland. The best points of entry into Poland were considered to be the Carpathian mountains and Pomerania. Poland would be liberated from the west and the south. In addition troops would move into Poland from either Finland or the Baltic states. The Balkan and the Baltic fronts had the advantage of facilitating the establishment of Polish control over non-Polish territories which would have been occupied by either Germany or the Soviet Union.

On 15 April 1940, in anticipation of the imminent creation of the Middle Eastern and Balkan fronts, these ideas were further developed by General Bronisław Regulski, Commander of the Polish Mechanized and Armoured units in Avignon.[51] In his opinion the South-eastern front would give the Poles an opportunity to prepare for future allied action south of Poland and in Russia, to participate in joint action with the Allies and finally to encourage partisan action and launch a national uprising which would assist the incoming Polish troops. According to Regulski, the defeat of the Soviet Union would be accompanied by simultaneously pursued military action and a propaganda campaign which would destabilize the southern regions of the Soviet Union.[52] He considered that the Georgian, Cossack and Ukrainian populations were most likely to succumb to Polish propaganda efforts.

In the closing section of the exposé Regulski referred to one of the imponderables which clearly preoccupied Polish military and political leaders. On the one hand there was a temptation to allow the Allies to do the fighting and to defeat the enemy, which would leave Polish troops to enter Poland and place the exile government in power. On the other hand the allied willingness to assist the Poles, it was believed, could only be guaranteed if the Poles were seen to be fighting partners in the war. Regulski suggested that the dilemma could be resolved by the Polish exile army assisting in the formation of units consisting of other nationalities since these 'would symbolize the Polish contribution to the allied action against the Soviet Union'. In this way, he implied, Polish units could be kept out of battle for the more important task of capturing power in liberated Poland.

The issue of the degree to which the government-in-exile was willing to co-operate with the allied war effort was one which cropped up frequently in the quarrels between Sikorski and his opponents within the army and the political leadership. It nevertheless remained an unresolved dilemma. In April 1940 Sikorski was challenged by his Chief of Staff, Colonel Alexander Kędzior. The latter suggested that putting the newly formed units into action carried the risk of their being depleted. Kędzior had earlier criticized the government for allowing the French to plan for the use of an inadequately trained Polish brigade in Finland.[53] He considered that the most important aim of the Polish army-in-exile should be the liberation of Poland and not co-operation with the Allies.[54] He accepted that undeniably the defeat of Germany had to come first but he also maintained that the main role of the army, once it arrived in Poland, would be to create preconditions for the extension of the army and to defend the state. Kędzior based his analysis on the assumption that the Allies would only be concerned with the defeat of Germany and would proceed no further. Therefore the continuing fight against the Soviet Union would be faced by Poland alone and that task would have to be held in mind throughout the war.

To Sikorski such ideas were pure treason. He was distressed by

Colonel Kędzior's statements not just because he was publicly raising doubts about the allied commitment to Poland but also because this was done at a press conference on the eve of the Norwegian campaign, in which Polish units were scheduled to participate.[55] Claiming that similar ideas had been responsible for the September disaster, Sikorski attacked the very notion that political influence could be obtained without direct military commitments. As he put it, 'An army which avoids its duties on the front would fail to fulfil the mission which is expected of it in this historic moment ...'.[56] When in May Sikorski allowed Gamelin to use another inadequately trained Polish unit Kędzior resigned.[57]

Clearly what the Polish leadership was grappling with was the need to try and draw a clear distinction between the use of the army for the liberation of Poland, on the one hand, and for the purpose of co-operation with the Allies on the other. The realities of the war and the Polish conviction that political influence would only be obtained as a result of military co-operation rather than by using diplomatic skill precluded such a clear distinction from ever being made.

Even before the fall of France the obsession that 'perhaps all roads lead to Poland' had firmly taken hold. This is exactly what happened in the case of the French decision to station troops in the Middle East. To the French this was obviously in defence of French North African possessions. Why the Poles considered it desirable to go in with the French is less obvious. But as Sikorski was heard reasoning, 'it is not possible to say which road to Poland will turn out to be the longest and which the shortest'.[58] It was difficult to identify a direct link between participation in allied strategy in the Middle East and the liberation of Poland.

The Poles, trying to anticipate the future course of the war, tried to resolve this by envisaging the development of a Balkan front. Since that would hinge on the attitude of Turkey, the Polish government took an interest in its view of the war. But the Polish Ambassador to Turkey, Sokolnicki, who was extremely well informed of the complexities of that country's foreign policy, warned that it was not possible to think of a limited war.[59] Turkish co-operation with the Allies would only come about as a result of major events and political shifts, in which case the Balkan front, so advantageous to the Poles, would most probably be the least of the Allies' concerns. Sokolnicki advised that the government should look at the direction in which allied thinking was developing and not view minor military theatres in separation from the whole.

His perceived need to place Polish units in geographical locations which could serve as a springboard for the Balkan front led to Sikorski's efforts to create a number of Polish units, including an air force, in the Middle East. This was encouraged by General Weygand's nomination to the East Mediterranean theatre. French plans for a Levantine front raised Polish hopes of a campaign against the Soviet Union.[60] On 2 April Sikorski authorized the creation of the Brigade of Carpathian Fusiliers. Commanded by Colonel Kopański, the brigade was based near Beirut. It was hoped that it would expand to 7,000 men. In fact by the time of the fall of France it numbered less than 3,000.

The Poles saw the German attack on France as the long awaited opportunity to rout the enemy and to liberate Poland. They had thrown in their lot with the French ally and Sikorski was confident that the outcome was a foregone conclusion. In that they were not alone. The British Chiefs of Staff had in the early spring of 1940 been confident that the French army was capable of withstanding a combined German and Italian attack.[61] Full economic and military cooperation had apparently been achieved, as well as an uneasy understanding about the aims of the war.[62] The defeat of France was not seriously considered.

Lord Gort, the Commander-in-Chief of the British Expeditionary Force, started having doubts about the French defence capabilities as early as 15 May.[63] On 28 May, Sikorski still deluded himself that France and Britain were determined to resist at all costs.[64] On 15 June the French Prime Minister Reynaud informed Zaleski that he was planning to evacuate his government to North Africa.[65] He advised the Poles to move their government and troops to Great Britain. Fortunately for them the British had already decided to facilitate the removal from France of as many troops as possible. Thus when Sikorski came to Britain and met British military and political leaders on 19 June, he was assured that every endeavour would be made to bring to Britain the greatest possible number of Polish troops.[66]

The evacuation of Polish troops was made difficult, among many other reasons, by the fact that from the onset of German–French hostilities they had been committed to fighting and no plans had been developed for the eventuality of France's defeat. In most cases Polish commanders neither wanted nor were able to extricate Polish units from the ongoing battles against the invading German troops. Although Sikorski issued radio instructions to the troops to make their way to the nearest port from which they could be picked up, military activities and the general disorganization which prevailed in the wake of the German attack made it impossible for orderly transfers to take place.

Four Polish units, at various stages of training and organization, had been committed to the French war effort. The 10th Armoured Brigade fought in Champagne. On 18 June, when all fighting had ended, it was dispersed in order to avoid capture by the Germans. Most of the men tried to make their way individually to southern ports from which a number were subsequently brought to Britain. The 1st Grenadier Division fought in Lorraine with the French 2nd Army Group. When the German troops broke through the Maginot Line on 12 June and moved north and north-east, the Polish units heeded Sikorski's instructions and dispersed to move south. The fate of the 2nd Infantry Division was the most prosaic. This division fought in Alsace and with French units crossed into Switzerland on 19 June. The Swiss decided to treat them as part of the French 45th Corps and briefly threatened to return the Polish soldiers to occupied France. Only as a result of determined negotiations by the Polish commanders and the Polish representatives in Berne was this threat averted. The 11,000 men were nevertheless disarmed and their equipment was handed over to the German authorities in accordance with agreements signed by the Vichy authorities and the German government.[67] They remained in Switzerland throughout the war, in spite of repeated and strenuous efforts by the Polish government-in-exile to have them released. Polish troops in the region of Coetquidan had been mobilized to defend Brittany. Most did not go into battle but were moved to the coast and evacuated to Britain.

Sikorski was subsequently criticized for having failed to assert clear leadership during the fraught days of the French defeat. Between 11 and 17 June he was negotiating with the French government and was out of touch with his own government. Then suddenly on 18 June he was airlifted to Britain where he secured British support for the arrival of the Polish government-in-exile and all troops which could be saved. The evacuation of troops was left in the hands of subordinates. Bitter criticism of his role was fuelled by the realization that only 23.5 per cent of previously enlisted men, 27,614 in all, had arrived in Britain. 16,092 men were taken prisoner and 54,647 remained either in Switzerland, France or were known to be making their way to Spain.

The fall of France was a tragic setback for Sikorski's hopes of making a major military contribution to the war. The army which had been painstakingly built up, and on which hung such important and grandiose hopes, was now scattered. All of Sikorski's political and military plans had been based on the assumption that a direct contribution would be made to allied fighting. More importantly, the illusion of a swift reversal of fortunes and of a victorious return to Poland was gone. The defeat of France also shattered the conviction that the war could essentially be confined to the European theatre.

Until June 1940 Britain was viewed as a secondary ally. Now she became the principal and the only patron. In the elaboration of war plans imperial and global interests would inevitably take priority over European interests. There was no reason for the Poles to think that Britain would take as lively an interest in the East European balance of power as France had. It could be argued, as the Poles did, that France's interest in East European affairs was never constant; nor was it necessarily favourable to Polish interests. Nevertheless, French foreign policy and strategic priorities always took into account the need for some form of Eastern front. During the inter-war period this might not have been successfully translated into direct economic assistance or military co-operation but it clearly was there and that always gave rise to hopes that France's European war would facilitate Polish aims and aspirations. After the fall of France, the fate of Poland became associated with Britain, a country whose interest in European politics had frequently been of a transitory character and which furthermore had shown scant interest in East European politics. British territorial and economic aims were unlikely to coincide with those of Poland, and the need to defend the economic and political interests of the British empire was likely to be a powerful distraction from the perceived parochial demands of a minor European state.

2   Britain and German expansion in Eastern and South-eastern Europe

In 1939 a war in Central and Western Europe could not be viewed by a British government as a conflict to which it should devote all of its military and economic potential. But German aggression in Europe clearly could and did pose a threat to Britain and its globally scattered interests. Nevertheless the defence of these would always involve the defence of imperial priorities, naval communications and economic links with British markets. The inevitable conclusion of this dilemma was a preference, at least in London, for seeing Europe primarily as a French effort to which the British would make a contribution, while proceeding with training and equipping its own army, which was not expected to be ready until 1941.

By the beginning of 1939 Britain took a direct interest in French plans against Germany and Italy. This concern was affirmed by the course of military planning and co-operation, pursued by the British and French military staffs since February 1939. By May plans for the despatch of the British Expeditionary Force to fight with the French in Europe evolved in greater detail. Not only were the French assured of the presence of thirty-two British divisions on French soil by the end of the second year of war, but these were also to be provided with the latest and best equipment.[1]

Far more telling was an analysis of what the British had decided not to pledge to the European war. In the first place they had refused to bow to French pressure to use the bulk of the Royal Air Force (RAF) in defence of France. Nor would Bomber Command authorize attacks on German cities and industries, unless the Germans first bombed the British Isles. Clearly Britain hoped that Germany would be defeated by French forces.

When war broke out, the view that the French were in command of that side of the ship was maintained by both political and military leaders in London.[2] Britain's limited contribution to the continental war effort made it impossible for British politicians and generals to assume the initiative in that region. The establishment of the Supreme War Council, a body which was to direct the course of Franco-British military action, added nothing to the reality of the relationship. It was in practice no more than a forum for debate and discussion and assumed no effective control over joint military plans, since these plainly did not exist. Most importantly the Allies had no plans for assuming the initiative against Germany. The Supreme War Council became a forum for airing of plans for a number of peripheral campaigns: the Balkan campaign was discussed on 15 September, the Soviet attack on Finland in November and allied assistance to Norway in April 1940.[3] The Western front, the main one in Europe, continued to be the subject over which General Gamelin retained control and therefore was not discussed at the meetings of the Supreme War Council.

Although the British political and military leadership could cover up their inactivity with the explanation that they were waiting for the French to assume the initiative in fighting Germany, the French could not evade the issue so easily. They had to think of their security. A psychology of caution and foreboding paralysed the French High Command. General Maurice Gamelin, the French Commander-in-Chief, appeared to see himself as the custodian of France's long-term military potential. His conviction in the long, drawn-out war, for which he believed to be preparing France, did not permit him to authorize the squandering of valuable and scarce French resources on military operations which might not directly contribute to the ultimate defeat of Germany.[4] Unlike the British, Gamelin knew only too well the French army's shortcomings and was sensitive to the limited British contribution to the defence of France. In these circumstances, the German attack on Poland did not lead to the emergence of new military plans for action against Germany.

In the first months of war, the western Allies, far from posing any form of challenge to Germany, did all possible to reassure Germany that they should not be viewed as posing a threat. Rolling on to their backs, to display their soft underbellies to the potential aggressor, both hoped to gain time, rearm and launch an attack, not then, but later.

On 1 September the ferocity and success of the German attack on Poland forced British politicians to face a dilemma which they had earlier recognized, but not yet fully resolved, namely how to respond to German aggression in Eastern Europe. German claims on Czechoslovakia in 1938 had caused the British government to move away from the previous policy of detachment from that region. Not entirely unwillingly Chamberlain was drawn into the Czechoslovak–German conflict mainly in order to forestall a major European conflagration, but also in order to assume some control over French involvement in East European politics. France's commitment to defend Czechoslovakia was linked with the Franco-Soviet agreement. In the early months of 1938 few international statesmen doubted that the consequences of a German attack on Czechoslovakia would be Europe-wide. France's support for that state would have resulted in the Soviet Union coming to Czechoslovakia's aid. Britain could not have stood apart from such a serious conflict, and would no doubt have assisted France in her actions against Germany. But the Soviet Union's need to cross Polish or Romanian territory to assist Czechoslovakia militarily would have been an added complication. In 1938 it was predicted that Poland would most likely throw in her lot with Germany. Her economic and political ties with Hitler's regime were strong, notwithstanding the unresolved problem of the Free City of Danzig.

This line-up of protagonists was avoided. The Munich conference, initiated by Neville Chamberlain's personal diplomacy, dispelled the crisis by allowing Germany to claim Czechoslovak territories. The French commitment to Czechoslovakia was replaced by a vague reference to the need for the four Munich conference powers to guarantee the integrity of the now renamed Czecho-Slovakia. In the opening months of 1939 Britain's focus of attention shifted to the threat of a German invasion of the Low Countries, only to be drawn back to the east by rumours of a planned German attack on Danzig in early March and fears of Germany assuming control over Romanian oil.

Thus, in the crisis month of March 1939 Britain was forced to accept that German aggression in Eastern and South-eastern Europe was a matter of direct concern to Britain because it threatened European stability. British responses nevertheless were ambiguous. In 1938 the Foreign Office had become alarmed at the extent of German economic, and consequently also political, influence in South-eastern Europe. This development had already been noted in 1936 and had been monitored by the French and British ministries responsible for these matters. In the autumn of 1938, after extensive consultations had taken place between the Foreign Office and the Treasury, the matter was discussed by the Foreign Policy Committee of the Cabinet. The outcome of these consultations was a Cabinet decision that, although it was undesirable, the growth of German influence in that part of Europe could not be counteracted without a major programme of investments, subsidies and grants or at least credit guarantees. Since these were not readily available for South-eastern and East European states, with which Britain had only limited commercial and economic contacts, the Foreign Office accepted that the British government's desired objective of retaining some pro-British orientation in that region could not be secured.[5] Arguably this decision meant that Britain would not seek an open confrontation with Germany in the region.

Britain's equivocation was tested in the first half of March 1939 by three events that followed each other in rapid succession. The first was the German occupation of Prague on 14 March and the creation of the German protectorate in Slovakia a few days later. These were closely followed by extremely worrying rumours, whose origins were confused, of German pressure on Romania to secure a monopoly of that country's oil production. Finally, British politicians became aware of the possibility that Germany and Poland were heading for a confrontation over German claims to Danzig. The last was particularly worrying because Britain, in its capacity as member of the League of Nations, was one of the guarantors of the Free City of Danzig. The result of anxious Cabinet deliberations which took place daily, and at times twice daily, in the second half of March was that Chamberlain approved the Foreign Office's initiative to try to build an anti-German bloc in Eastern Europe.[6] A British guarantee to defend Poland against German aggression, made by Neville Chamberlain in the House of Commons on 31 March, was followed by an undertaking to Romania.

Nevertheless these gestures were not backed by decisions and policies which would have left no doubt in the minds of the German policy-makers and assured the recipients of the British guarantees that Britain was putting the full weight of her military and diplomatic weight behind an anti-German bloc in the east.[7] Even though in the course of future months the British and French governments agreed to make available aid for investment in the Romanian oil industry, this was never enough to overcome the serious doubts and divisions which existed within the Romanian army and Romanian royal household on the subject of opposing Germany. Indeed, efforts to assure Germany that Romania was not committed to the British side remained the most notable feature of Romania's communications with German officials.[8] A similar situation prevailed in Poland. Even though the Polish Minister for Foreign Affairs, Józef Beck, was willing to accept a British commitment against Germany, he still continued his own efforts to reach an accommodation with Germany and rejected all attempts to induce him to agree with Romania and the Soviet Union on a joint response to German aggression.[9]

At the root of both Romanian and Polish policies lay Britain's failure to convince both that it was in their best interests to enter into agreements which could be interpreted by Germany as hostile. As long as British financial and military plans for action in Europe were confined to the Western front both Romania and Poland were keenly aware of the fact that the burden of building and sustaining an Eastern front against Germany was going to be shouldered by them.[10] The result was that while both took seriously into account the possibility of a German attack in the near future neither was going to throw away recklessly even the slimmest chance of negotiating their way out of trouble. Accordingly, between April and September 1939 the Romanian government kept open diplomatic lines with both London and Berlin. The Poles, fearful of the growing stalemate over Danzig, assumed that German aggression was likely to occur in the near future and went ahead with plans for war, confident that France and Britain would come to their aid.[11] Nevertheless they too sought to keep open channels for the resumption of negotiations.

When the Germans attacked Poland, British politicians proved unwilling to re-examine fully the dilemmas which they had been facing and coping with on a piecemeal basis since at least March 1939. All decisions on any action which they considered necessary had already been implemented or were in the process of being implemented: a minor Act of Parliament allowing conscription during peacetime had been approved in April; staff talks with the French had been taking place since April; the re-equipment of the British Expeditionary Force that was to be sent to the Continent had already been given priority;[12] new investments in armament and munitions industries had been approved in February 1939, though these were constrained by strict budgetary limits.[13]

Basing itself on the experiences of the First World War, the Chamberlain Cabinet decided on 23 August to consider broadening its political appeal in the event of war breaking out.[14] The result of deliberations, and behind the scene negotiations, was singularly unimpressive. Neither the Labour nor the Liberal Parties were willing to join a government so little changed from the one which they believed to have been responsible for the failed policy of appeasement. The only two interesting additions to the previous team were the inclusion of Winston Churchill as First Lord of the Admiralty and Anthony Eden with responsibility for Dominions affairs. Most importantly Chamberlain and Halifax remained in control, facing little opposition within the House of Commons and none from their own team. In these circumstances it is not surprising that no review of previous policies was undertaken. Foreign policy and military priorities remained as before, and merely adjusted to the new situation. It would take more than the defeat of Poland to cause a major political shake-up in the government.

In Britain, from the very beginning, the war was not seen as a struggle to liberate Poland but as one to defeat Germany. This distinction, which was made openly by British politicians, would make a great difference to the Poles and Czechs. It meant that at least until German aggression was seen to affect British interests directly, politicians and leaders alike were in a quandary as to whether and what actions should be taken in response to the German initiatives.

In the first months of the war, Cabinet discussions were dominated by three areas of concern which were not always clearly formulated. They were the implications of the Polish defeat, the future role of the Soviet Union and the need to prevent Germany from obtaining access to raw materials. Deliberations about them tended to be uneasy and inconclusive. By the end of September, when the defeat of Poland by German and Soviet troops was confirmed, the need to prevent Germany restocking in oil from Romania and other vital raw materials from other European states came to be seen as the most important issue.

One of the key factors which had earlier constrained the development of any military plans for assisting the Poles was the lack of direct lines of communication with Poland. In any case, it had been decided in the course of the Franco-British Staff talks in May 1939 not to attempt to give Poland direct military assistance in the event of a German attack.[15] Not surprisingly, therefore, the September discussions of the Polish ability to resist Germany tended to produce sentiments of support rather than effective decisions. British inactivity in the face of a concerted and increasingly successful German war in Poland nevertheless did cause some disquiet within governmental bodies. There existed some embarrassment about the lack of response, since neither politicians nor military leaders could plead ignorance about the nature of the war. But this unease never gave rise to an open admission of the obvious conclusion, namely that Britain was not going to take action herself.

On 8 September, the Cabinet was informed of a report which had been received from General Carton de Wiart, the Head of the British

Military Mission to Poland. Carton de Wiart, a colourful character who had earlier retired to live in Poland, spoke Polish and had excellent contacts within the Polish military leadership. His reports were authoritative and well informed. At this early date he informed the Cabinet that Polish resistance was faltering.[16] The next day the Cabinet once more discussed news from Poland, this time a report by Captain Davis of the British Military Mission. The need for military assistance was stressed by Davis, as it had been in the earlier report.[17] The British Ambassador to Poland, Sir Howard Kennard, accompanied the Polish government when it left Warsaw and throughout was able to keep his government informed of the extent of German action against Poland. He particularly drew attention to the fact that he, together with members of the diplomatic community, saw German aeroplanes bombing civilian targets. In a report filed immediately after he had left Polish territory he summarized his impressions on the subject.

Commenting on this the Foreign Office drew attention to the potentially embarrassing implications of the information which had been received from Poland. Were the Foreign Office to acknowledge publicly that it was aware of indiscriminate German air attacks, there could be a public outcry with demands for Britain to do something to stop German bombing. Since neither the fact of German troops attacking Poland nor the nature of the warfare was going to change the government's policy of non-involvement in the Eastern front, dissemination of this information was not welcome. But, the Foreign Office reasoned, in future hostilities a situation might arise in which there might be a need to refer to Germany's actions in Poland. An admission would then have to be made that German atrocities had been known of and ignored. It was clear that excessive knowledge of German actions in Poland could be embarrassing to the British while being unlikely to affect policy-making.[18]

Obviously, once war started, Britain could do little militarily or politically to prevent the fall of Poland. Before the German attack on Poland it was realized that supplying Poland from the west would be an impossible task, in particular since the Baltic was to all intents and purposes going to be closed. The subject was discussed on several occasions, notably during the Franco-British Staff talks and the British–Polish Staff talks. The only possible route for overland transit to Poland was from the Mediterranean through Romania. The speed of German victories rendered the conclusions of these talks obsolete even before the ships could be loaded. General Mieczysław Norwid-Neugebauer, the Head of the Polish Military Mission which arrived in

Britain in August, found the British military authorities very reluctant to provide any equipment. In spite of having asked for Hurricane fighter aircraft, anti-aircraft guns and quantities of ammunition, he obtained very little. He was merely promised 10,000 Hotchkiss guns and 15–20 million rounds of ammunition, and even then the consignment was to be completed in six months' time.[19] However, by mid-September, four ships were ready to leave British ports with the aim of delivering supplies to Poland along an overland route through Romania. By then Norwid-Neugebauer had obtained 44 planes and 5,000 Hotchkiss guns. But on 14 September, the Deputy Chiefs of Staff were considering 'what action should be taken as regards various consignments of war stores which are already on their way or about to be despatched to Poland'.[20] The military situation in Poland was so uncertain that even though it was decided to allow the ships to sail to the Mediterranean, the captains were not to be given further instructions until they neared the Dardanelles. The Deputy Chiefs of Staff report concluded, 'If, when the time came, Poland had been completely over-run it was for consideration whether these armaments should be diverted to Romania, Turkey, Greece or Egypt'.[21] The truth of the matter was that Britain simply did not have spare equipment. Her own rearmament programme, which had only been initiated in the spring of 1939, meant that British services were experiencing serious shortages. The supplying of an ally, who was in any case likely to be defeated, had to be balanced against British long-term needs.

In spite of their unease about their own inaction, neither the political leaders nor the military chiefs were prepared to recommend a change in British policy, although they did seek to reassure themselves that they had done all that was possible. On 10 September the Cabinet was informed that the Chiefs of Air Staff were to look at the possibility of 'sending high flying aircraft over Germany in daylight with a view of upsetting German industry by causing air raid alarms'.[22] On the following day the Foreign Secretary Lord Halifax reported that leafletting was apparently not making a great impression in Germany, 'but that anything in the shape of news was eagerly awaited'.[23]

The Polish Ambassador in London and the Head of the Polish Military Mission in London persisted in requesting that Britain take action against Germany. In Poland, the British Ambassador Howard Kennard and his French counterpart Léon Noël were acutely aware that British and French military action was anticipated in Poland as the only means of averting defeat. During the night of 6 to 7 September, Beck defined the main aim of his diplomatic endeavours as putting diplomatic pressure on the two western Allies to commence aerial action against Germany.[24] In these circumstances it was considered inadvisable to state openly that such action would not be initiated even though it had already been decided during the course of the Franco-British military talks that there would be no direct military involvement by either in the Eastern front. It was left to the Head of the British Military Mission to Poland and the British Ambassador to offer the Poles reassurance while making no promises.

On 8 September Kennard was furnished by the Foreign Office with information which he was to use in discussions with the Poles. He was advised to try to skirt around the painful and embarrassing question of whether the British or the French were responsible for lack of British aerial action against Germany on the Western front. He was to deny that British anxiety about American public opinion was in some way influencing decisions about bombing German territory. Most emphatically, Kennard was to persist in refuting any suggestion that Britain had failed to assist Poland. The Foreign Office telegram to Kennard concluded by stating that Britain's very declaration of war on Germany had already rendered Poland assistance. The Poles were to appreciate that the ability of British warplanes to fly over German territory and the consequent threat of British air strikes against German bases and aerodromes had 'contained' the German air force. According to the Foreign Office, up to 50 per cent of the German aerial capacity could have been considered to have been thus immobilized. Finally, Kennard was to point out that, were it not for the threat of British action, these aeroplanes would have been used against Poland.[25]

Poland's brief semblance of holding out against Germany was not enough in itself to cause a change of policy. On 8 September, having considered General Carton de Wiart's report, the Cabinet members agreed once more that the only way Poland could be given assistance was by 'waging war on Germany until Poland was rehabilitated'. In other words the defeat of Poland was accepted as a foregone conclusion even before that occurred. It was furthermore agreed that the liberation of Poland would only be possible after the ultimate defeat of Germany.[26]

Thus the joint Anglo-French decision to remain passive while Germany attacked in the east was not altered by the course of the German–Polish war. During the First Meeting of the Supreme War Council, on 12 September, Chamberlain restated this point. He spoke of the inevitability of the Polish defeat. Had British supplies been available to the Poles, according to Chamberlain, their resistance would have been strengthened and perhaps prolonged. But their ultimate defeat could not have been avoided. At this early stage in the war, the British Prime Minister maintained that 'the only real help to Poland lay in winning the war'. Not interfering with Germany while she was occupied in Poland appeared to offer Britain the advantage of being able to continue undisturbed preparing for the inevitable future confrontation. The possibility that the RAF's actions over Germany might involve civilian casualties was considered to carry the risk of alienating neutral opinion, notably in the United States where Chamberlain hoped Roosevelt would be able in due course to persuade Congress to repeal the neutrality legislation.[27]

Whichever way Chamberlain looked at the subject of Poland, it was obvious that he saw no reasons for altering Britain's policy of military inactivity. This was made clear once more by Chamberlain in one of his regular letters to his sisters. Writing on 17 September, he mused upon the course of past and possible future events:

> Poland is about finished now and Hitler will very soon be in a position to move his aircraft and part of his Eastern Army elsewhere. What will he do? Some, including I think our own HQ expect him to build up forces for an attack in the West. I cannot take that view myself. I see no possibility of his scoring a major success in the West and surely he must have one to keep up the spirits of his people and encourage neutrals to take his side.[28]

On 9 September a new issue had been introduced to the Cabinet. Under the heading 'Anticipated Duration of War' Chamberlain opened a discussion on war aims. Information had apparently been received suggesting that Hitler might succeed in exploiting British and French inactivity to induce the Poles to surrender. Chamberlain was not prepared to be drawn into making any statements on the subject. He nevertheless appreciated the necessity of defending the position of the government. At the same time government thinking on the subject of the duration and the course of the war needed to be clarified.[29] Immediately after the meeting a declaration was made to the press stating that the government was operating 'on the assumption that the duration of the war would be at least three years'.

In the House of Commons Chamberlain was challenged on several occasions to make a statement on Britain's war aims. In each case he refused to be drawn. Explaining that fighting was still taking place in Poland, Chamberlain avoided committing himself to any territorial promises. There was a general agreement both within the government and the House of Commons that during the First World War commitments of this type had been a mistake. They had made wartime diplomacy difficult and had hindered the peace process at the end of hostilities.[30]

The government's acceptance that the defeat of Poland could not be averted did not mean that British politicians and civil servants had removed Poland entirely from their considerations. On 6 September the Cabinet was informed by the Chancellor of the Exchequer that the Bank of England had made appropriate arrangements to secure control of funds which the Bank of International Settlement was holding on behalf of a Polish bank. This was done in order to prevent the German authorities gaining access to Polish accounts.[31] The loan and credits of £5 million, which had been only grudgingly offered to Poland during peacetime, and which had been rejected by the Polish Minister for Foreign Affairs, Colonel Józef Beck, as derisory, were now once more offered. On 7 September the Treasury completed arrangements for £5 million to be granted to Poland in order to facilitate purchases of war materials.[32]

The Treasury's attitude towards Poland generally, and towards the question of financial assistance for strengthening Poland's fighting capacity in particular, remained consistent with views expressed during the negotiations in the summer. It could be suggested that it remained in line with the government's policies towards the Eastern front at the time. Robert Waley, Principal Assistant Secretary in the Treasury, minuted on 1 September his regret that the indiscreet British Ambassador in Warsaw had given the Poles the opportunity to reopen the question of financial assistance. Equally, he regretted that it was impossible not to offer now the loan which had been made available to the Poles in July.[33]

The speed of Germany's military victory brought to the fore another subject. Earlier the Poles had let it be known that some form of exile authority would be set up in the event of a defeat in the war. The attitude of the Foreign Office had been that there would clearly be some advantages in such a government being brought together outside occupied Poland. It was nevertheless assumed that its role would be limited. Again, lessons were drawn from the experiences of the First World War. While the desirability of establishing some Polish authority abroad was accepted, it was assumed that its role would be purely symbolic.

In a message to Sir Reginald Hoare, the British Minister in Romania, a country through which the bulk of fleeing Poles were likely to pass, the Foreign Office wrote on 16 September that it was considered very important for a Polish government to continue *de jure* 'wherever they may decide to go'.[34] Behind this support for the maintenance of a Polish authority was the generally positive British response to informal Polish suggestions that naval units, airforce crews and soldiers could be used by the British in the continuing war. This subject was already being discussed in British military circles.

In the message of 16 September, Hoare was asked to ascertain the likelihood of the Polish troops being able to cross into Romania. With a complete lack of understanding of Romanian–German relations, the Foreign Office put it to Hoare that the Romanian government might have some use for the Polish troops, which they were otherwise likely to intern. Romania's military capacity had never been highly rated by the Chiefs of Staff. Their acquisition of Polish equipment was considered by the Foreign Office to be a very good idea. It was believed that, if the Germans subsequently attacked Romania, it would welcome the military assistance of Polish soldiers and would make good use of the scarce equipment thus obtained.[35]

The reality of the situation in Bucharest was totally different from that assumed in London. The British and French hope that Romania would at least try to deny Germany access to oil reserves was based on an incorrect analysis of the strength of the pro-western faction within the royal household. At the beginning of the war the Prime Minister managed to persuade the King not to declare neutrality, which could have been viewed by the western Allies as a sign of hostility, by 5 September. But, threatened by Hungarian troop concentrations and menaced by Ribbentrop's warnings, the Crown Council issued a declaration which indicated a preference for a policy of neutrality.[36] The Romanian government still tried to argue briefly with Germany that this neutrality was not infringed by supplies routed through its territory to Poland. When Poland's defeat appeared imminent, Romania's neutral stance became noticeably more benevolent towards Germany. The foolish notion that Romania might disagree with, let alone fight against, Germany originated in the Foreign Office and the British Ambassador in Bucharest had to argue against it. On 18 September the Romanian government, having first allowed members of the Polish government to cross the border, interned them.

British diplomatic pressure on the Romanians to release the Poles was bound to be unsuccessful. It was left to Hoare to disabuse the British government of its conviction that it still had some leverage with the Romanian government. The Foreign Office had instructed him to press the Romanians to allow the Polish government to leave. Hoare was to warn the Romanian authorities that a refusal to let the Poles depart would create a bad impression in European capitals. Replying on 19 September, he questioned the likelihood of this type of argument carrying weight in Romania. 'Does anybody in England or France imagine that a "deplorable impression" has not been created in every country in Europe by the absolute and complete failure of the French and British to afford the Poles even a few days breathing space in which to check German pressure?'[37]

The British Minister in Bucharest felt it necessary to make these points in so forceful a manner because during September, as the focus of attention moved away from the inevitable fate of Poland, new plans to limit Germany's military capacity emerged. Romanian oil became one of the commodities which the British hoped to deny Germany. Unfortunately Britain's presence and British prestige in Romania were slight, and the pace of events was clearly being set by Germany.

That September King Carol of Romania, never a man of great resolve, came increasingly under the influence of the pro-German wing of his court advisers. His own anxieties about the German–Soviet *rapprochement* were heightened by the apparent absence of British resolve to assist Romania. The belief that Turkey and the Soviet Union, both potentially Romania's enemies, were the two focal points of British and French diplomacy, made it easier for pro-German elements to persuade the King not to follow pro-British policies.[38] As a result, at the end of September, the Romanian government sought an accommodation with Germany.

The Romanian government was nevertheless still keeping open other options, having made no clear commitments. Efforts were made to open talks with the Soviet Union aimed at resolving disputes over Bessarabia, and hopes were still harboured that perhaps Britain, and maybe also France, would reconsider their policy of only partial involvement in Balkan affairs.[39] The extent of British influence and prestige remained unclear. Unless some major policy initiatives were made in the direction of assisting militarily the Balkan states, that influence and prestige were likely to wane. Decisive military and political action by Britain then could still have prevented Romania from assuming a pro-German policy. Such action was not forthcoming.

The Romanian decision to intern the Polish government effectively ended that government's hopes of transforming itself into an exile authority. The French, on whose territory the government was to be formed, took a direct interest in the matter.[40] The British assumed that the Polish government-in-exile would neither settle in Britain nor seek financial assistance from Britain. British politicians therefore viewed the matter as essentially a French problem. On 27 September Clifford Norton, until recently the Counsellor of the British embassy in Warsaw, wrote that the French government should be allowed to assume control over issues relating to the future Polish government-in-exile. He argued that the government would most likely reside in France and the French would be responsible for organizing its military resources. The Polish government-in-exile would clearly be a French problem.[41] Discussing the desirability of having General Wieniawa-Długoszowski, the Polish Ambassador to Rome, at the head of the exile government, Alexander Cadogan, the Permanent Under-Secretary of State at the Foreign Office, agreed with the views expressed by Norton. These comments reveal the degree of British disinterest in Poland and its government-in-exile. Cadogan regarded the lack of French consultation as more of an issue for British foreign policy than the question of who would lead the new Polish government.[42]

On 26 September the Polish Ambassador in London, Count Edward Raczyński, informed the Foreign Secretary, Lord Halifax, of the decision to form a government-in-exile based in Paris and headed by Wieniawa-Długoszowski. On receiving the Polish Ambassador's note, Halifax is quoted as asking 'what was expected of him in connection with this matter?'.[43] The diffidence of the British contrasted with the swiftness of the French objection to the Polish choice of President. As Raczyński was leaving, Cadogan handed Halifax a note from the French government stating that it had refused to recognize a Polish government headed by Colonel Beck's old crony. Within the Foreign Office and the military committees no views were expressed about the choice of men who were to form the Polish government-in-exile. In fact, few personalities were known in London. Early in the war the French authorities had identified General Władysław Sikorski as the man they wanted to see in charge of Polish affairs in exile. In London he was unknown. Even in June 1940, when Sikorski had been the Prime Minister and Commander-in-Chief in the government-in-exile for nine months, Peter Wilkinson of the British Military Mission, who organized Sikorski's departure from France, was still to feel that the Polish leader was entirely unknown outside the Foreign Office. More importantly he was unknown in the War Office, even though agreements for the use of Polish air crews and few surviving naval units had been made in September.[44]

The British government might have been uninvolved in the controversies surrounding the creation of a Polish government-in-exile, but it was not indifferent. On 21 September the Cabinet discussed the desirability of a Polish government remaining in existence. The main reason given for supporting the creation of a Polish government was the need for it to assume control of Polish resources. These were listed as 'a large sum in gold, certain naval units, a large Polish man-power capable of being organized into Divisions for use on the Western front'.[45] The use of Polish manpower was of some, though not yet major, interest.

In spite of the lack of political commitments, plans for the utilization of Poland's armed forces in the western war effort developed decisively and with tangible results. Initial suggestions for joint military action in the west came from the Poles. Proposals for military co-operation were made even before the outbreak of the war. On 25 August Kennard reported from Warsaw that Admiral Jerzy Świrski had requested the departure from the Baltic of three Polish destroyers to operate henceforth with the British navy, from Leith.[46] This proposal had the approval of the highest Polish military authorities and was based on a realistic appreciation of the fact that the Polish navy could not operate against Germany in the Baltic. More importantly, it shows how the idea of waging a war against Germany was seen by the Poles in a very broad European context, even before the defeat of Poland.

On 11 September the Admiralty received a note from General Norwid-Neugebauer, Head of the Polish Military Mission to Britain, about extending the scope of naval co-operation.[47] He was concerned that Polish material and manpower resources available outside the Baltic should be used in the common effort. Additional naval units, destroyers and submarines would in due course, he anticipated, make their way out of the Baltic. Finally a hope was expressed that the Royal Navy might make available some ships to be manned by Polish sea cadets presently stranded in Casablanca, seamen from merchant ships, and Polish naval reservists in England. This proposal contained all the ingredients of future Polish military co-operation. It offered co-operation with a common aim and signalled Polish determination to continue the fight against Germany irrespective of the outcome of the German offensive in Poland.

On 13 September Kennard, who was still in Poland, informed the Foreign Office of Beck's proposal to him and the French Ambassador that spare airforce personnel should be sent to Egypt or Syria to be 'made use of on any front that might be agreed upon'.[48] As was shown in the previous chapter, the Polish government was then in retreat and Beck was seeking to prolong the fighting, while defeat was swiftly becoming a reality. Plans for the abandonment of Polish territory were being justified by the need to conserve resources in order to win the European war. Although Beck seemed to be making an offer of Polish trained manpower to the west, he still hoped that the Polish military campaign against Germany would continue and that, once equipped, the Polish airmen would either return through Romania back to Poland to take part in the war or stay with the western forces and participate in the western campaign to defeat Germany.

For the British authorities, these early suggestions of military co-operation offered an opportunity to deal with their own shortage of trained manpower. The responses of both the government and military authorities to the Polish offers were therefore positive and encouraging. But from the start the Poles expected their co-operation to be balanced by political co-operation on the part of the British and neither the British government nor its military leadership took that into account. This difference of outlook lay at the root of all future difficulties between the Poles and the British.

On 16 September the Cabinet took note of the Chiefs of Air Staff decision to consider the Polish proposal that the RAF should employ a number of airmen presently undergoing training in Britain.[49] The Foreign Office was subsequently pleased to hear that the Poles hoped to increase the numbers of personnel available.[50] By 24 September a telegram was despatched by the Foreign Office to British legations in the Baltic states and South-eastern Europe instructing them to assist the passage of Polish pilots and technicians to ports from which they could be transported to France and Britain.[51] Henceforth British consulates and embassies secretly assisted the passage of appropriately qualified Poles through neutral countries, providing them with funds and tickets. In the spring of 1940 the present author's father is listed as having received the assistance of the British consulate in Athens, where he arrived on foot from Poland, to board a ship which was to take him to Britain to enlist with the Polish bomber squadron there.

By the time a Polish government was formed in Paris on 30 September, the British government had already acknowledged the Polish desire to continue military action against Germany and work was in progress to establish the legal basis for this co-operation. The decision to use Polish manpower was made without considering the lack of political agreements about war aims and the long-term implications of military co-operation between a Polish government-in-exile and

Britain and France. Polish willingness to continue fighting and British shortages of flight and ground personnel for the rapidly expanding air force provided, at this stage, ample scope for Anglo-Polish military co-operation.

The entry of Soviet troops on to Polish territory on 17 September and their occupation of the eastern regions of Polish Byelorussia and Ukraine briefly disrupted the uneasily prevailing British consensus about not getting directly involved in the Polish–German military confrontation. It also caused British politicians and military leaders to return to the uncomfortable subject of the Soviet Union and its role in European politics. During the course of the Anglo-France-Soviet military talks in August 1939, with which the Poles refused to have anything to do, the Soviet delegation had pressed the western Allies to explain how they would be expected to engage Germany militarily without the right of entry on to Polish territory. This question challenged the very idea of an Eastern front. Admiral Drax, the Head of the British delegation to Moscow, therefore directed an enquiry to Halifax. In response the Foreign Secretary advised that the British government did not want to become involved in Polish–Soviet relations.[52] During the tense days before the collapse of the talks with the Soviet Union the British and French governments briefly considered putting pressure on Poland. This was done unconvincingly. Neither material aid nor military support were used as bait to draw in the Poles. While it can be argued that the Poles were as unlikely to yield to such pressure as they were unrealistic about the extent of their military strength against Germany, it is worth noting that in any case British ministers did not want to pursue the Soviet enquiry.[53]

When the Soviet troops entered Polish territory on 17 September, that possibility had not been anticipated by the Poles.[54] At this stage Poland's defeat was assumed by the British to be a foregone conclusion. Therefore, on its own account, this new aggression did not cause any major revision of policy. Indeed, it is remarkable how little it seemed to have mattered to Halifax that Germany and the Soviet Union were acting jointly. When Raczyński called on the Foreign Office with a suggestion that the Polish government considered clause 1(b) of the Anglo-Polish Agreement, which referred to aggression by a 'European Power', as relating to the possibility of aggression by the Soviet Union, Halifax's response was straightforwardly hostile.[55] He told Raczyński: 'As regards Soviet aggression we were free to take our own decision and to decide whether to declare war on the USSR or not'.

Continuity with the policies pursued before the outbreak of the war was also maintained in Cabinet deliberations. During discussions on 18 September Cabinet members expressed a certain amount of abhorrence of Soviet actions nevertheless mingled with a keen appreciation for Britain's long-term objectives. The Prime Minister suggested that the Cabinet agree a statement condemning Soviet entry on to Polish territory. This statement, according to Chamberlain, was to confirm that Soviet action did not affect 'or weaken the obligation which we had solemnly undertaken towards Poland'. Finally, a commitment to the restoration of Poland after the war was to be repeated.[56] The Secretary for War felt that the crisis required a statement of some substance. He declared that '... the Empire was faced with a situation of grave peril, and he thought that the country should be stirred to make far greater efforts and submit to far greater sacrifices than were at present contemplated'.[57]

In reality, nothing was done. A British declaration of war on the Soviet Union could not have saved Poland anyway and, as far as British ministers were concerned, there was nothing to be gained from getting involved in a confrontation with the Soviet Union at this stage. Furthermore, the Soviet Union's economic potential and usefulness to Britain could not be disregarded. But even now British politicians and military leaders could neither fully comprehend the implications of German–Soviet co-operation nor speculate on the role that the Soviet Union might have in the future war. The Chiefs of Staff had a very low opinion of the Soviet military capability and their views reinforced the government's indecisive attitude towards the Soviet Union. As a result the government uttered only general statements of condemnation. It was felt that such statements left open the possibility of initiating future talks with the Soviet Union aimed at gaining access to Soviet economic resources.[58] It is clear from the course of the political and military discussions pursued by the government that once Poland fell attention was being focused not on the Soviet Union but on South-eastern Europe.[59]

Politicians in London were not oblivious to the fact that British inactivity in the face of German and later Soviet attacks on Poland was likely to be interpreted as a sign of weakness by neutral countries. The long-term objective of securing American support also meant that American public opinion had to be taken into account. The dilemma was not easily resolved. Reckless military assistance to Poland would have impaired Britain's future fighting potential, or so it was assumed. Aerial attacks on Germany carried the risk of drawing upon Britain the full might of the German bomber force, at a time when it was pre-sumed that the RAF Fighter Command was unlikely to be able to defend the British Isles. A public condemnation of the Soviet Union by the British government could have led to an irrevocable deterioration in British–Soviet relations, and this would affect adversely trading relations between the two countries. This in turn would weaken Britain's ability to pursue the long-term objective of defeating Germany.

The other side of the dilemma was that inactivity was leading to the collapse of Britain's standing in the eyes of the neutrals, of which Italy, Spain and Romania were considered to be of key importance. British politicians preferred to resolve their predicament by ignoring it and proceeding with short-term and piecemeal decisions in which British military and economic potential was only used with extreme caution. That very quandary and the inability of British statesmen to break away from traditional ways of thinking and approach the question of German aggression afresh is illustrated by an exchange between Lord Perth, the Minister of Information, and Alexander Cadogan, the Foreign Office Permanent Under-Secretary on 5 October. Lord Perth wrote:

> May I urge that the time has come to make known the existence of the secret protocol between Poland and ourselves, by which we were freed from the obligation to fight for Poland if she were attacked by Russia.
>
> In the first place I believe that the knowledge of this protocol might have a considerable effect on the Russian Government, who it seems to me are somewhat anxious that part of our war aims may be the return of the Polish state with the boundaries which it had previous to the outbreak of the war ... Secondly it would strengthen our moral position in various countries, particularly in the United States and Spain.[60]

Cadogan's response to this was to minute, perhaps a bit wearily, 'I think this might make our position a little better – only a little'.[61]

The British response to Soviet occupation of Poland's eastern terri-tories could not be seen outside the context of Britain's relations with other Central and South European states. At this early stage the question posed was what would be the consequences of a further deterioration in Britain's relations with the Soviet Union rather than what policy should be pursued. The British Ambassador in Moscow is quoted as saying that such a deterioration 'would benefit Germany without helping Poland'.[62] A hope emerged that the removal of the buffer which had hitherto existed between the two and the establishment of direct territorial contact between the Third Reich and the Soviet Union would precipitate a war between them. This much was said in a circular telegram to the Colonies and India, dated 19 September, explaining the attitude of His Majesty's Government towards the progress of the war. In it the Foreign Office went to great lengths to suggest that the Soviet entry on to Polish territory had not been an entirely unexpected event and that it should not therefore be seen as a deterioration in the situation and 'may well lead to a sharp conflict between Germany and Russia'.[63] Nevertheless, no study was undertaken of the possibility of joint action against Germany by Britain and the Soviet Union. Few British politicians had moved that far. Anxiety was expressed about future Soviet policy, in particular after the Soviet–German Agreement of 29 September. Political and military considerations were confined to the discussion of the implications of future Soviet actions for Afghanistan, the Balkans and finally Romania, which were regarded as areas of consequence for British trade and security.[64]

The inconsequence of British policies towards the Soviet Union was to a large extent caused by both Chamberlain's and Halifax's reluctance to adjust to the exigencies of the war. Bad leadership allowed the conflicts of interpretation which naturally prevailed within the Foreign Office to paralyse decision-making. Two contradictory views emerged there. On the one hand, Rab Butler, Parliamentary Under-Secretary of State, advocated a conciliatory approach towards the Soviet Union, based on the view that its assistance would be needed in the future. On the other hand, Cadogan took a less benevolent view of Soviet aims.[65] But as long as there was the slightest hope of persuading Stalin to join the anti-German bloc Britain could not commit itself to view the Soviet Union as Germany's ally, and Britain's enemy.[66]

A third factor affecting British–Soviet relations influenced the British government in assuming a pragmatic approach to the Soviet question. At the time of the Soviet entry on to Polish territory it would appear that the need for Russian timber made Britain reluctant to embark on a policy of symbolic gestures of condemnation of the Soviet Union. These would have been token gestures that were all that Britain could have done to show her disapproval. Britain was neither able nor willing to take action against the Soviet Union in defence of Poland. This impotence had already been exhibited in the German attack on Poland. By mid-October, trading agreements came to be the only subjects of direct communications between the Soviet Union and Britain.[67]

The indecisiveness of British policy and the inability of its ministers to determine exactly what they wanted from the Soviet Union was further manifested when an attempt was made to use Turkey to entice the Russians away from Germany, even if not into direct agreements with the Allies. Since a direct association with the Soviet Union was considered politically undesirable, it was decided in September to try and bring the Soviet issue into the current Anglo-Franco-Turkish talks. These were conducted with the aim of forging an alliance which would guarantee the security of the Balkans and the East Mediterranean. The Turks were simultaneously conducting talks with the Russians. In London it was hoped that encouraging the Turks to continue with these and assuring them that they would not be expected to go to war with the Soviet Union could start a diplomatic opening to the Soviet Union.[68] The ultimate objective was to reduce German influence in Turkey and the Soviet Union. This contrived plan failed when the Soviet–Turkish talks collapsed. The Turkish side had been willing to act as a linchpin between the Soviet Union and Britain and France. Unfortunately Stalin refused to use the Soviet–Turkish talks to reassure Turkey and indirectly also Britain and France that the Ribbentrop–Molotov Pact only related to Poland.[69] During his visit to Moscow in October the Turkish Foreign Minister was pressurized by Molotov to weaken Turkey's only recently initialled agreement with Britain and France. Since the Turks were not prepared to forgo their independence to so obvious an extent, their talks with the Soviet Union collapsed.[70] As a result British hopes for an indirect Soviet commitment to British interests were also thwarted.

The alternative to challenging Germany militarily was the pursuit of war by means of economic sanctions. In 1939 British politicians deluded themselves that much could be achieved to limit German strength through economic warfare: once key war materials were identified and denied to Germany, Britain would gain the upper hand in preparations for the final confrontation with Germany.[71] South-eastern Europe was considered a crucial area from which Germany was deriving vital raw materials. With few exceptions British politicians and military leaders believed that this type of warfare offered a cheap and reliable, as well as inconspicuous, method of curbing Germany. Unfortunately there was a visible dearth of realism and sound planning.

In early September limited plans were made for denying Germany oil from Romania. Pre-emptive purchases were made of stocks and future output from Romanian oil wells. These efforts were closely linked to hopes for the establishment of a neutral Balkan bloc. Since 1936, when it noted the growth of German economic and political influence in the Balkans, the Foreign Office had advocated that the British government should offer money to these states in the form of subsidies for trade, loans and bribes. In this way they hoped to 'purchase' a pro-British orientation and secure political influence in the Balkans. Before the outbreak of the war the Treasury successfully opposed these plans.

In September 1939 British official policy had once more changed. The realization that Germany's influence in Europe as well as her belligerence were extending made the government now view in a more sinister light what, when first recognized by the Foreign Office in 1936 and again in 1938, had been seen initially as a desirable process. In September 1939 British policy changed to a more active pursuit of influence in the Balkans. Within the Foreign Office the opinion was expressed that the limiting of German economic influence in the Balkans was of crucial importance, possibly the only way of combating the aggressor in Europe. At the same time it was assumed that there existed a residual pool of goodwill towards Britain in the region which only needed to be activated.[72] It was also hoped that, by remaining neutral, the Balkan countries would deny Germany their resources. It followed that Balkan neutrality would be beneficial to Britain while being injurious to Germany's interest. Apparently in the world inhabited by British politicians, trading partners, in particular Balkan ones, did not cheat and most certainly did not take advantage of diplomatic suitors to increase the price of goods.

On 18 September the Cabinet outlined its position on Balkan neutrality:

(a) It was desirable to secure Balkan neutrality if this were practicable, but we should keep ourselves free from unnecessary commitments as to our attitude in the event of a conflagration in the Balkans.

(b) If war broke out in the Balkans this country would want all the friends she could get, and it would be essential that we should be free to send aid to those countries which sided with us.[73]

In order to achieve these policy objectives the issues of British policy towards the Soviet Union and aid to the Balkans had to be resolved. The failure to address them inhibited the success of any plans and schemes which further undermined British influence and prestige. This was most apparent in the case of Romania, the central theatre of British economic warfare against Germany.

The Romanian government had good reasons to presume that

German–Soviet co-operation would lead to an agreement between the two powers over the disputed areas of Bessarabia. The Romanians' main concern therefore was to obtain British support for a gesture of warning to the Soviet Union. They feared that, like Poland, they would fall victim to a Soviet revision of territorial grievances, which would obtain German acquiescence. Therefore on 28 September Virgil Tilea, the Romanian Minister in London, met Cadogan to enquire whether the British commitment was also valid against the Soviet Union. Cadogan's answer spanned the contradictions in his government's policy. He assured Tilea that the British guarantee could not be invoked against the Soviet Union. But he asked that this issue should not be raised publicly. Both men agreed that were these points to be raised officially, British dissociation could be seen as an incitement to Soviet aggression.[74] Tilea returned to the subject in a conversation with Halifax on 17 October. The British view was that no purpose 'would be served by starting hostilities with an additional enemy in the shape of the Soviet Union'.[75]

Such frankness was to have predictable consequences. Any attempt to limit the growth of German influence and to undermine her war capability by economizing on the British commitment could not succeed. Britain was then heavily involved in pre-emptive purchases of Romanian oil and was dependent on Romanian goodwill to withhold from Germany as much of her output as possible. In addition a scheme was devised whereby barges and rolling stock were chartered to prevent Germany from transporting oil out of Romania.[76] Military plans were being developed for mining oil wells in the event of a German incursion into Romania.[77] In both schemes the British depended heavily on Romanian co-operation since British troops were not going to be sent to Romania, either to implement these plans or to defend Romania in the event of a confrontation with Germany. By 13 November the Cabinet Committee which had been established to deal with oil admitted that the policy of pre-emptive purchases from Romania had been a failure and that British political influence in the Balkans was negligible.[78] Britain's policy in South-eastern Europe was indeed 'a story of last-minute improvisations and the undertaking of commitments without the resources to fulfil them'.[79]

In the north, the idea of restricting German access to vital raw materials led Britain into negotiations with Sweden. Even though the Baltic and the Scandinavian states, notably Norway, were suppliers of materials to Britain at the beginning of the war, British diplomatic efforts, constrained as they were by the German blockade of Scandinavian trade with Britain, went in the direction of preventing Germany increasing her supplies from that region rather than enhancing British purchases.[80] Likewise the British–Swedish gentlemen's agreement, negotiated between September and December 1939, only committed Sweden not to exceed pre-war levels of exports to Germany.[81]

Romanian oil and Swedish iron ore were two items on the Foreign Office's long list of goods to be denied to Germany. Other items and other countries were drawn into this policy. An important feature of these arrangements was the limited degree of British involvement while not pledging Britain's resources. Britain had access to considerable resources from the empire and the Commonwealth. This, it was believed, was secured through Britain's 'command of the seas'. 'But the maintenance of that command absorbed a high proportion of the resources which it made available'.[82]

The defence of British trading routes required control of the Mediterranean. Turkey was identified as the only state likely to be able to mount a defence of that region. But an effective defence required a major financial and military contribution from the British and French to prepare Turkey for that task. The western powers might have preferred Turkey to remain neutral, but ready to assist either Romania or Greece in accordance with agreements signed earlier with both states. For her part Turkey was anxious about Italy and did not share the British conviction that Italy was likely to remain neutral.[83] In the end their anxiety about defence of the Middle East was so great that the British and the French bowed to Turkish demands and signed an agreement promising extensive economic assistance to Turkey in return for nothing more than a commitment to neutrality.[84] At the end of December the Supreme War Council confirmed that all diplomatic efforts were to concentrate on keeping Italy out of the war and on committing the Balkan states to neutrality. Henceforth the attitudes of Italy and Turkey would be the key factors in the discussion of the Balkan front.

The idea of a neutral Balkan bloc took into account the possibility of Britain having to take action to destroy Romanian oilfields. If this happened Turkish and Bulgarian neutrality would have to be retained. In the case of Bulgaria British and French diplomacy seemed to have had some limited success in so far as King Boris accepted a British declaration that Bulgarian neutrality would be maintained if the British had to intervene militarily in Romania.[85] In reality British influence proved to be too tenuous to persuade Boris to maintain a pro-British neutrality. At the beginning of 1940 Bulgaria started to move towards the German camp, a move that accelerated after the fall of France.

By the end of 1939 Turkey, the linchpin of Britain's Balkan policy, also seemed less open to British influence. It had been hoped that the Turks would permit the establishment of a British naval base on the Turkish coast. These plans came to nothing in spite of Turkey being in receipt of extensive British credits and military supplies.[86] Notwithstanding diplomatic and military efforts, by the end of 1939 the concept of a Balkan front seemed more distant than it did in September.

At the root of Britain's inability to build a pro-British bloc in the Balkans lay the simple fact that Britain did not have the resources either to station troops there or to build up the military strength of the Balkan states. In any case territorial and ethnic conflicts would have created insurmountable obstacles in any attempt to create a united Balkan response to German aggression. The lack of resources effectively doomed all plans. During the meetings of the Supreme War Council it quickly became apparent that Chamberlain had hoped that the French would take the lead in building a Balkan front. It was also felt by the British that France had already established some links by opening talks with the Balkan states. The French Prime Minister Edouard Daladier had apparently considered the key issues and, at the second meeting of the Supreme War Council on 22 September, advanced developed plans for stationing troops either in Salonica or Constantinople.[87] Even then he admitted that the troops available would amount to no more than a token force.

At the fourth meeting of the Supreme War Council on 19 December Daladier informed Chamberlain that sending an expeditionary force to the Balkans 'would be a dangerous mistake'.[88] By then the French admitted, and the British concurred, that diplomatic efforts in the Balkans had not been successful and that the question of the Italian response to their efforts paralysed any initiatives. Until the German attack on France, as a result of which Italy also declared war on France, both British and French statesmen continued to hope that Italian neutrality could still be secured. Any precipitous action in the Balkans, it was feared, could give Italy the wrong signals and force her into Germany's arms. The British and French delegations to the Supreme War Council agreed that neither would despatch armed forces to the Balkans and that military contacts would not be extended beyond those which had already been taking place.[89]

By December Britain's short-lived involvement in Eastern Europe had effectively come to an end. British plans for the future war focused on the Western front, economic warfare and naval action. The Eastern front, which had only been considered since March 1939, now became a vague and unreal concept. The Soviet Union, events in the Balkans, and by November the question of Finland, were worrying but still distant issues.

A consequence of Britain's failed attempts to constrain Germany by diplomatic and economic means was to confirm the British reluctance to view European security as a priority. British politicians broadened their perspective rather than focusing it on the German question, and increasingly viewed the war in terms of supplies and supply lines. Guaranteeing these was a global and complex undertaking which came to dominate military thinking, making European considerations peripheral. Before the war the diplomatic focus had been global, while the first months of the war were marked by diplomatic blunders and plain misjudgments. When the moment would come to speak of the liberation of Europe, Britain was going to have to build new bridges and to court new elites. For small neutral states, be they Scandinavian or Balkan, Britain could not have been an obvious ally. To the Poles, it was natural to look to the French, in the hope that their military plans for fighting Germany would offer Poles an opportunity for military co-operation with France. A Franco-Polish alliance was more likely to support pre-war Poland's post-war territorial objectives and political aspirations.

3   Britain's only fighting ally

The Polish government-in-exile's ambition to be accorded the status of a major ally was achieved ironically, and briefly, during the period between the fall of France and the German attack on the Soviet Union. For one whole year, the Poles felt that they and Britain faced the German menace united in purpose. Furthermore, as they were wont to stress in future war years, Poland was then Britain's only fighting ally. The government-in-exile failed to note that this prestigious association had only come about in the wake of the defeat of France. The very exclusiveness of the alliance at that time decreased the likelihood of the Polish exile army fighting on the continent of Europe. As long as there had been a hope of France leading the struggle to defeat Germany, the Poles could plan for continental action and direct participation in the liberation of Poland. In 1940 Britain, with a penchant to plan for the defeat of Germany by indirect means and an unwillingness to address the question of the Soviet Union, was the worst of the two possible Allies for the Poles. Between the summer of 1940 and the summer of 1941, the status and recognition obtained by the Poles was achieved at the expense of their stated military and political objectives. Within two months of the outbreak of the war most British politicians had consigned the fate of Poland to the distant outcome of that war. The Balkan front too appeared to have become less of a reality than it had been in September.

Attempts to stem the continuing growth of German power by encouraging other states to oppose the aggressor were doomed to failure unless Britain and France were themselves seen to be taking action. Accordingly, even when Britain and France were willing to assist Germany's potential victims they were to find that neutral countries preferred to accommodate German demands, rather than receive western aid. The very concept of a French- and British-led European campaign became hazier as the German army appeared unwilling to follow up the Polish victory with an attack west. While the initiative remained firmly in German hands British and French differences increased, culminating in the misconceived Finnish campaign and the failed Norwegian one.

The Finnish issue is a good illustration of the way in which the various British government and military authorities disagreed over the fundamental and general question of how the war should be pursued. In October 1939 news was received that the Soviet Union proposed to the Finnish government an agreement whereby the Soviet government would lease military bases in return for areas of Soviet Karelia. In London these events were analysed in the context of the ongoing British–Soviet trade talks. The Cabinet believed that these would offer the Soviet Union an opportunity to distance itself from Germany.[1] The nature of Soviet–German co-operation was little understood in London and its economic consequences were underestimated. In any event no one within the British government sought a confrontation with the Soviet Union. During the following months the escalating Finnish–Soviet conflict gradually changed this view. The Northern Department of the Foreign Office advocated a policy of encouraging small neutral states to stand up to the aggressors. There was also strong public support for Finland. By 30 November, the date of the Soviet attack on Finland, the British Cabinet had come to view the Finnish problem from the perspective of British interests in the Baltic. The much debated, but as yet not very successful economic warfare against Germany was introduced into the debate. The reasoning went along the following lines: Soviet control of Finland combined with the possibility of a German attack on Norway and Sweden would establish enemy control over the Swedish iron-ore mines and the supply routes through the Norwegian port of Narvik.[2]

The French saw the Finnish–Soviet conflict as an opportunity that was too good to be missed. Unhampered by British anxiety about alienating the Soviet Union, the Daladier government sought to mobilize forces for a major war of intervention. Its objectives had less to do with the defence of Finland and more to do with the opportunity it offered for an attack on the Soviet–German alliance.[3] Their ultimate objective was a major continental offensive, which would draw in Britain and cause wavering neutrals to overcome their doubts and throw in their lot with France and Britain.

From December 1939 onwards the British and French argued in the Supreme War Council over their plans. The French championed aid to Finland, whereas the British sought to use the conflict to draw neutral

Sweden and Norway into their fold in return for the defence of their territory against a possible German attack. The British assumed that Sweden and Norway would be eager to obtain allied aid and would be only too happy to defend Finland if assured assistance against Germany. On 12 March Finland and the Soviet Union signed a peace treaty thus ending allied debates on whether or not to take action. Even though the Finnish issue appeared to have resolved itself plans for intervention in Scandinavia survived while the question of what could be done to disrupt the supply of Swedish ore to Germany remained very much on the agenda of allied discussions.

The western Allies did not fully realize that neutral governments had their own ideas on the desirability of being seen to co-operate with Britain and France. In particular neutral states were unwilling to allow British and French troops and naval units to operate on their territories. Therefore, if the Allies wanted to secure the ore fields and the supply routes to Narvik they would have to take military action against Norway and Sweden. During the course of the Finnish–Soviet war both Scandinavian governments made it clear that they neither welcomed British suggestions that they should defend Finland nor were they willing to consider offers of assistance against Germany.[4] Hoping that the Scandinavian countries would nevertheless come round to the British view the Allies started laying mines in Norwegian territorial waters on 8 April 1940. A day later Germany attacked Norway. Only then did the Norwegian government reluctantly permit allied action on its territory. But in spite of embarking on a military campaign which escalated from a commitment of 8,000 to one of 60,000 men, little could be done to prevent Scandinavia succumbing to Germany. Within weeks Norway was occupied, and Sweden chose strict neutrality.

The Finnish–Soviet conflict and the Norwegian campaign were clearly military campaigns for which the British had not been prepared. Both offered limited scope for action since the background and implications of hostilities were extremely complex. In any case the Baltic and Scandinavia were peripheral to British military priorities.

The same cannot be said of the Franco-German campaign. French and British inactivity in the east since September 1939 was explained by the allied governments' preoccupation with the Western front, its military demands and the continuing need to build up resources for the German attack in that direction. The alliance with France had been the central plank of Britain's European policy. Detailed staff talks which had been conducted jointly since May 1939 were aimed at defining the precise contribution of each side to the forthcoming war. Naturally, it was understood that France was going to shoulder the burden of land fighting. The British Expeditionary Force scheduled for action in France, though a small one in relation to French needs, represented the maximum contribution which could be made at the time. By April 1940 four British divisions were in place in France. Further Territorial divisions were to follow.[5]

The biggest bone of contention between the two Allies was the question of the use of the RAF in the planned French campaign. In September 1939 the British Chiefs of Staff had planned to use the ten available squadrons of the British Advanced Air Striking Force to bomb German communications and industrial installations. The French, seeking to avoid provoking a German air strike on French cities, insisted on using the air force only to support land operations.[6] At the time of the German attack on the Low Countries on 10 May, Franco-British discussions on the use of British bombers operating from France were inconclusive and the French preference for not taking action against targets in Germany remained the agreed joint policy.[7]

Behind these discussions lay the British conviction that the French land forces were capable of defending the Western front. British commanders generally believed that the French were up to the task. Indeed, as they openly admitted, they had no choice but to cling to that conviction, for they knew their own resources to be inadequate. British military plans assumed that Britain's role was to build up and assist the French war effort.[8]

The Franco-German war went disastrously wrong for the Allies from the beginning. By 15 May 1940 Churchill, who on 10 May became Prime Minister, instructed his Chiefs of Staff to consider the possibility of a French defeat. The conclusions that he and the military leaders came to were brutal. Britain was prepared to back France fully but only to a point where Britain's capacity to continue the war was not affected.[9] With the fall of France Britain's continental policy, hitherto based on the assumption that any fighting in Western Europe would be a French affair, was in tatters. Henceforth Britain's war against Germany was to be concentrated on retaining control of the seas and aerial command over Britain.[10] Future plans for action in Western Europe were left vague and complicated by the conflicting policies towards the Vichy government. In the short term the British were anxious to prevent the resources of the French empire and the French navy being used by Germany. In the long term plans for the liberation of Europe assumed that some co-operation from the French people would be vital.[11] Throughout the remaining months of 1940 and 1941 a variety of initially official and later unofficial attempts were pursued by the British government to establish links with the Vichy government. None of them were successful and the question of the liberation of France was relegated to plans for a post-war Europe.[12] In any case neither in 1940 nor in 1941 was it possible to plan for a new Western front. With that plans for continental action were temporarily shelved. To the Polish government-in-exile which arrived in Britain after the fall of France this meant the conclusive relegation of any plans for the liberation of Poland to an increasingly distant future. The Sikorski government had assumed that its troops would enter Poland from the west and south. The shelving of plans for a Western front at a time when the Balkan front appeared to be a hazy and increasingly unreal prospect reduced all its military options to only one, namely military co-operation with Britain on fronts which might have more to do with British imperial considerations and broad strategic needs. The commitment to the stated British objective of the ultimate defeat of Germany now meant that the Polish military contribution could no longer be tied to liberating and assuming control over Poland.

In British relations with the Polish government-in-exile Britain's policy towards the Soviet Union would become the most contentious issue and the most obvious obstacle to Poland being granted full recognition as an esteemed and valued partner. At least that is how it seemed. The apparent unwillingness of the British government to champion the Polish cause seemed to be connected with Britain's determination to seek co-operation with the Soviet government. The reality was much more complex since the Soviet issue too often offered an obvious explanation for British unwillingness to show appreciation for the Polish ally and the Polish military contribution to the joint war effort. A closer scrutiny of British policies towards the Polish question in general and the Polish government in particular shows that at least two, sometimes more, strands of policy evolved between 1940 and 1943. On the one hand there were not always consistent attempts to seek the Soviet government's collaboration with the British war effort. On the other hand a realistic appreciation prevailed within the Foreign Office and the government ranks that at the end of the war Britain was unlikely to assume the initiative in Eastern Europe. They were therefore unwilling to encourage excessive political and territorial hopes among the exile governments. At times these two policies were interdependent. But British determination not to encourage the Poles and not to give in to their demands was not always linked to the course of British–Soviet relations.

The Soviet Union occupied the attention of British politicians and civil servants, albeit in an inconsistent way, throughout 1940 and the first half of 1941, and thus even before the German attack on Soviet territory. The variety of attitudes and approaches to the subject of the Soviet Union within the government has already been mentioned. When the extent of Soviet diplomatic pressure on Finland became known in November 1939 some within the Foreign Office favoured direct intervention against the Soviet Union.[13] Others were not convinced of the need to consider the Soviet Union as a potential ally. Orme Sargent, the Deputy Under-Secretary of State, reflected the confusion of ideas which prevailed within the Foreign Office when he indicated that it was not clear to him what Britain's policy was towards the Soviet Union. Rab Butler, another Under-Secretary, strongly advocated long-term co-operation with the Soviet Union. Sir Robert Vansittart, the Diplomatic Advisor to the Cabinet, saw Soviet policy as nothing other than naked aggression and accordingly advised that the destruction of the Soviet Union should be one of Britain's aims.[14] The Chiefs of Staff on the other hand discouraged the belief that a swift knock-out attack against the Soviet Union was possible.[15] But within the War Office there were those who felt that the bombing of the Baku oilfields offered an easy way of destroying Soviet oil production and with it stopping Germany from obtaining vital raw materials.[16] At the same time the Cabinet was willing to heed a suggestion made by the Soviet Ambassador in London, Ivan Maisky, that trade talks between Britain and the Soviet Union should continue.[17]

This divergence and the resulting confusion of ideas had arisen because no consistent attempt had been made to analyse the role of the Soviet Union in Britain's war against Germany. As a result each issue was analysed in isolation from the broad problem of the war and was viewed merely as a difficulty, be it of the supply of timber or oil for Germany, or the need to protest or otherwise at the Soviet occupation of Polish or Baltic state territories. In some cases there appeared good reasons for taking action against the Soviet Union. In others there were equally valid reasons for moderation and circumspection.

There is a general consensus among historians that the despatch to Moscow of Sir Stafford Cripps, a well-known Socialist and Labour MP, in May 1940 did not mark a new orientation in the British government's policy towards the Soviet Union.[18] This had not been a government initiative in the first place. Cripps had put forward the idea of going there without any prompting from either Maisky or any of the British politicians. Nevertheless by the time he returned from his private and unexpected visit to Moscow in April 1940 his advocacy of the need to renew relations with the Soviet Union coincided with ideas which had been voiced by a number of other individuals.[19] These ranged from Andrew Rothstein, a journalist member of the Communist Party, on one political extreme, to the Beaverbrook press on the other. In common with others they expressed unease at the possibility of war being fought without Soviet assistance.[20] According to Gorodetsky, the reluctant appointment of Cripps as Ambassador to Moscow 'sealed the debate raging in the Foreign Office through the 1930s on the advisability of improving relations with Russia . . .'.[21]

The fall of France gave an additional impetus to the change of attitude which was emerging very slowly within the Foreign Office. When in May the Cabinet appointed Cripps to go to Moscow, it was with the aim of smoothing the way for barter agreements.[22] Only after his departure for Moscow was it decided to upgrade the appointment to ambassadorial rank. The Foreign Office had not considered the question of Soviet policy objectives to be a high priority. Other, more pressing issues, most notably military developments in France, preoccupied British politicians.[23]

The circumstances of Cripps' appointment and the conflict between his own clearly stated objective of securing Moscow's trust and the Foreign Office's unfocused approach to the Soviet question explain why throughout his stay in the Soviet Union Cripps frequently appeared to be pursuing unauthorized initiatives. In most cases his differences with the Foreign Office were not over key policy objectives but over how best to approach a given problem. Cripps was determined to persuade the Foreign Office to come round to his view that the Soviet Union was willing to enter into talks with Britain. He believed it to be his role to create preconditions for the Soviet leadership to abandon its alliance with Germany.[24] Halifax and the Foreign Office assumed that pragmatism was causing the Soviet leaders to continue co-operation with Germany. They were therefore less inclined to depend on persuasion as a means of drawing the Soviet Union towards Britain.[25]

The result was that while Cripps aimed at developing the basis for long-term relations with the Soviet Union the Foreign Office remained reluctant to assume the initiative. Departmental heads were only too well aware that there was nothing Britain had to offer the Soviet Union and therefore there were few reasons for it to co-operate with

Britain. In any case Soviet actions did not indicate any willingness to break with Germany. The occupation of the Baltic states and subsequent action in Bessarabia in the summer of 1940 added to the potential sources of distrust between Britain and the Soviet Union. Cripps' attempts to explain the Soviet perspective were not heeded by Foreign Office civil servants or the Foreign Secretary.

On 22 October 1940 Cripps communicated to the Soviet government an unusual statement in which to some extent he exceeded Foreign Office instructions. He stated that Britain would be prepared to recognize *de facto* Soviet occupation of the Baltic states, Bessarabia, Bukovina and the Polish eastern regions recently incorporated into Soviet territories. In addition the British government would undertake not to enter into anti-Soviet agreements for the duration of the war. This initiative was badly thought out. Cripps had earlier been putting pressure on the Foreign Office to address issues to which the Soviet Union was sensitive, most notably post-war territorial readjustments. His efforts were rewarded in so far as he received a vaguely worded authorization to open discussion with the Soviet leaders on these subjects. Cripps exceeded even these instructions. Although he had not been authorized to raise the question of Polish borders, he did so. The Soviet view was that the lack of precision in issuing directives to Cripps was evidence of the lack of importance attached by the Foreign Office to the proposal.[26] There is no doubt that Halifax had hoped for improved relations between the Soviet Union and Turkey, believing that this process would assist the British in their negotiations with Turkey. Halifax's reasoning was that if Turkey's anxiety about the Soviet Union could be allayed, Turkey would be less dependent on Germany and therefore more willing to associate with Britain. In any case the British–Turkish talks were inconclusive and Cripps' startling proposal to discuss the Polish border rectifications remained unanswered until February 1941 when it was rejected by the Soviet authorities.

The change of leadership was an additional factor in the inconsistencies of British policies towards the Soviet Union and Eastern Europe as a whole. Chamberlain's hostility to the Soviet Union was legendary. Hence, little guidance was given to the Foreign Office in its search for a definition of British interests in Eastern and Central Europe. Churchill's feelings about the Soviet Union and Stalin were considerably more complex. Without pretending to be impressed by Soviet achievements, Churchill was capable of appreciating the stark reality that Soviet participation in the war on Britain's side would make Britain's task immeasurably easier. On assuming the leadership of the British government, Churchill took a wide interest in all matters of the conduct of the war. His comments figure clearly on Foreign Office memoranda and his instructions tended to be precise and emphatic. Unfortunately while Churchill's interest in certain subjects was keen, he could be equally negligent of other matters. His initiatives and sporadic enthusiasms were not always helpful in the conduct of foreign relations.

Poland and matters relating to the Sikorski government did attract his attention. As a result, Churchill's instructions and comments frequently appear on files about relatively routine matters. This can give the impression that Churchill attached importance to Poland whereas, in reality, he maintained a sympathetic interest in the Polish government-in-exile, rather than support for the Polish cause. Sikorski enjoyed relatively easy access to Churchill. This was irksome to the Foreign Office since the Poles frequently went to the very top, rather than availing themselves of the usual formal channels of communication through the British Ambassador to the Polish government. Although Churchill's interest in Soviet and Polish subjects was inconsistent it was nevertheless noticeable and lively. That they were at least heeded was an illusion to which the Poles easily succumbed, as might any historian of the subject. As a consequence the Polish government's disappointments were readily linked to the British government's increased preoccupation with the Soviet Union, even when this was not the case.

In the autumn of 1940 Britain's attention was forcefully diverted from European issues to the Balkans and Asia Minor. The Italian attack on Greece on 28 October came at a time of intense discussions within the War Office and Cabinet on the desirability of taking action against Italy in North West Africa. At stake were not merely British communication lines through the Mediterranean but also the position of Turkey in the war. Once more the question of a Balkan front surfaced. Anthony Eden, who had already taken an interest in the Middle East in his capacity as Minister for War, a post to which he was appointed on 12 May 1940, supported the idea of a Balkan front. On 23 December 1940 Eden took over the Foreign Office. He advocated the idea of a Balkan front, disingenuously hoping to bring Turkey closer to Britain, but he was unsuccessful.[27] On 6 April 1941 Germany attacked Yugoslavia and Greece. Bulgaria in the meantime had gone over to the German side. Eden's extensive negotiations had failed to convince any of the Balkan states of the need to oppose Germany and to aid Greece.

The failure to draw Turkey into an anti-German agreement was the most important diplomatic failure of the first months of 1941.[28] The loss of Greece and the evident British inability to impress the Balkan states would blight any future plans for a British-led Balkan war of liberation as well as Polish hopes for a return to Poland from the south. The loss of the Balkans, like the fall of France, further emphasized that the liberation of Poland, placed in the midst of enemy territory, would have to await the final and total destruction of the German empire.

Developments in South-eastern Europe gave Churchill an early opportunity to try to persuade Stalin that Britain should be trusted. Having learned from Enigma de-crypts that prior to moving into Yugoslavia Germany had moved troops to the border with the Soviet Union, Churchill instructed Cripps on 3 April 1941 to inform Stalin of these developments.[29] The initiative failed when Stalin did not respond. Churchill's motives were revealed a few weeks later. In a House of Commons speech on 9 April he explained that were Germany to gain control of the Ukraine and Caucasus she would obtain raw materials vital to the defeat of Great Britain.[30]

The British establishment rightly assumed from the outset of the war that the Poles would be difficult Allies. As will be shown, on arriving in Britain Polish politicians and officers proceeded loudly and very publicly to fight each other. This undoubtedly explains why on 9 July 1940 Victor Cazalet, Conservative MP for Chippenham, was appointed Political Liaison Officer to General Sikorski. In April 1940 Cazalet had visited Polish units in France as part of a parliamentary group. He was enchanted by them. Within the next few weeks a deep and lasting friendship developed between Sikorski and Cazalet who became his champion in Britain.[31] According to Cazalet's biographer his role was to 'smooth relations between the British Government and the Poles, and also to reduce the tensions and animosities within the ranks of the Free Polish Government'.[32] This was an unusual appointment since, in addition to direct contacts between the British government and the Polish government-in-exile, the usual consular staff continued to function. It could be claimed that Cazalet's appointment reflected the importance attached by Churchill to the Poles. It is more likely that the perceived need to accommodate and soothe a rather difficult ally justified it. In any case, neither the Foreign Office nor the War Office welcomed the appointment. There was a feeling that Cazalet was unduly sympathetic to the Polish cause. Frank Roberts minuted on the 9 July, 'The War Office take a very gloomy view indeed of Major Cazalet's functions, and insist that they are purely political. This means that we shall have to be very careful that he does not interfere too much in diplomatic matters'.[33] Colonel Bridges had already been appointed Military Liaison Officer with the Poles, a post he continued to hold.

Immediately on arrival in London, various members of the Polish government proceeded to wage a bitter war of attrition against particular individuals and groups, but most notably against the Prime Minister, Sikorski. Sikorski responded in kind, preparing plans to purge the ranks of government employees and the officer corps of supporters of the pre-war government. The first public sign of internal friction was noted when President Raczkiewicz and his entourage arrived in London on 21 June 1940. He was not met by Sikorski, whose absence was justified by the need to rest after the ordeals in France. During the next few days no attempt was made by Sikorski to see the President or the Minister for Foreign Affairs, Zaleski.[34] Raczkiewicz responded by dismissing Sikorski and appointing Zaleski as his successor. The crisis dragged on for a month, in the course of which more individuals pitched their own particular grudges into the simmering pot of disunity. The protagonists were divided into the supporters of Sikorski and his policies on the one hand and representatives of the pre-war government and bearers of assorted grievances on the other hand. The impasse was ended when a number of officers from Sikorski's entourage visited Zaleski and threatened physical violence unless he declined the President's request to form a new government. The *pronunciamento* overcame the present difficulty without resolving anything. But the crisis signalled to British civil servants and politicians the need to pay attention to Sikorski's relations with the army. It also alerted them to Sikorski's precarious position within his own government.

Attacks on Sikorski continued from several quarters. The most serious accusation concerned his initiative in relation to the Soviet Union. During a lightning visit to London, at the time of the French armistice talks with Germany, Sikorski instructed his friend Stefan Litauer, the head of PAT (the Polish news agency in London) to prepare a memorandum to Churchill summarizing the Polish attitude towards possible contacts with the Soviet Union. Sikorski handed this memorandum to Halifax. The most controversial point in it was a declaration that the present government would be prepared to consider certain territorial adjustments on the border with the Soviet Union.[35] As if that were not startling enough, the memorandum proceeded to suggest that in Soviet-occupied Polish territories a Polish army should be raised which would co-operate with the Red Army. The crisis which ensued in the Polish government during the following months tested the limits of Sikorski's authority and for the time being ended any hopes of establishing indirect contacts with the Soviet authorities.

The most important question asked by historians since then is what Sikorski hoped to gain by making such a suggestion at a time when the Soviet Union was clearly Germany's ally and one of the two occupying powers. It has been claimed that Sikorski believed incorrectly but nevertheless sincerely that the Soviet Union had recently signalled its willingness to re-establish relations with Poland. That was what he had told Kennard, the British Ambassador.[36] It is difficult to see how he had arrived at such a conclusion. The most obvious explanation for Sikorski's willingness to seek a *rapprochement* with the Soviet Union is that he wanted to recruit the Polish men there into the exile Polish army.[37] This suggests that Sikorski did not have a realistic appreciation that the Soviet Union was likely in due course to become Britain's ally. He merely wanted to gain access to Polish manpower in order to establish in Britain the political authority of the exile government by creating a strong and numerous Polish army-in-exile. His initiative was premature and other Polish politicians were able to forestall it.

Opposition to Sikorski spread beyond the relatively small circle of government ministers. His enemies made a conscious effort to undermine military discipline and to mobilize the officer corps against his policies. On 8 June Łukasiewicz sent an open letter from Paris in which he accused Sikorski of having divided the *émigré* community and, most critically of all, of having lost the whole of the Polish army so painstakingly built up in France by his bad military judgment.[38] Łukasiewicz was a prominent member of the Piłsudski faction. His attack was seen as the first shot in an open war against Sikorski. Copies of this letter were circulated among Polish army officers who had managed to get to Britain and had been moved to Scotland. This letter was distributed together with another one, written by General Dąb-Biernacki, one of the commanders in the September campaign. Dąb-Biernacki had been particularly badly treated in France by Sikorski who had had him imprisoned in the penal camp at Cesiray. He accused Sikorski of failing to build on the achievements of the Piłsudski period and subjugating himself and the Polish army-in-exile to French needs.[39] Both letters were used by the President to attack Sikorski and galvanize the supporters of the old regime. More worrying to Sikorski was the ready audience that both letters found among disgruntled army officers and government officials.

The Polish infantry which had been rescued from France had been moved immediately to the region of Perth. The officer corps, mostly followers of Piłsudski, had succeeded in making their way to Britain, as they had previously to France, in disproportionately larger numbers in relation to non-commissioned officers and other ranks. Accommodation was rudimentary and discontent was widely voiced. Failure to obtain commissions, the general insecurity and demoralization led to a high degree of politicization. Although Sikorski was committed to building a new Polish army, there were few if any areas where recruitment could take place. For the time being grandiose plans for assembling the First Polish Army Corps in Scotland had to remain on paper. Opposition among the officer corps was tackled by creating a place of compulsory settlement for officers in Rothesay on the island of Bute. Officially the officers sent there were merely surplus to current requirements and were awaiting commissions. But it was well known that Rothesay was a detention camp for officers who opposed Sikorski.[40] By the autumn of 1940 two additional centres, essentially military penal camps, were set up by the Polish government in mainland Scotland at Kingleddors and Tainachbrach, the latter for 'moral deviants'.[41] Unfortunately for the Poles rumours started circulating within the British labour movement and Jewish communities that the bulk of soldiers incarcerated there were Communists and/or Jews. An army commission was set up by the Poles to investigate these rumours. It was somewhat puzzled to find among the camp inmates an articulate and astoundingly fluent English-speaker, 'for a Jew' as the commission noted, who turned out to be Isaac Deutscher, a recent volunteer to the Polish army. When finally released from the Polish army Deutscher returned to London to write for *The Observer* and *The Economist*.

But Sikorski had to contend not only with attacks from within his own community. When he arrived in London he had no assurance that the British government would agree with Polish territorial and political objectives. Anxiety over British motives seems to have been ever present in Sikorski's mind and explains some of his initiatives. During the conversation which Sikorski had had with Halifax on 19 June 1940 the latter broached the subject of allied relations with the Soviet Union. Halifax informed the Polish Prime Minister that Cripps had been despatched to Moscow with the aim of 'finding some basis for agreement which might contribute towards weakening the Soviet

Union's co-operation with Germany'.[42] No offer was made by Halifax for Britain to take up the Polish case over the Polish territory occupied by the Soviet Union. Instead he made a rather detached suggestion which implied that Polish–Soviet relations were entirely a matter for the Poles. Halifax noted this as follows: 'If the Polish Government for their part were able to take parallel action with a view to winning the goodwill of the Soviet Government I felt it would be all to the good'.[43] Sikorski did not have to be a very perceptive listener to hear in these pronouncements a hint of opportunism. The Soviet Union had gone to great lengths to give legitimacy to their occupation of Polish Ukraine and Byelorussia by holding elections in those territories. It was obvious that the question of British recognition of the Soviet acquisition of those territories was going to arise in any diplomatic talks between Britain and the Soviet Union.

War aims were the subject of frequent discussions within the Polish government during the autumn of 1940. There was an obvious need for the Poles to obtain some commitments from the British government to the restoration of territories occupied by the Soviet Union. They notably failed in their efforts to obtain this. The most that the British had been prepared to commit themselves to was expressed in the Military Agreement signed by both sides on 5 August. This was a statement of joint 'determination to prosecute the war to a successful conclusion'.[44] The matter was made worse by Churchill's assurance in the House of Commons on 5 September that Britain had not made any commitment to post-war borders.[45] When rumours reached the Poles about Cripps' approach to Stalin they decided to challenge the British. In an interview Zaleski had with Halifax on 18 November the Polish Minister sought to elicit a sympathetic response to the Polish aims. Zaleski tersely told Halifax:

> His Government ... had consistently tried to facilitate the task of His Majesty's Government, since Great Britain was not at war with the Soviet Union, by not making too much of the fact that Poland on the other hand was; and they for their part had been under the impression that, whatever policy His Majesty's Government might be forced to adopt towards the Soviet Union in the course of the war, no definitive proposals would be made to the Soviet Government without previous consultations with the Polish Government as between Allies.[46]

Following this approach, the Poles presented a memorandum summing up their war aims.[47] In it they expressed the hope that after the war Britain would seek to maintain a counterweight to Germany in

Europe and would therefore support a Middle European Federation dominated by Poland and Czechoslovakia. The Soviet Union was dismissed by the Poles as a state with 'Asiatic interests' whose potential, they believed, had clearly been overestimated. Therefore they suggested that a strong (Polish dominated) Central East European Federation would offer a guarantee that Russia would be excluded from Europe.

From the outset the Foreign Office was wary of the danger of being drawn into discussions of this sort. On the one hand, as Frank Roberts, Head of the Central Department of the Foreign Office, put it, it was only to be expected that Polish ambitions could not be satisfied. On the other hand, a clear statement to this effect would discourage the Poles and a confrontation with an ally was to be avoided. Frank Roberts was reputed to be sympathetic to the Soviet side, whereas in reality his comments and advice tended to be dispassionately realistic. The Polish memorandum travelled around the Foreign Office over a period of time, clearly attracting anxious comments. On 25 January 1941 Eden, now Secretary for Foreign Affairs, commented upon the Poles' conviction that after the war the Soviet Union's main interests would be Asian. He clearly doubted that they would be and therefore assumed that Poland and the Soviet Union would be in conflict in the future, a possibility which the Poles had been at pains to avoid mentioning.[48] Not all within the Foreign Office took so charitable a view of the Poles. William Strang, Assistant Under-Secretary, wearily wrote to Cadogan describing the memorandum as 'tiresome'.[49] Whether tiresome or realistic there is no evidence that the Polish attempt to limit British initiatives in relation to the Soviet Union were anything other than dismissed from the beginning.

Publicly at least, Sikorski remained unswerving in his loyalty to the British and never voiced open criticism of their policies. Some of his aides and political Allies were less constrained. Colonel Leon Mitkiewicz, Head of Polish Military Intelligence and Sikorski's delegate to the Supreme Allied Executive, noted on 4 July 1940 his own belief that Britain was increasingly seeking a basis for co-operation with the Soviet Union. In these circumstances he felt that Poland should guard against becoming isolated.[50] Mitkiewicz remarked that when he had discussed this point with the newly appointed Chief of Staff, Colonel Tadeusz Klimecki, the latter agreed with him. In a memorandum submitted to Sikorski on 1 July 1940 Klimecki drew attention to two possibilities. One was that of Britain being forced to accept German–Italian peace proposals. The other possibility was that Britain's inevitable defeat would be postponed by the German attack east. In either case he believed that Poland would be sacrificed by the British in order to negotiate their way out of the war or to obtain an essential alliance with the Soviet Union.[51] According to Mitkiewicz Sikorski agreed with this analysis.[52]

It is therefore likely that Sikorski felt the need to seek contact with the Soviet government in order to forestall a British accommodation with the Soviet Union at Poland's expense. This suggestion was made by, among others, Adam Pragier, one of the exiled leaders of the PPS (Socialist Party) who would not have lightly associated with groups opposed to Sikorski. Pragier felt that Sikorski should not trust the British. He believed that since Britain was trying to loosen German–Soviet ties she would no longer raise objections to Soviet long-term aims in relation to Poland.[53]

Sikorski's attempt to resume a dialogue with the Soviet Union was also contrary to the principles on future foreign policy which the Cabinet Committee of the government-in-exile approved on their arrival in Britain.[54] It had been agreed that for reasons of state Poland had to participate in fighting the aggressors, rather than allowing the defeat of Germany and the Soviet Union to be secured by Britain using her own and her empire's resources. This was one of the key points reiterated by General Kazimierz Sosnkowski, one of Sikorski's rivals who was at the time responsible for communication with occupied Poland. This and other issues dealing with the post-war balance of power was presented by him in a memorandum to the Cabinet Committee and subsequently approved by it when the government arrived in Britain. The return of France to the position of a European power was described as being in 'Poland's political interest' since it was believed that France would have the main say in 'matters relating to the political organization of Europe after the war'.[55] Like the British government, the Polish one was at this stage unsure about the future course of the Vichy government's policies. When in due course de Gaulle tried to obtain Polish recognition for the Free French he found the Poles unresponsive. Gladwyn Jebb of the Foreign Office's Economic and Reconstruction Department recorded in January 1941 that Sikorski had 'complete contempt for the majority of de Gaulle's supporters, though not for de Gaulle himself'.[56] There was another reason for Sikorski's government to show reluctance to enter into close political relations with the Free French. About 500,000 Poles were known to be living in unoccupied France. There was a need to protect them. It was also hoped that they could be recruited into the Polish army in Britain.[57]

The Polish government formulated its clearest guidelines in relation to the Soviet Union. The return of territories occupied in 1939 and the liberation of the Baltic states, which were defined as a Polish sphere of interest, were considered the minimum that the Polish government would demand in any future co-operation. The Polish Cabinet accepted that future developments might require Britain to ally with the Soviet Union. In these circumstances the attitude of the Polish government-in-exile was that the confrontation with the Soviet Union would be necessarily postponed. Nevertheless a clear definition of Britain's obligations towards its Polish ally after the defeat of Germany had to be obtained as soon as possible.[58] In the following months the exile government developed links with Lithuanian, Estonian and Latvian exile political groups, in the belief that they were likely to share Polish opposition to Soviet aggression and German tutelage after the war.

The policy of raising Polish fighting units in exile was defined as a means of putting pressure on the ally and a means of obtaining political influence, as it had been earlier in France. Sikorski therefore could not afford to allow the army to continue as a hotbed of intrigues and political dissent. In the end its main role was to secure political influence for the government. Without a military contribution, Sikorski reasoned, the exile government's role would be insignificant and it would be incapable of securing for post-war Poland the territorial and political advantages due to it as a victorious allied power. In order to secure a degree of understanding and co-operation from the Polish soldiers and officers Sikorski visited Polish troops in Scotland at the end of August 1940. This was a trip earnestly encouraged by the British authorities who were also aware of the boredom and collapse of morale among the idle Polish soldiers stationed there after their rescue from France. During a meeting with the commanders of units Sikorski explained the role of the army during the war and after.[59] He pointed out that the army had and would continue to have two main roles. The first was to form the cadre of a future great Polish army, which would restore order in Poland after the end of hostilities and, as Sikorski ambiguously explained, 'It might so happen that a few hundred people then utilized, used in an appropriate way, might put things in the right track and orientate things in the right direction'. Sikorski was alluding to a future political mission of the army in controlling revolutions and ethnic dissent. The army's second role was to establish a reputation for Polish military endeavour in order that 'friends be certain that Poland is really a first class ally, one that will never fail'.

Stripped of its hyperbole, the speech assured the Polish officers that the government's policy was to develop a stock of goodwill and build up a debt of gratitude in the west and to use the army in future not only to liberate Polish territories but also to establish political order.

Once more the building up of the Polish military units was being used to obtain political leverage. During their sojourn in France the Poles had had the opportunity to discuss with the British their military plans. They did not find British politicians helpful or encouraging. While still in France Sikorski's government sought British aid in putting pressure on the Canadian government to allow the recruitment of Poles from Canada. The proposal met with little understanding within the Foreign Office. As one Foreign Office civil servant put it to Raczyński on 30 January 1940, 'from the point of view of the efficiency of the allied war effort, it was much more important to rescue and embody the destitute Poles in various parts of Europe rather than up-root Canadian Poles from their employment'.[60] The Foreign Office evidently overlooked the fact that the Poles did not view their plans for the creation of a fighting force as 'rescuing destitute Poles'. The insult would have been felt poignantly by the Poles.

The British government's attitude of maintaining a distance from Polish plans for the formation of fighting units in the west continued until the fall of France. Strang told Raczyński as much on 9 February when Raczyński met him to urge the British to complete the drafting of military agreements. Raczyński admitted that the idea of forming two divisions in Canada had been abandoned and instead it was hoped to bring Polish recruits to Europe to join the Polish formations there.[61] Strang had been authorized to say that 'it would not be possible for any part of the Polish land forces to be formed, equipped or trained in the United Kingdom. As the Polish land forces were ultimately to form part of the Polish army in France, it was natural that they should be equipped, formed and trained on the French model'. British disinterest in Polish military plans did not confine itself to the question of models and types of equipment. British finance was not available to assist in the transport of Polish volunteers to Europe. Payment of any expenses incurred by the Poles was not to be postponed until the end of the war but cleared against credits already agreed.

During the talks which were conducted over the following months another problem was added to the strained discussions between the Poles and the British. This related to the extent of Polish jurisdiction over Polish nationals living in Britain who refused to join the Polish units. The Poles wanted total control over Polish citizens resident in Britain while the Foreign Office was unwilling to allow the government-in-exile such wide-ranging authority.[62] In time the problem acquired a different dimension. A number of Poles who had for a variety of reasons been stripped of their Polish nationality during the 1930s objected strongly to being called up by the Polish authorities. They appealed to the British to allow them to enrol in British units. The fact that most of them were Jews, whose passports the Polish authorities had refused to renew as part of anti-Semitic policies of the Sanacja government, only made the matter more embarrassing. Between August and November 1940 a number of agreements, Parliamentary Acts and an Order in Council clarified the extent of the exile government's jurisdiction over its citizens and servicemen. Generally speaking, matters relating to military issues and discipline were dealt with by the Polish authorities in accordance with Polish military law whereas matters coming under the jurisdiction of civil courts were dealt with by British courts.[63]

From the beginning the British authorities expressed concern about stateless aliens becoming stranded in Britain. The British were not only anxious that they would become Britain's responsibility at the end of the war. They were also unhappy about the possibility that allied governments might deprive their citizens of their nationality as a penal sanction, thereby saddling their British hosts with responsibility for people punished in this way. This explains why legislation was introduced allowing exile governments extensive control over their citizens, in particular those who were liable to military service, and also why provisions were made for the British civil and military authorities to assist them in exercising that control.[64] Subsequently British civilian authorities were frequently to find themselves drawn into clashes between aliens and their exile governments. The most numerous seem to have been cases of Polish Jews and Communists, and Greek Communist sailors opposed to their own exile royal government.

From 16 May 1940 discussions within British government and military committees on the possibility of France's collapse inevitably addressed the question of how Britain could alone withstand a German attack. Deliberations concerned a Chiefs of Staff paper entitled 'British Strategy in a Certain Eventuality' which had been circulated on 19 May. Their unquestioned conclusion was that sea and aerial power had to be built up in preparation for Britain's lonely stand. As the fall of France became more of a reality in the following days, British military leaders became increasingly concerned with Britain's manpower and equipment shortages.[65] On 15 May the Ministry of Aircraft Production and Air Staff agreed to concentrate on improving production of equipment, aircraft and on training and obtaining trained crews.[66]

The Poles immediately benefited from this change of policy. The previous detachment from the Polish government's plans for building up an exile army rapidly turned to direct interest and involvement. As French resistance ceased, Churchill personally intervened in response to Sikorski's request for assistance in evacuating a number of units from France.[67] Polish troops were rescued from the French coast together with British ones. The willingness of the British government to do this created a strong impression on Sikorski and seemed to herald unity of purpose between the two Allies.[68] In reality, support was being given to the Poles because they represented a resource, namely trained manpower. In an interview with Sikorski on 19 June 1940 Halifax voiced the government's concern that Britain might not secure the means with which to continue the war. He recorded his words to Sikorski as follows: 'I was sending a telegram instructing Sir R. Campbell to point out frankly to the French Government the necessity of everything possible being done to help the Polish Government and Polish troops to leave France. I felt that I need hardly add that HMG agreed that it was absolutely essential that they should not fall into the hands of the enemy'.[69]

After the French Armistice Anglo-Polish military co-operation was quickly formalized. In the Anglo-Polish Military Agreement of 5 August 1940 it was accepted by both sides that the units already available would form the nucleus of a future Polish military force. Article I of the agreement stated:

> The Polish Armed Forces shall be organized and employed under British command, in its character as the Allied High Command, as the Armed Forces of the Republic of Poland allied with the United Kingdom.[70]

The Polish Air Force, in accordance with Article II of the same agreement, did not come under the direct command of the Polish authorities but became part of the RAF. Although provisions were made to guarantee a distinct character of the Polish squadrons their use was clearly defined by Article III of Appendix I of the Anglo-Polish Agreement:

> Except as provided in Article II for the employment of a Polish Army, Co-operation Squadron, operational control of the Polish Air Force units will rest entirely with the Royal Air Force Command to which they are attached.[71]

The decision to place the Polish Air Force under British command was a concession to British requests for a unified command. The British attitude towards the question of the use of Polish servicemen had earlier been ambiguous. This had most probably been caused by the changing needs of the RAF. Before the fall of France the Air Ministry was very reluctant to make provisions for the receipt and training of Polish airmen. In October 1939 it appeared that Britain could use Polish flight personnel to form two bomber divisions and two reserve divisions.[72] Negotiations dragged on until 11 June 1940 when an agreement was signed by Sikorski which defined the conditions under which the RAF was allowed to use Polish pilots. Only small concessions were made and those related to the right of Polish inspection and emblems, leaving the substance of the British command structure unchanged.[73]

The rationale for this and the clauses incorporated in the agreement of 5 August 1940 can be generally explained by the Air Ministry's low opinion of Polish pilots. The RAF did not understand Polish qualifications and expertise.[74] There are also suggestions that the Polish government's bargaining position was weak and that British law did not permit the employment of foreigners in any capacity other than in the RAF Volunteer Reserve Corps.[75] Neither of these explanations is correct. In fact the Air Ministry received damning reports about the organizational efficiency of the Polish air force and the quality of the officer corps. A representative and by all appearances an influential report was submitted in March by Group Captain Davidson. This included a variety of opinions, all emphatically advocating that the RAF should under no circumstances relinquish control of the Polish Air Units. Group Captain Davidson wrote:

> Both Polish organization and discipline leave much to be desired and the experience of the last three months suggests that without extensive British control it will be impossible to form efficient Polish Air Units ... Neither Polish officers nor NCOs have the authority with their men necessary to create the discipline as known in the British Air Force ... Since the Polish Air Units' decisions with regard to rank and promotion often appear to be affected by favouritism it would seem essential that all such decisions should finally rest in British hands ... even though outwardly the impression might be maintained that the Poles themselves had the final word.[76]

Polish success in getting a large number of pilots out of Romania enabled Sikorski to request the British to increase the number of pilots they were prepared to train. Confusion about this sudden piece of good luck was apparent in the Air Ministry. It was recognized that this was a windfall, but it was not clear what use could be made of it. The feeling that 'the Pole was an individualist and that an aircraft like the Wellington with a crew of six, was not really suited to their temperament, whereas Blenheims would be more suitable' came with a frank statement that there simply were not sufficient numbers of Wellingtons to equip the Polish units.[77]

But the Air Ministry's failure to make use of Polish personnel not only caused irritation to the Poles. It also became an issue within the Air Ministry. According to a report written by Wing Commander C. Perri dated 24 May 1940, the duties performed by Polish pilots to date seemed to have consisted of drill and lectures. 'Multiplicity of Air Ministry branches ... insufficiency of suitable aerodromes ... insufficiency of instructional equipment ... inability to obtain authoritative decisions' were reasons given for the failure to make proper use of Polish pilots.[78] The debate on whether Poles should be trained better to use British equipment or whether equipment appropriate to the Polish temperament should be found was cut short by a sudden influx into Britain of pilots from France and North Africa and by an RAF decision that it needed to expand rapidly the fighter units.

On 14 July a conference was held at the Air Ministry to discuss the disposition of allied air force personnel now in the United Kingdom.[79] The Chiefs of Air Staff had approved the formation of two fighter squadrons and two bomber squadrons from Polish personnel and plans were made for the formation of further squadrons as trained men were becoming available. Air Chief Marshal Sir Hugh Dowding of Fighter Command now stated, 'It had already been decided that 10 more fighter squadrons were to be added to Fighter Command as quickly as possible and we were finding it not too easy to find the personnel'. Furthermore, 'The Air Chief Marshal was emphatic that these Czech and Polish formations would receive every encouragement and all possible help from Fighter Command'. Once British military needs were defined there appeared to be no obstacles, either of equipment or temperamental compatibility, to the full utilization of allied air personnel.

Military co-operation at the beginning of their exile in Britain gave the Polish government good reason to hope that their co-operation with the British war effort would yield political results. The participation of Polish fighter squadrons in the Battle of Britain gave the Poles the type of publicity they sought and believed would benefit their cause. The two squadrons 302 and 303 took part mainly in the defence of London where they claimed to have shot down no less than 203 German planes. By October 1940 Polish pilots in Polish and British fighter divisions made up a fifth of Fighter Command.[80] Although public and official recognition of that contribution was enormous, there is no evidence that the feeling of gratitude was in any tangible way translated into a sense of political obligation.

Less known but of equal importance was the participation of Polish soldiers in fighting in Syria and Egypt. In this case Sikorski, having retained direct control over the land forces, attempted from the outset to obtain political influence and recognition. The number of Polish soldiers in the Middle East under British command was small. In December 1941 it numbered 348 officers and 5,326 ranks. They were organized in the Independent Polish Brigade which had previously been called the Carpathian Brigade. Its importance lay in the fact that at a time of extreme danger to Egypt it was available to defend Alexandria and thus came to symbolize British–Polish co-operation. Polish expectations were inflated even more in the spring of 1941 when it seemed that the hoped-for Balkan front would be opened and the route back to Poland would thus be breached. While still in France the Poles had harboured great hopes of being able to liberate Poland by marching up through the Balkan peninsula.

The Carpathian Brigade had been formed in Syria and Beirut under French command and was supposed to be part of General Weygand's Middle Eastern Army which planned to move into Europe through the Balkans. The full development of the Polish Brigade had been constrained by a shortage of manpower. Since it had been based in Homs in Syria it had not participated in German–French hostilities. Nevertheless its commander, General Stanisław Kopański, was anxious that his men should not be forced to accept the armistice signed by the French commanders. He therefore sought instructions from his government. Sikorski informed him that if the French decided not to fight on he was to place himself at the disposal of British military authorities in Palestine.[81] When the moment came to part company with the French units, General Mittelhauser, the French commander, and General Kopański failed to come to an agreement. Briefly it looked as if Polish troops would have to fight the French soldiers in order not to become prisoners of their previous ally. The matter was resolved and when the Polish units departed their feelings of pride were enhanced by the fact that their numbers were swollen by French soldiers and pilots who had refused to accept their government's withdrawal from the war.[82]

Until December 1940 the Polish Brigade was stationed near Alexandria and was used to reinforce and build up the defence of the city against the anticipated Italian attack. In December a decision was made to use the Poles to guard Italian prisoners of war captured in battles on the Libyan front. But on 24 February Kopański was informed that the Brigade was to be sent to Greece to reinforce the Balkan front. On 9 April 1941, after another reorganization, the troops were loaded on to ships destined for Greece. That same day they were informed that plans had been changed and they were now to be deployed in Libya.[83] Then that decision was changed and the Poles returned to Alexandria. In June there appeared a possibility that they would be used to fight the Vichy units in Syria, a confrontation which Sikorski tried to avoid.[84] Several times the Polish units were re-equipped and retrained, depending on whether they would be deployed in the mountainous regions of the Balkans or the sands of North Africa. The Polish soldiers were first taught to use mules for the Balkans and then were equipped and reorganized to become a mechanized unit for the desert. On 15 August 1941 Kopański was unexpectedly informed by Auchinleck that the Polish Brigade would go to relieve Australian units in Tobruk.

It was only to be expected that in these circumstances problems of strategy would arise. Sikorski tried several times to co-ordinate plans for the use of the Brigade in such a way that would enable them to participate in the final liberation of Poland. The Balkan front was favoured both by Sikorski and Kopański. There was also the need to retain some political independence, hence the reluctance to be drawn into direct military conflict with Vichy France and Italy. Finally, there was the irresistible desire to be needed by the British, hence the inability to exercise control over the destination of the Polish Brigade once its use was requested, irrespective of previously made decisions.

Kopański, who had witnessed the changing military fortunes of the British in the Mediterranean, felt throughout that firmer political guidelines were needed. In July 1940 he informed Sikorski that it was vital that a military person be posted to the Middle East who was 'experienced in military, political and diplomatic matters to whom all military attachés, diplomatic representatives and Polish consulates in the whole of the East would be accountable and who would co-ordinate their activities and would represent Sikorski and the allied government here'.[85] Sikorski tried to obtain permission to visit troops in Egypt in January 1941 but was discouraged by Churchill.[86]

In February 1941 Sikorski informed the British that he wanted to appoint General Sosnkowski as his representative in the Middle East. While Sikorski wanted to get rid of a strong and popular critic of his foreign policy, he also wanted to assert the Polish government's authority. Sosnkowski's instructions spoke of the hopes attached to the use of the Independent Brigade in the Balkans. It was to be Sosnkowski's duty to ensure that the Brigade was used to serve Polish interests.[87] Sikorski hoped that Turkey would decide to make a direct commitment to the war since Soviet–German machinations might make her willing to enter into agreements with Poland. In that event the Brigade would be a direct Polish contribution to the joint effort and thus would symbolize Polish–Turkish–British unity. Sosnkowski was to ascertain whether Polish units could be introduced into the Balkan battle-zone, if that possibility were reconsidered. Sikorski reiterated the need to emphasize as strongly as possible the Polish contribution to the war. Sosnkowski's mission was aborted when the British authorities refused to accept the nomination of a Polish representative from London.

In his conversation with Churchill on 16 February Sikorski obtained an assurance that if the Balkan front were reopened in Turkey, Polish units in Egypt would be freed to go there.[88] He nevertheless handed over the Brigade to the British commanders, clearly intending that it should be part of the great British military effort in the Middle East. When on 14 March 1941 Churchill requested that the Brigade stay in the Middle East Sikorski agreed, 'but asked that the Brigade, which was one of the few remaining embodiments of Polish nationality, should not be lightly cast away or left to its fate'.[89] Churchill was not unsympathetic to the Polish appeal and advised his commanders to hold this point in mind. But he and his military leaders refused to concede the appointment of Polish officers to GHQ Middle East. The decision not to give way to Sikorski over this was as much for political as it was for military reasons. British military and political leaders did not want to have their hands tied over policy relating to the Middle East.[90]

In a speech to the soldiers of the Independent Brigade made while visiting the Middle East in November 1941 Sikorski said:

> When three months ago I asked the British government to send you to Tobruk, I was motivated exclusively by considerations relating to our state. The most vital Polish interests required that the alliance of

25 August 1939, an alliance which was one between two free and
independent nations, now find its expression in our presence at this
front.[91]

Allowing the Independent Brigade to become part of the British
forces in the Middle East went counter to Polish objectives in more
than one way. In addition to the possibility of the Brigade being used
in African fighting at a time when the Poles would have preferred to
keep open an option on the Balkan front, there was the unwanted
military confrontation with Italy. Polish unwillingness to confront
Italian troops adversely affected their standing in the eyes of the
British commanders in the summer of 1940. At the time the Brigade
had been established under British command in Palestine. Not until
December were plans made for its reorganization and rearming. While
the official reason given was that the legal framework for Polish–
British co-operation was still unclear, misunderstandings had arisen
because of Polish unwillingness to declare war against Italy. Having in
mind the possibility of Poland and Italy jointly dominating the Balkan
region after the war, Sikorski had refused to declare war on Italy in
June 1940. Instead he merely broke off diplomatic relations. This
manoeuvre backfired. The British Chiefs of Staff simply concluded that
the Poles were not willing to take offensive action against Italian
troops and therefore refused to rearm them.[92] In his talks with
Kennard, Sikorski tried to resolve the dilemma by stating that he
wanted to see the Brigade used but that the political issues had to be
resolved beforehand.[93] Whether Sikorski was referring to his government's Italian dilemma or the need to obtain a *quid pro quo* from the
British is not clear. Neither problem was referred to again by the
British political leadership and the Brigade languished in inactivity.
Only when the matter was clarified by Sikorski's unambiguous state-
ment that the Brigade could be used against Italian troops did the
Brigade receive the equipment to transform it into a mechanized unit.

Since September 1940 developments in the Middle East had con-
fronted the British with painful choices. The Italian attack on British
possessions in North Africa, launched on 13 September, although
stalled, made it painfully clear to the British Chiefs of Staff that the
defence of that region and protection of vital communication routes
through the Mediterranean could not be assured until Italian troops in
Libya and Eritrea had been defeated. In January 1941 German involvement in the Balkans and assistance to the Italian campaign in Africa
were added to the already formidable list of threats to British security.[94]
In January the Chiefs of Staff reversed the previous decision to

allow General Wavell, Commander-in-Chief of the Middle East, to concentrate on the Italian threat. Instead he was instructed to proceed with the offensive in Libya but only as far as Benghazi and to prepare troops for action in Greece.[95]

Britain's hoped-for mobilization of the Balkans failed both diplomatically and militarily. Turkey's unwillingness to receive British aid merely confirmed that country's reluctance to be drawn into the anti-German camp. Militarily the British fared even worse. On 6 April 1941 the German offensive against Greece started and was impressively successful. On 24 April British troops were forced to evacuate the country. Soon after Crete was abandoned. The strategic consequences of these victories were critical to the British. Not only was the Mediterranean now accessible to the Luftwaffe, but the defence of the Middle East and Egypt forced the Chiefs of Staff to make painful decisions about the desirability of retaining in Britain troops, naval units and an air force for the defence of the British Isles. Although by July 1941 Italian action in the Red Sea region and in Abyssinia had been conclusively ended, Wavell was only too well aware that the Western Desert was defended by a totally inadequate number of troops. These were the circumstances in which the use of the relatively small Polish Independent Brigade was requested by the British. While the Polish political leadership in London was only too delighted to see Polish soldiers given an opportunity to prove their valour, they immediately tried to fit these plans for the Brigade into their own strategy. Since the Balkan front, rather than the Middle East and Africa, remained their preferred zone of operation, they concentrated on the contribution that fighting in North Africa could make to that plan. When Sikorski was asked by Churchill to allow the Brigade to be used in Greece, Sikorski enthusiastically telegraphed Kopański:

> The formation of a new war front in the Balkans lies in accordance with our political and strategic interests and brings us nearer to Poland. It provides conditions for a future offensive on the continent.[96]

But the military situation was changing too rapidly. While the Poles had their sights fixed firmly on the Balkan region, the British Middle East Command analysed the Balkans as part of their Middle East and Mediterranean strategy, and therefore were liable to drop the idea of the Balkan front if communication routes and North Africa became a priority. These were considerations which the Poles were liable to ignore. In the end they deluded themselves. General Kopański's soldiers acquitted themselves bravely. But the North African campaign was not a central consideration in the complex global designs of the British.

For all his hopes that Polish soldiers would be seen assisting Britain at a difficult time, Sikorski failed to admit, or perhaps even appreciate that he had obtained no political concessions or commitments as a reward for this sacrifice. It is difficult to say whether he believed at this stage that the debt of gratitude thus accrued would naturally be discharged at the end of the war or whether he realized that he had no choice: to refuse Churchill's request for the use of the Brigade could have jeopardized the co-operation with Britain that by his reasoning was the basis for future British assistance to Poland. In any case in the autumn of 1941 relations with the Soviet Union came to overshadow all other considerations.

4   Britain, Poland and the Soviet Union: June–December 1941

On 22 July 1941 the much-anticipated German attack on the Soviet Union finally took place. On the evening of that day Churchill made a radio broadcast in which he publicly extended a hand of friendship to the soldiers defending the Soviet Union. The speech was conspicuous in stressing all that united the British and Soviet nations and leaving unmentioned all the issues which might have divided them. The Prime Minister's failure to make British–Soviet co-operation conditional on a Soviet commitment to restore Polish territories was deeply meaningful to the London Poles, whose ears were finally tuned in to the possibility of betrayal. During the following month the politicians of the government-in-exile were no longer divided by the question of whether to re-establish relations with the Soviet Union. They all accepted the necessity for that. They now contended how to force the British and American governments to make their assistance to the Soviet Union conditional on the latter showing goodwill to the Poles. The failure of the two western democracies to champion the Polish cause became the most obvious sign of the rapidly diminishing importance of the Poles in allied diplomacy.

During July 1941 the Polish Prime Minister, following the policy approved by the Council of Ministers, opened talks with Maisky in order to arrive at a mutually acceptable treaty. This was finally signed on 30 July. Brief as it was, the most important point was contained in Article 1 which merely stated that the Soviet–German treaties of 1939 had ceased to be valid. Poland assured the Soviet Union that it was not allied with any anti-Soviet power. Both parties agreed to co-operate with the aim of defeating the Nazis and to that end a Polish army was to be created in the Soviet Union.[1] There was no Soviet commitment to the restoration of occupied Polish territories nor any undertaking regarding future Polish–Soviet borders. The agreement was a bilateral one that did not involve the United Kingdom, which had signed its own agreement with the Russians on 12 July. To Sikorski this was the maximum he could obtain from the Soviet side and represented the minimum personally acceptable to him. He had wanted a British guarantee of the treaty, and had unsuccessfully sought from the Soviet side a commitment to the restoration of Polish territories. His opponents, led once more by Raczkiewicz, Sosnkowski and Zaleski, regarded this minimum as unacceptable, and therefore no more and no less than a betrayal.

From the start of the Polish–Soviet talks the Poles sought signs of Soviet goodwill, and at the same time a British commitment to Poland. The Soviet reluctance to accept Polish demands can be explained in a variety of ways, the most obvious being that the Soviet Union was not dependent on Polish goodwill or co-operation, and therefore was in a position to reject inconvenient demands.

It is more difficult to understand why British politicians appeared so ungenerous towards the Polish ally at a time when they presumed that the Soviet Union would need British assistance. The key to understanding British policy towards Poland in the period after the German attack on the Soviet Union lies in a British attitude towards the Soviet Union that was never free of ambivalence. The nature of the Anglo-Soviet relationship that developed during the next three years was always complex because British determination to co-operate with the Soviet leadership was motivated by a variety of considerations. It has been suggested that Churchill's reasons for making the famous speech of 22 June, which came to symbolize the spirit of British co-operation with the Soviet Union, 'served his own domestic needs, Soviet expectations, and American demands while concealing the absence of any tangible undertaking'.[2] The suspicion that Britain was seeking an accommodation with Germany at Russia's expense was never to leave the minds of the Soviet leaders. The conciliatory gestures that followed from London were efforts to allay Soviet suspicions. With such a tenuous basis for trust, the residence in Britain of the Polish government-in-exile, and the associations of so many of its members in some way or another with the pre-war government and its ideology could only heighten Soviet suspicions. From the outset therefore Churchill, who was determined to draw the Soviet Union into co-operation with Britain, would not permit Polish issues to distract Soviet leaders from the need to establish relations with Britain.

The Anglo-Soviet agreement signed on 12 July was very simple and had been signed by Molotov, the Soviet Commissar for Foreign Affairs, and the British special envoy in Moscow, Stafford Cripps. Britain and the Soviet Union committed themselves to assist each other in the present war and undertook not to sign separate treaties with the enemy.[3] During the following months attempts were made by both sides to add substance to the statements in the signed agreement. But from the outset there existed serious doubts in Britain about the desirability of British–Soviet co-operation. In addition to the ban on the use of the word 'alliance' to describe the nature of the relationship, there were officially and unofficially stated apprehensions about the degree to which it was desirable to co-operate militarily[4] and about the ideological and political implications of assisting a Communist regime.[5]

It has been suggested that the group most resistant to the need for co-operation with the Soviet Union were the military men who felt that the losses incurred by the British Imperial Forces in Greece and Crete meant that Britain could not and should not get involved in aiding the Soviet Union. In fact, prior to the outbreak of the war, British–Soviet military contacts had been non-existent and therefore there was nothing to build on. The political and military arguments for concentrating on British priorities seemed perfectly sound, so that only a very far-sighted military man could have persuaded himself of the need to make aid to the Soviet Union a priority. A Soviet defeat was regarded as a foregone conclusion and the military therefore strongly advised that Britain should prepare for the German invasion of the British Isles, which they thought would inevitably follow the fall of the Soviet Union.[6] The Joint Intelligence Committee maintained that the Soviet war effort would fold in a few days, while the Chiefs of Staff were plainly loath to enter into any contact with representatives of the Red Army.[7] Anti-Soviet prejudice played a significant role in this singular approach to Britain's long-term objectives.[8]

There is another plausible reason for the British failure to build up Soviet trust. The course of British–Soviet negotiations in July 1941 was tortuous for both sides due to their inability to resolve questions of detail rather than of substance. A key element was the difference between Cripps' approach to the Soviet leadership and that of the Foreign Office. The latter felt that the Soviet Union should be required to make concessions in order to prove its willingness to co-operate. This was most apparent in relation to the recognition of the Soviet annexation of the Baltic states, which both Cripps and the Foreign Office were willing to concede. But the Foreign Office nevertheless believed that some gesture of goodwill should be required from the Soviet Union before the British could let themselves be seen acquiescing to Soviet demands.[9]

The differences between the two governments were not confined to the Baltic states. The establishment of co-operation between Britain and the Soviet Union meant that both sides had to address themselves to the Polish dilemma. Even if it was not yet central to either side's military effort the issue was nevertheless unavoidable. To start with the absence of an agreement between Poland and the Soviet Union would have impeded the course of British–Soviet relations. The Soviet Union would have inevitably demanded that Britain prove her commitment by dissociating herself from Poland which was invariably seen as a thorn in the Soviet Union's side by the Soviet leadership. It is more difficult to ascertain the importance that British politicians attached to Poland in general, and its place in British–Soviet relations in particular. The absence of major Cabinet and Foreign Office discussions of the desirability of making the agreement into a tripartite one suggests that, at the time, the Soviet Union was considered to have been the more important partner, while Poland was of less significance.

No direct pressure was put by the British government on the Poles to re-establish relations with the Soviet Union. Nevertheless Eden and the Foreign Office took an interest in the matter, thus implying that Britain wanted and expected the Poles to abandon their previous attitude of implacable hostility towards the Soviet question. They were also willing and keen to assist in the process of reconciliation. Eden even modified Sikorski's first public pronouncement on the subject. On 23 June Sikorski made a radio broadcast to Poland explaining the Polish government's response to the German attack on the Soviet Union. The Polish Council of Ministers had earlier approved the text of the broadcast. Under pressure from Eden, Sikorski altered it to remove any belligerent tone and confined himself to stating blandly a hope that the Soviet Union would consider its treaty with Germany of 1939 as not having taken place.[10] When reporting back to the Council of Ministers on 25 June Sikorski made clear his assumption that the British government would undertake to assist the process of reconciliation between the Poles and the Soviet Union along Polish lines. The least the Sikorski government expected was a Soviet repudiation of the Polish eastern border which had been imposed in September 1939 and the release of the Poles from Soviet prisons and camps.[11]

But British politicians went further than just encouraging the Poles. Both Churchill and Eden had been sufficiently well informed on divisions within the Polish ranks to appreciate that Sikorski's ideas coincided with their own to a larger degree than did those of the

President and the Minister for Foreign Affairs. The Polish Ambassador to London, Edward Raczyński, suggested that the British made sure that preliminary contacts between the Poles and the Soviet Ambassador would be conducted in a spirit of reconciliation by talking directly with Sikorski rather than the President August Zaleski, who was strongly opposed to the re-establishment of relations with the Soviet Union without a prior British and American commitment to the restoration of Poland in pre-war boundaries.[12] Cadogan noted on 5 July that Zaleski's presence at the opening of talks between Sikorski and Maisky 'wouldn't help matters'.[13] Victor Cazalet recorded in his diary on 14 July, 'Anthony Eden came to lunch last week and was overwhelmingly charming. The real problem at the moment is to get the Polish–Russian agreement. Sikorski has behaved with the utmost common sense and statesmanship. Both the P.M. and Anthony are loud in his praises'.[14]

Within the Polish community it was generally believed that Eden was guiding the Poles towards the *rapprochement* with the Soviet Union at all costs. The Head of Polish Military Intelligence, Leon Mitkiewicz, whose anti-British views have already been noted, felt that Sikorski had been pressurized. Not unusually for a man of his background he concluded, 'The main role leading to the conclusion of the agreement between Poland and Russia was played undoubtedly and officially by minister Anthony Eden. Unofficially, behind the scenes, perhaps by the "masons".'[15]

This background but nevertheless tangible pressure which the British were known to be exerting was to become a source of embarrassment to Sikorski who became very keen in future to assert that British influence had not been a key factor in his decision to negotiate directly with the Soviet Union. During his trip to North Africa and the Soviet Union in December 1941 Sikorski used several opportunities to justify his actions retrospectively to the Polish Ambassador to Turkey. He told Sokolnicki:

> Contrary to the rumours circulating, I state that it was not the English who manoeuvred me into the Polish–Soviet talks, but I manoeuvred Eden into them, in order that Great Britain take part in them next to us. There was no English pressure on us in that matter, but there was my pressure on England.[16]

In a further conversation Sikorski suggested that, in the event of Russia 'winning too early' and entering Polish territory in advance of allied armies, the agreement was intended to give Poland leverage, presumably against the Soviet Union. As Sikorski mused, 'in that event will the agreement not have any meaning? ... No I do not say that I will [be able] to stop them, but in any case we will have something to base ourselves on, there will be grounds for us to demand something ... and the allies would be witnesses ...'.[17] Sikorski's words to Sokolnicki should be interpreted carefully. The signing of the Sikorski–Maisky agreement had led to another crisis in the Polish government, as a result of which Sikorski was even more acutely aware of the need to refute suggestions that he had allowed himself to be exploited by the British and lost sight of Polish interests.

While the Poles were given clear and unambiguous hints as to what was expected of them, British politicians insisted on keeping their own talks with the Soviet Union distinct from the agreement which they wanted the Poles to conclude. Colonel Mitkiewicz drew attention to the fact that in official communications with the Polish government, and in the parliamentary statement at the time of the signing of the agreement, no undertaking on any Soviet–Polish pact was given by Britain.[18]

In fact Churchill and Eden were wary of Polish attempts to get them to make commitments to Poland. Sikorski's opponents within his own government tried to draw the British government into their intrigues. Zaleski saw Eden on 8 July and gave him a memorandum in which he implicitly criticized Sikorski. Eden pacified him by uttering a particularly ambiguous reassurance:

> If as a result of any arrangement we could arrive at, we could show that Poland and Polish interests were being fairly treated by Russia, we should give satisfaction in many countries where Poland was as much liked as Russia was disliked.[19]

While the British political leadership viewed the matter as an issue which needed to be resolved, in accordance with their own objectives but without British involvement, the military authorities saw clear benefits to be derived from gaining access to the pool of Polish trained personnel now interned on Soviet territories. On 24 June Sikorski wrote to the head of the British military mission in Moscow, Lieutenant General F. N. Mason-Macfarlane, to tell him of the latest developments and of the suggested use for Polish troops in the near future.[20] Sikorski informed him that until the Soviet Union reversed the territorial changes of September 1939 and until it recognized Polish rights as defined in the Riga treaty, he planned not to leave Polish manpower in the Soviet Union but to evacuate it. Until the above conditions were satisfied, and as long as agreements for the formation of Polish units in the Soviet Union were not completed, manpower would be concentrated in areas from which it could be moved out. Four evacuation routes were identified:

> the Caucasus (Baku), Iran to Palestine
> the Turkmen Republic (Lutfabad), Iran to Palestine
> Vladivostok to the Polish camps in Canada
> Archangel (but only occasionally).[21]

On 3 July the Commander-in-Chief, Middle East, wrote to the War Office conveying General Kopański's request that the British authorities use their influence to move Polish volunteers presently in the Soviet Union to the Middle East. The War Office had to inform him that they could not proceed but that the matter would in due course be resolved.[22]

British policy-makers were not alone in their anxiety not to be drawn into detailed discussions on the subject of post-war territorial adjustments. Roosevelt too had to take into account internal opposition to his policy of involvement in Europe.[23] He was also warned by Adolf A. Berle Jr, the Assistant Secretary of State, of the disastrous effect wartime commitments had had on the European balance of power after the First World War.[24] As a result of these considerations a message was sent by Roosevelt to Churchill on 14 July cautioning him against entering into any premature commitments.[25] It was not a coincidence that the American initiative had taken place at the height of negotiations for an agreement between Britain and the Soviet Union. Within the State Department strong suspicions had been voiced about any British–Soviet understanding which would exclude the United States from influence in post-war Europe. The State Department therefore was determined to caution Churchill lest Anglo-Soviet co-operation relegated the United States after the war to the role of a passive supplier of economic assistance.[26]

To the Polish government in London the British appeared singularly ungenerous towards their Allies. American politicians did not inform the Poles that they were putting pressure on the British not to enter into excessively binding agreements with the émigré governments. The Poles were allowed to assume that America was Poland's friend and supporter, whereas Britain was not. In July 1941 at the height of the Polish government crisis which nearly ended in Sikorski being dismissed by the President, Sikorski told Strang that Jan Ciechanowski, the Polish Ambassador to Washington, was taking Zaleski's side and that 'they are criticizing HMG for failing to give support to the Polish Government'.[27] For his part, Ciechanowski claimed that in an interview he had with American Acting Secretary of State, Sumner Welles, on 27 June, he was told that the American government shared his apprehensions about the degree of British willingness to conciliate the Soviet Union. Subsequently, he wrote, Welles stated that, 'at the appropriate moment the President would certainly agree to use his influence on behalf of Poland, and the appropriate time for such a step would be when Moscow applied to the American Government for Lend-Lease'.[28] During the American–Soviet economic negotiations Ciechanowski asked Welles for Roosevelt to use his influence to obtain concessions from Russia. Welles then declared that no opportunity had arisen to allow the Americans to press the issue.[29]

In its communications with the British the State Department denied that it wished to influence the course of Polish–Soviet talks. At the same time the British government received a direct assurance from the United States that no attempt would be made to interfere in the course of Polish–Soviet talks. During an interview with Halifax, by then the British Ambassador to Washington, Welles assured him that the Poles had been told 'that the US government would be glad to see agreement reached between the Poles and the Soviet but that they thought that any necessary detailed discussions should take place in London, where they had already been in progress'.[30] This statement was intended to assure the British that the United States government was leaving the Polish issue to them.

As has been mentioned already, the degree to which Sikorski was prepared to go along with Soviet demands, even though no assurances were given to restore Polish frontiers to the pre-September 1939 state, caused a major crisis in the Polish government. The background to this intra-governmental conflict is far from simple. Criticism of Sikorski, his style of governing, his alleged submissiveness to the British, his imprudence and haste in negotiating with the Soviet Union, had been voiced earlier. This particular crisis was considerably more dangerous because the President appeared to have sided with ministers who disagreed with Sikorski. The Minister for Foreign Affairs, August Zaleski, and two important ministers, Marian Seyda, a representative of the extreme right National Democratic group, and General Sosnkowski, a much-liked and respected military personality, tendered their resignations.[31] The quarrel was public and deeply acrimonious with both sides attempting to obtain British support. When President Raczkiewicz stated that he would not grant Sikorski powers to sign the agreement with the Soviet Union, the crisis within the Polish government threatened to become a diplomatic embarrassment and upset British plans. Cecil Dormer, the British Ambassador to the Polish government-in-exile, had an interview with the President to persuade him not to create obstacles. A variety of arguments were used, all of which were general and oblique in their commitment to Poland. The suggestion that 'a better agreement would not be obtained by waiting and that if this chance was missed it would not recur later' was supported by a statement 'that in the opinion of His Majesty's Government the Soviet Government had met the Polish desiderata on all essential points; otherwise I said they [HMG] would not be now pressing the Polish Government to agree'.[32]

But, however desirable it was, from the British point of view, that Polish–Soviet relations be put on a less acrimonious footing, British independence of action was not to be limited by unnecessary commitments. All Raczkiewicz was to be promised in return for not creating difficulties for Sikorski was an assurance that 'Poland was our first ally, was fighting side by side with us and in a common cause and we must see to it that we kept the cause constantly before our eyes'.

Sikorski's hand was strengthened by an unusual comparison with Cripps' powers to sign that was made by the Foreign Office. In a conversation with Sikorski's confidant and political advisor, Józef Retinger, Strang explained Cripps' situation. This was intended to encourage the Polish Prime Minister to defy his President's refusal to authorize the signing of the agreement. There is another interpretation which can be put upon the matter, namely that both agreements were viewed as being of a limited validity. This is suggested by Strang's words that Cripps, who signed the British–Soviet treaty at a time when he had no powers to sign treaties, did so 'by authority of His Majesty's Government'. Strang stressed that the Polish–Soviet treaty was, like the British agreement, no more than a joint declaration.[33] Retinger took this to mean that the President's opposition would not, in British and Soviet eyes, invalidate Sikorski's signature. When the agreement was thus signed by Sikorski, opposition within the Polish Cabinet was irrelevant. Unfortunately, as a consequence of this procedure, Sikorski was henceforth under relentless personal pressure to show that the agreement was of great advantage to the Poles, which was not always easy to prove.

The crisis in the exile government was further defused by the President being forced to dismiss Zaleski together with General Sosnkowski and the Minister of Justice, Marian Seyda. But Sikorski was still not to feel secure. The signing of the agreement with the Soviet Union was added to the stock of political grievances that preoccupied the

Polish community. Nor did the joint agreement to create Polish fighting units in the Soviet Union help Sikorski. As will be shown, the formation of these units created a new source of political challenges to him personally and his authority as Supreme Commander.

The conclusion of the Polish–Soviet agreement led to the establishment of a Polish army in Russia. That in turn raised the government's expectations in relation to Britain. Despite its fears that Poland was disadvantaged by the entry of the Soviet Union into the war, the Polish government-in-exile hoped that its importance could be maintained and even enhanced because of the increased military contribution which could now be made by the Poles. Immediately after the British and Polish agreements with the Soviet Union, British politicians tried to reassure the Poles that relations between them were unchanged. On 30 July Eden handed Sikorski an official note intended to assure the Poles that no separate agreement concerning Poland had been made by the British with the Soviet Union.[34] In addition it confirmed that the British government had not recognized the Soviet territorial revisions which had taken place in September 1939. This negative formulation could not mean that the restoration of Poland to her pre-war borders was one of Britain's war aims. Within the Foreign Office lingered a reluctance to get involved in the complexities of Polish politics. Oliver Harvey's diary testifies to the extremely unflattering view of the Poles which prevailed in British government, and particularly in Foreign Office circles. Writing on 12 July he noted, 'The Polish–Soviet conversation on treaty went fairly well. M[aisky] agreed to most of the Polish points ... There is also an ugly snag in that the Polish political prisoners whom the Poles want released and who are believed to have been "liquidated" ...'.[35] Writing a few days later, Harvey felt free to blame the Poles for the slow progress of the talks.[36] The Poles were generally seen as likely to try and create a situation which would embroil Britain in unwelcome commitments. In October Harvey commented:

> We must be careful of the Poles. They are most insinuating. We must guard against the mistake of the French in the last war who by their infatuation for the Poles and support of their wildest claims, sapped the foundation of the Peace Settlement.[37]

Cadogan was more explicit. On 27 July he wrote in his diary, 'Saw A[nthony Eden] and Strang about Polish–Russian business. Both sides are crooks, but it looks as if we may get a signature this afternoon'.[38]

Sikorski's attempt to present the Polish–Soviet agreement as a factor strengthening Poland's role in the war was rendered even more difficult by the publication on 12 August of the British–American agreement which came to be known as the Atlantic Charter. The high moral tone adopted in the declaration made it impossible for the Poles to publicize their desire to incorporate in their borders territories to which they had dubious ethnic and historic claims, but which they considered vital to Poland's future security. Plans for the incorporation of East Prussia and the retention of the eastern regions were thrown into doubt by the Charter's statement that territorial aggrandizement was not sought by the signatories of the Charter and that the rights of the inhabitants to decide their fate would be respected.[39] The Poles regarded the declaration with deep anxiety. They knew that it would be difficult to justify keeping within Polish borders Byelorussian and Ukrainian minorities whose hostility to the Polish state had been clearly manifested during the September campaign. Polish politicians felt betrayed by such a public dissociation by the United States from the future fate of Poland.[40]

On 18 August Cecil Dormer, the British Ambassador to the Polish government-in-exile, reported an interview with Raczyński, the newly appointed Polish Minister for Foreign Affairs and Polish Ambassador to London. Acting on Sikorski's instructions, Raczyński explicitly linked the agreements with the Soviet Union and the United States. Dormer was told that the Poles felt neglected: the Polish–Soviet agreement appeared to have resulted in their negotiating position being weakened. They also felt that the Anglo-American declaration had established a principle of self-determination which could result in their hopes for changes on their western frontier being defeated.[41] Raczyński tried to induce the British Foreign Office to make a separate statement qualifying the application of the Atlantic Charter to the Polish case. The British government should, he suggested, state that it believed that Poland

> cannot emerge from this war reduced in strength. Consequently the future frontiers of Poland should not in any case embrace a territory less important than that which Poland possessed before the German aggression, her frontiers should be drawn so as to safeguard the country's security as a part of the general security of Europe, they should assure Poland's vital needs of a wide access to the sea adequately protected from foreign interference, and her economic necessities proportionate to the number of her population.[42]

The Polish request was unacceptable to the British. It would have implied a commitment to the maintenance of Polish territorial integrity after the war and to supporting Polish aspirations in that part of Europe. For Churchill the Atlantic Charter, despite its unwelcome references to peoples' rights to 'self-determination', was a major achievement in relation to the United States. It was a success in that it bound the United States to the British war effort at a time when that country was still a neutral state.[43] Additionally, during the meeting at which Churchill and Roosevelt agreed on the text of the Atlantic Charter, a decision was made to assist jointly the Soviet Union, a contribution which Churchill considered vital if Germany was to be defeated.[44]

But Churchill's satisfaction at having obtained a partial, nevertheless crucial, United States commitment to the war did not mean that he was insensitive to the possibility of the allied small states being unhappy about the substance of the Charter. In a letter to Attlee, dated 11 August, the day when the negotiations of the text were completed, Churchill admitted that he considered the Charter as no more than an 'interim and partial statement of war aims designed to reassure all countries of our righteous purpose and not the complete structure which we should build after the victory'.[45]

The Poles did not understand the complexities of Anglo-American relations and understandably but vainly sought to obtain some reassurance that the British had not lost sight of Polish objectives. The Political, Economic and Legal Office of the Polish government wrote to Sikorski warning him that the Atlantic Charter, if implemented, would make it impossible for Poland to obtain Danzig, East Prussia and Oppeln Silesia.[46] The other point stressed in the memorandum was the fact that no mention was made of the need to force the aggressor states to compensate their victims. The idea of Poland receiving territorial compensation in Prussia and the west had been toyed with by Sikorski in 1940 and was virtually accepted by the Poles as a logical consequence of Germany's defeat.[47] This very point was put by Raczyński to Eden at a meeting on 18 August and in a subsequent memorandum.[48] The Poles argued that the signing of the Polish–Soviet agreement had put them at a disadvantage in future negotiations over Poland's eastern frontier. The Atlantic Charter now raised doubts about Poland's future position in relation to Germany. They therefore wanted a declaration from the British government that the self-determination principle would not be applied rigidly, to the exclusion of economic and defence considerations.[49] This request was vehemently rejected by Frank Roberts of the Foreign Office with Eden agreeing that it was impossible for Britain to put a gloss on the recently signed agreement.[50] Thus, while the establishment of closer British–Soviet relations diminished Poland's importance to Britain, increased British–American co-operation further reduced it.

The Poles nevertheless hoped that this state of affairs would be reversed because, with the establishment of Polish–Soviet relations, the Polish military contribution to the war effort stood to be dramatically increased. On 14 August 1941 a Polish–Soviet Military Agreement was signed. This specified conditions for the creation of Polish armed forces in the Soviet Union. Units thus formed were to be part of the Polish army, under the authority of a Polish commander, but operationally they would come under Soviet control.[51] Polish naval and air force personnel in Russia were to be sent to join Polish units in the west. Furthermore Sikorski and the British military leadership in the Middle East hoped that Polish soldiers could be moved from the Soviet Union to replenish the Independent Brigade in the Middle East. When making plans for the creation of military units in the Soviet Union Sikorski thought of strengthening the exile government's negotiating position and of building up the future Polish army. He did not entertain the possibility that that very army and its officer corps would become his most bitter opponents and would assume an independent political role, negotiating directly with the Soviet government and British military leaders in the Middle East.

From the moment of their formation it was impossible for Sikorski to impose his authority upon the military leadership of the Polish units in Russia for a number of reasons. There were communications difficulties. But more important was the nature of the army. It was made up of soldiers who had been trapped in the eastern areas by the advance of the Soviet army into Poland. All of them had experienced imprisonment and incarceration during the past two years. It was difficult to persuade them of the need to reconcile themselves with the Soviet Union, and to abandon hopes of settling old and new grievances. A high proportion of the officer corps had been educated before the First World War in the Polish regions which had been under tsarist control. They therefore spoke fluent Russian and presumed themselves to have a unique insight into the 'Russian mentality'. A number of officers had even been in the tsarist army. General Władysław Anders, Sikorski's appointee as Commander-in-Chief of Polish units in Russia, had been brought up in Russian Poland and spoke fluent Russian. The military's tradition of involvement in politics, established by Piłsudski and fostered by his successors, made it impossible for these men to understand Sikorski's admonitions that they should keep out of politics and concentrate on military issues. In their perception, these two issues were not separate, but interlocking.

The above factors all contributed to make it impossible for Sikorski to enforce his decisions on the political issues which surfaced as the Polish units were organized in the Soviet Union. The tenuous nature of his authority over Polish officers in the Soviet Union was exposed in particular when he faced opposition within his own government, where the President remained his main enemy, and when British commanders in the Middle East made arrangements directly with Anders, in preference to agreeing matters with the Polish Commander-in-Chief in London.

Sikorski was aware of the possibility of losing control over political and military developments within the Polish army in the Soviet Union. He tried to prevent this happening by appointing a trusted friend to the post of ambassador. That man was Stanisław Kot. His main qualifications for the post were his support for Sikorski and his loyalty to him. He was not a diplomat and had no knowledge of Russian affairs. Unlike Anders he did not speak Russian. But, according to Kot himself, Sikorski believed that the officials in the Ministry for Foreign Affairs opposed the Polish–Soviet agreement and would sabotage it. In Moscow Sikorski wanted someone whom he could trust and not someone who would make and pursue his own policies.[52] Kot's role was confined to communicating to the Soviet authorities as instructed, and not making his own judgments. Indeed no specific instructions were given to the new ambassador because Sikorski wanted to retain absolute control over all communications and decisions concerning the government's relations with the Soviet Union. According to Kot, Sikorski believed that policies were made either in Washington or London and it was there that one had to be present and vigilant.[53] Unfortunately for Sikorski, Kot proved very unpopular with the Poles in Russia who found a way of sidestepping him. He retaliated by immersing himself in intrigues, seeking to expose supporters of the previous government, thereby making himself thoroughly disliked. The Soviet leadership found him equally unpalatable and this only increased their inclination to deal directly with Anders, further lessening Sikorski's influence.[54]

One of the most intractable dilemmas of Polish–Soviet relations at the time was whether the Poles, in forming military units in the Soviet Union, ever intended them to be used to support the Soviet fight against Germany. Sikorski appears to have been extremely circumspect in his statements on the subject. Initially his attitude towards the

Soviet–German front and the Polish units being formed in the Soviet Union appears to have been in line with his previously stated views. He believed that the defeat of Germany and Italy would take place in the west and that Britain and the United States would have a decisive say in post-war settlements. Therefore he sought anxiously to have the Polish contribution to the war noted by those Allies. But unlike his opponents within the *émigré* circles, most notably the President and, in due course, General Anders, he believed that Poland should take part in fighting in the east. This is not to say that he necessarily wanted Polish soldiers to assist the Soviet army in resisting the German attack on Russia. He believed such resistance was of no direct concern to the Poles. What mattered was to stake a claim to a presence at the future armistice table.

A fundamental assumption repeatedly made by most of the Poles in the west was that Soviet military action was not going to be either lasting or conclusive. Even Sikorski believed that the Soviet army would, at best, defend Soviet territories against Germany and that British and United States military successes would finally lead to the defeat of Germany.[55] Instructions issued to Stanisław Kot on 28 August show that in forming an army in the Soviet Union the possibility of a swift Soviet defeat was always held in mind. It was also feared that the Soviet authorities might renege on their arrangements with the Poles. Therefore the option of withdrawing the Polish army from Soviet territories would have to be held open. Were the Soviet Union to collapse, the Polish units leaving Russia would be used to create an army which would co-operate with the British army.[56] Persia, Palestine, Afghanistan and India were considered to be likely routes for the possible evacuation of units out of Russia.

But Sikorski also believed in the need to establish a relationship with the Soviet leaders if only to maintain Poland's position within the circle of fighting Allies. Anders, by contrast, seems to have always doubted the need to take the Soviet Union into account as an ally. His aide-de-camp, Jerzy Klimkowski, stated that as early as 5–6 August 1941 Anders was planning not to allow Polish troops to take part in the Soviet–German war but to hold them ready until, after the defeat of the Soviet Union, he could lead them out of Russia.[57] Cripps confirmed this view. After dinner with Anders in Moscow on 3 September 1941 Cripps recorded in his diary the latter's conviction that the Soviet war effort would be over unless the Poles in the Soviet Union were armed. Anders' conceited conviction was that the Russians could not win the fight against the German forces unaided.[58] This belief in the imminent failure of the Soviet military effort seems to have been held by Anders steadfastly in the face of evidence to the contrary. In the course of an after-dinner speech in Palestine, when he met Kopański in September 1942, Anders reiterated his conviction in the ultimate defeat of the Soviet Union by Germany.[59] He had been deeply affected by his knowledge of the hardships experienced by Poles in the Soviet Union. As a result Anders remained unable to comprehend or heed Sikorski's more subtle approach to the Soviet ally.

On 1 September 1941 Sikorski, in a letter to General Anders in Russia, outlined the main principles of future foreign policy of the government-in-exile.[60] In it he admitted that the German attack on the Soviet Union offered a good opportunity for the establishment of contacts with the Soviet leadership. He wrote, 'One has to agree to more than one tactical manoeuvre in international relations'. He believed that the Soviet Union would respect the spirit of the agreement but stressed that Poland must retain total independence of action and should not allow itself to be used by the big powers. According to Sikorski, if the Polish army then being formed in the Soviet Union were to realize its role it would have to be used as a whole, not as individual units, and only when it had completed its training.

But of course the key issue was where the Polish army was to be used. Sikorski continued, 'As far as this point is concerned, I wish it [the Polish army] to be used, on the one hand, in the direction in which it will be able to play an independent role in the context of the whole war effort, but on the other hand, that it should co-operate as closely as possible with our British ally'.[61] Thus, already by September Sikorski had identified the area in which the Polish army formed in the Soviet Union was to make its future military contribution as the Caucasus and Iran, 'where, in addition to taking part in the direction of prime strategic importance, there will be an opportunity of extending a helping hand to our British Allies and at the same time of fighting side by side with the Russian Allies'. In conclusion Sikorski instructed Anders that he did not wish the Polish army to be used in the Soviet thrust west as it would 'be absorbed in the Russian front, would be broken up and would play a secondary role. These negative consequences would not be compensated for by an eventual earlier entry into Poland'.[62]

In this letter Sikorski once more alluded to plans for the army to play a political role in Poland after hostilities ended. He warned against political disunity which he saw as having been the source of the earlier difficulties in France. 'The army being formed and commanded by you', Sikorski wrote, 'must retain total moral health and must become a true and reliable instrument of the Polish government. It must be ideologically united. Because of this it should keep away from politics'.[63]

From the outset Sikorski attempted to communicate to the British military and political leaders the message that the Polish army in the Soviet Union should be viewed not as a purely Polish matter but as an allied concern. The British occupation of Iran in August 1941 and talks conducted within British military circles on the desirability of defending the Russian oilfields in southern Russia seemed to offer an opportunity for a Polish initiative. This very point was therefore put to Churchill by Sikorski on 11 September.[64] Churchill was told that Anders had been instructed 'to gravitate southward with his forces': an oblique hint was thus made about the possible usefulness of Polish forces in defending the newly acquired routes between the Persian Gulf and the Caspian Sea, and between Russia and India. This point was reiterated four days later during a meeting Sikorski had with Roger Makins, Head of the Central Department of the Foreign Office.[65] While expressing a very pessimistic view on Russia's fighting capacity Sikorski stressed that 'whatever happens in Russia, and particularly if things go badly, a well equipped and homogeneous Polish force will be able to play a role out of all proportion to its size'.

Another reason why the Poles were seeking to make the Polish army in the Soviet Union an allied concern was to secure equipment and basic necessities. In spite of initial hopes that the Soviet side would honour the spirit of the Soviet–Polish agreement and facilitate the creation and equipment of as large a Polish force as possible, by September 1941 it was realized that Soviet supplies were meagre and that the Soviet authorities were restricting the flow of equipment to the Poles. Sikorski had believed that Anders would be able to call up at least 100,000 Poles. A military contribution of that magnitude would present a decisive argument in Poland's favour in any future political discussions. In September it was realized that the army could not be formed, trained or equipped without direct allied assistance. The quandary could be resolved if the Poles could persuade Britain and the United States that they needed these men. Failure to do so would leave the Polish army in Russia as a purely Polish–Soviet matter which would not offer the Poles the opportunity to assert themselves in inter-allied negotiations. Dependence on Soviet supplies would also allow the Soviet authorities to limit the size and potential for expansion of the Polish units for economic, military or even political reasons.

On 24 September Sikorski conveyed through Cripps a message to General Zygmunt Szyszko-Bohusz, Head of the Polish Military Mission in Russia. Szyszko-Bohusz was instructed to seek an opportunity for the Poles to participate in the defence of the Caucasus oilfields.[66] But the proposal was not to be put to the Russians. Instead he was to ask the British representative in Russia to suggest the idea to the Russians. The aim of the message could not have been merely to signal the willingness of Polish troops in Russia to go into battle. Sikorski was anxious lest the request to move Polish units to the south be interpreted by the Russians as an attempt to avoid fighting Germany in the east. Soviet suspicions of Polish motives were easily aroused. The German thrust into Russia was now so serious that the Caucasus was not the only area requiring reinforcements. In any case the south was not an obvious zone of operation for the Poles who had been concentrated in the Kuibyshev and Saratov region. But, as Sikorski wrote, the participation of Polish troops in the defence of southern Russia would offer an opportunity to 'render a service to the Soviet Union and the Allies'.[67]

In October 1941 the Soviet leadership faced one of the most serious threats since the German assault in June. In August, on Hitler's instructions, the full weight of the German thrust in the Soviet Union was pushed not towards Moscow but north and south.[68] Once the blockade of Leningrad had been achieved the German generals in Russia were anxious to secure defensive positions before the onset of bad weather and therefore welcomed Hitler's instructions on 5 September which once more directed the main thrust towards Moscow.[69] On 30 September General Guderian's Panzer units attacked the Bryansk front south-west of Moscow and on 2 October the German army Group Centre fought for the Smolensk–Moscow highway.[70] By 14 October German troops captured Kalinin ninety miles north of Moscow, threatening to encircle the capital and opening up defensive positions protecting central Russia. By mid-October the occupation of Moscow seemed inevitable. Nearly three million Soviet soldiers had been taken into captivity and the Soviet military initiative seemed to have ended.[71]

In southern Russia the military situation seemed just as perilous. The coal-mining district of Donbas and the town of Kharkov were captured by the German Sixth Army. Most of the Russian troops in the area were pushed down towards the Crimea and thus immobilized. By the end of October the route to Rostov and to the key area of the Don River seemed undefended.[72] Control of the Don regions would have meant easy access to the oil-producing region of the Caucasus and a possible link up with Iran. Were this to happen the Turkish government's commitment to neutrality, already tested by British and Soviet occupation of Iran,[73] could have been undermined. The Turkish military leaders were assiduously courted by the Germans at the height of their military success in southern Russia.[74]

These military developments and the immediate diplomatic implications of further German advances might explain why the Soviet leadership changed its attitude towards the Polish troops. The fear that these could, at a critical time, become a force similar to the Czech Legion during the Civil War of 1917–20 could not have been discounted. As a result the Soviet authorities tried to limit the size of the Polish army and to move the already formed units into battle.

An attempt by the Russians to commit the Poles to joining the Soviet war effort was resolutely rejected by Anders in the autumn of 1941. This was justified mainly by pointing to the bad physical condition of the Polish soldiers. Sikorski concurred with this decision by reminding Anders forcefully of his absolute duty not to allow the units to be wasted.[75] However, while stressing the unpreparedness of the troops, Sikorski emphasized:

> The Polish Army in the Soviet Union has an enormous propaganda value for the Soviet Union in the whole world, but mainly in America. But if this army is to fulfil its propaganda value it must be used in battle as a whole.

While there can be no doubt that Anders was sincerely concerned about the health of his soldiers, who had only recently suffered the worst privations of the Soviet labour and prisoner-of-war camps, his reluctance to place the Polish units at Soviet disposal was politically motivated. In the end he had never wanted these men to fight for the Soviet cause but for the allied one. His next task therefore was to persuade the British military leaders that the fate of the Polish soldiers in the Soviet Union should be of direct concern to them, for they represented an opportunity too good to miss to increase the numbers of soldiers under direct and indirect British command.

From a purely manpower point of view, the British Chiefs of Staff needed little persuading that they could use the Poles. What proved more difficult for Sikorski was to explain how British use of Polish soldiers fitted into a global allied strategy. The signing of the Polish–Soviet military agreement, on which the creation of Polish military units in the Soviet Union was based, was a matter of some interest to the British Chiefs of Staff. In addition to the need to consider whether the Soviet authorities would be able to equip these soldiers there was the added prospect of some Poles being brought out to join units in Britain and the Middle East. The British Chiefs of Staff addressed themselves to these questions within days of the Polish–Soviet political and military agreement being concluded. In the course of a meeting on 11 August the Chiefs of Staff discussed supplies for the Polish army in Russia.[76] It was taken for granted that equipment would have to be sent by the British since the Soviet authorities simply did not have adequate resources to fulfil their commitments to the Poles. At the same time the Chiefs of Staff discussed how Sikorski's policy of mobilizing Poles in Russia into an army would benefit the British war effort. Since supplies were to be delivered by British ships to the port of Archangel, it was decided that Polish military personnel destined to leave the Soviet Union would be transported on the return journey in order that on arrival in Britain they be incorporated into units being formed in Scotland or even those in the Middle East. The Chiefs of Staff felt that they would want Polish personnel in the following order of priority: (1) airmen, (2) sailors, (3) infantrymen. The matter was conveyed to the allied Forces Committee which discussed the issue on 15 August.[77] At this stage at least it was understood that the Poles were not intending to remove all the newly formed units from Russia and the Air Ministry was the only one which clearly wanted to see the evacuation of Polish airmen to Britain. Generally it was felt that the matter was outside the scope of British policy. A reference to the advantage of raising the Polish Brigade in the Middle East to a division by incorporating an additional 15,000 soldiers from Russia clearly changed the tone of discussion. There was also an oblique comment by the Chairman 'that he understood that for other reasons, the War Office thought it might be useful to have part of the Polish forces assembled in the Caucasus'.[78] At the end of the discussion a clear recommendation was made to suggest to the Polish authorities 'that HMG would see some advantage in part of the Polish military forces being assembled in the Caucasus region with a view to their eventual transfer to the Middle East or for other purposes'.

Polish forces in Russia were again discussed by the Chiefs of Staff at a meeting on 18 September.[79] A War Office memorandum prepared in anticipation of the discussion made two unequivocal recommendations:

1. From a military point of view the Poles are probably better soldiers than the Russians, and if it were politically possible, it would be

preferable for the equipment which we are sending to Russia to be used to arm Polish Divisions.

2. If a decision is ultimately taken to provide equipment for some or all of the Poles, it is important that they should be concentrated in southern Russia ... Moreover, if Russia finally collapses, we may be able to get some of the Polish Divisions out through Persia or Iraq.[80]

Since no clear decision could be made, the whole matter was deferred until discussions on material support for the Soviet Union were completed. The Chiefs of Staff returned to the subject on 2 October. They were aware of the substance of Sikorski's communications with Anders in the Soviet Union and therefore knew of the Poles' willingness to fall in with British requirements.[81] During the discussion General John Dill, the Chief of the Imperial General Staff, presented a clear case for making use of the Poles. According to him they could be invaluable in the defence of the Caucasus oilfields and 'as a means of reinforcing our army in the Middle East without the cost of shipment'. He too repeated the suggestion that the Caucasus should be identified as an operational zone for the Polish troops because it offered the possibility of a swift departure from Russia, if the German campaign were successful there.[82] The Foreign Office was instructed to suggest to the British authorities in Moscow that they should support the Polish proposal for establishing bases in the Caucasus.

A memorandum submitted by Sikorski was discussed by the Chiefs of Staff on 25 September.[83] Sikorski reiterated his view of the Poles in Russia as a pool from which men could be brought to reinforce the army in Britain and the Middle East. Since at this stage equipment was the main issue for discussion it was decided to leave the matter to be dealt with at the forthcoming supply talks in Moscow. It is interesting to note that, at the Chiefs of Staff meeting on 25 September, the removal of the Poles from central Russia to the Caucasus was discussed as if it had already been agreed that this would facilitate their equipment and at the same time enable the British to skim off some of the personnel to Polish units already fighting with the British. The evacuation of all Polish units from Russia was opposed by none of the military leaders.

During this period differences between the respective plans of Sikorski and Anders came to the fore. Noting Anders' equipment requisitions, Sikorski wrote him a strongly worded note which was clearly aimed at bringing Anders into line.[84] Anders appeared to be thinking in terms of building up a big Polish army and seemed reluctant to evacuate certain categories of servicemen. According to his aide-de-camp Klimkowski, the decision to move the Polish army to southern Russia had been made by Anders after consultation with the Head of the Polish Military Mission, Szyszko-Bohusz, on 14 September 1941.[85] Anders based himself on the conviction that the German offensive was likely to be successful within a very short period of time and concluded that this would necessitate a rapid expansion of the army as there was little time to lose. According to him the removal of the Polish army to the border with Iran or Afghanistan would therefore be useful because:

1. In the event of the Russian front breaking down the Polish army will be able to cross to Persia and even in the final analysis through Afghanistan to India.
2. [It would be] easier and quicker to obtain supplies of ammunition, which could arrive there from the British.[86]

Anders also planned to disperse ammunition which had already been given to the Poles throughout the units moving south in order to train all men and not only the small groups which had already been formed into military units. In addition he stated that it would be necessary for the Poles being moved to the south to have guns for personal safety (presumably, while still in Russia, against Soviet attacks!). Finally he was committed to preventing the Soviet High Command moving already trained and equipped units to the front. He proposed to use the excuse that they had not been given sufficient ammunition to put them into battle.[87] According to Klimkowski, in the middle of September Anders decided to ignore orders from the exile government in London and to follow his own policy. Accordingly he deliberately bypassed Sikorski and entered into direct contacts with the British Military Mission in Russia.[88] There is no evidence that the British knew of Anders' aims at this stage and therefore they cannot be said to have encouraged him.

Sikorski objected to both of Anders' aims. He still spoke of Archangel being the main port through which supplies would be coming in. Differences between the two were potentially very serious. Sikorski was not sure why Anders appeared to be thinking of building up a big army in Russia. Anders did not inform London of his plans to evacuate the whole army out of Russia. Therefore his refusal to release men for evacuation to the Middle East and Britain was incomprehensible. Sikorski was also anxious about the implications of having in the Soviet Union a large and politically united army whose leadership could easily challenge his primacy in Polish politics. The Polish Prime Minister wanted the army in the Soviet Union to be a conduit for men being moved to the British zone of military operation, while retaining a presence in the Soviet Union. Therefore he put greater stress on Poland's military co-operation with the western Allies and not with the Soviet Union, which he considered politically less significant. He considered the evacuation of 10,000 servicemen to the Middle East to be much more important to the Polish cause than forming a big army in Russia.[89]

The main difference between the two leaders was over whether the Soviet Union should be regarded as of any significance at all in the war. As far as Anders was concerned there was no point tying any political and military hopes to the Soviet war effort. He wanted to gather his men and go to the front where the real fighting was taking place, namely with the British in the Middle East. Had Sikorski known of these ideas at the time, he would have been horrified, as he was when Anders succeeded in pulling the Polish divisions out of Soviet Russia in 1942. Sikorski believed in using the Polish units as part of a joint Polish–Soviet–British military effort. As far as he was concerned only such co-operation guaranteed maximum political recognition.

Sikorski's apprehensions about Anders were increased by developments in the Middle East. On 3 October General Kopański's Brigade relieved the two Australian brigades in Tobruk.[90] This was an opportunity for which the Poles had been waiting. They were given the task of defending an independent section in Tobruk, a highly visible contribution to the allied cause. This was also the first opportunity since the Norwegian campaign for Polish units to go into battle. Kopański noted with satisfaction that they would be fighting against not only Italian but also German troops. He and Sikorski were anxious that this chance to show a high profile in the British war effort should not be lost or diminished because of casualties.[91] There was an immediate need to organize reinforcements from the Soviet Union. Anders' unwillingness to settle for a symbolic army in Russia appeared to confuse military plans. More importantly it could jeopardize the political advantages of an alliance with the Soviet Union.

At the beginning of October Lord Beaverbrook went to Moscow to discuss the question of supplies to the Soviet Union. To the Poles the results of the mission were an unmitigated disaster which only increased British dissociation from the Polish cause. Unfortunately it also came to symbolize everything that was wrong in British relations with the Soviet Union and Polish dependence on the two Allies. The key weakness of Poland's position in British policy was succinctly exposed. The proposal that Britain and the United States would support the Soviet war effort had been agreed by Roosevelt and Churchill before the German attack on Russia and in advance of Soviet adherence to any agreement.[92] The initial objective had been to use supplies as leverage for political and military agreements. Cripps believed that supplies should be offered on the condition that the Soviet Union was seen to be acting as a partner.[93] Beaverbrook did not see himself as pursuing that aim. He was unequivocally in support of British assistance to the Soviet Union and felt that haggling over details and reciprocal commitments would only increase Soviet suspicions.[94] He therefore refused to link the issue of British supplies to the Soviet Union with the fate of the Poles there. He also did not insist that a certain quantity of supplies be reserved for the Poles. The Beaverbrook mission therefore did not strengthen the Poles' negotiating position and left their plans for the creation, equipping and supplying of the Polish units dependent on Soviet plans.

Beaverbrook's attitude also made it difficult for the Chiefs of Staff to pursue their aim of getting the Polish units to the Caucasus without having to depend on Soviet goodwill. Unfortunately for the Poles, the Americans were prepared to go to any lengths to aid the Soviet Union. Averell Harriman, the chairman of the American delegation which went to Moscow with Beaverbrook, believed that the President wanted at all costs the Russians to continue fighting the Germans. Since the defeat of Nazi Germany was Roosevelt's stated objective, the Soviet war effort was viewed by him as contributing to the achievement of American aims.[95] This view was supported by his most influential political and military advisers.[96]

Anders in the Soviet Union and Sikorski in London were equally disappointed by the failure of Beaverbrook and Harriman to take up their case with the Soviet leadership. The biggest blow to their hopes was the failure to earmark supplies for the Poles. Had this been done, it would have freed them from the constraints imposed by Soviet supplies and military priorities and given them an independent position in Russia. But Beaverbrook, who during his visit to the Soviet Union insulted and slighted everyone except Stalin, had made a deliberate decision on this point. In any case prior to his departure for Moscow Churchill had given him total freedom to negotiate with the Russians. The aim of the mission was to encourage Russian resistance and not to resolve disputes.[97] Not surprisingly Beaverbrook did not seek to argue the Polish case.

In October 1941 Beaverbrook became the chairman of the newly established allied Supplies Executive which henceforth would decide all matters relating to aid to the Soviet Union. This reduced the Foreign Office's and more importantly Cripps' influence on issues of supplies to the new ally.[98] It also meant that henceforth, in talks with Soviet politicians, it would be wellnigh impossible to link the question of aid to demands for political concessions.

Beaverbrook subsequently admitted that, 'It would be right to say that I refused to be caught up in the Polish negotiations at any time'.[99] In 1944, when public opinion was swinging against the Soviet Union and in favour of the 'gallant Poles', Beaverbrook tried to justify his position retrospectively by giving reasons for his neglect of the Polish case in 1941. Apart from the insalubrity of the pre-war Polish government and the activities of the Poles in Britain, Beaverbrook wrote, 'whatever the cause of the tragedy, the friendship of Russia is far more important to us than the future of Anglo-Polish relations'.[100] That was clearly the actual reason why in the autumn of 1941 Britain appeared to be neglecting her Polish ally.

The question of supplies for the Soviet Union, the use of Polish servicemen in the Middle East and the need to plan for the possibility of German victory on the Eastern front, were all related problems. They were additionally linked with the British occupation of Iran. So far there exists no entirely satisfactory explanation for the British decision to occupy that country in September 1941. The need to defend oil supplies on the one hand, and the desire to assure safe access to Russia for the purpose of supplying her with military aid on the other, have traditionally been offered as explanations.[101] Churchill's biographer suggests that British action in Iran was aimed at preventing a pro-Nazi regime from establishing itself there.[102] Gorodetsky puts forward an alternative theory. He believes that what started as a not clearly thought out need to defend oil supplies in July 1941 became, in September 1941, a vague desire to create a buffer zone between the area likely to be occupied by Germany and the British sphere of interest in the Middle East.[103] He emphatically rejects the suggestion that the move had been intended to cement British–Soviet relations by establishing direct areas of co-operation.

Within British political and military circles discussions about aid to the Soviet Union had been primarily about material and equipment. But on 19 September Churchill sought the approval of the Chiefs of Staff for sending two divisions to the Middle East. He considered it likely that they would take part in the defence of the Caucasus.[104] German successes at the beginning of October meant that the Caucasus ceased being a purely Soviet military dilemma. Churchill realized that a breakthrough could bring German troops closer to Britain's position in the Middle East.[105] He therefore saw the Soviet defence of the region as a matter of direct concern to the British. The Chiefs of Staff were not inclined to take the same view and on the whole seemed to favour limited involvement in the Caucasus.[106] When the Cabinet approved sending troops to the Caucasus this was made conditional on the availability of these troops. Nevertheless operation 'Crusader', the forthcoming offensive in the Western Desert of North Africa, took precedence over aid to the Soviet war effort.[107] During October Churchill urged his Chiefs of Staff, notably the Commander-in-Chief in India, Wavell, and the Commander-in-Chief in the Middle East, Auchinleck, to consider the matter. Auchinleck's postponement of 'Crusader' meant that operation 'Velvet', the code name given for aid to the Soviet Union, was also put off for the time being. In reality neither of the Chiefs of Staff nor Air Chief Marshal Tedder, Air Officer Commanding-in-Chief, Middle East, fearing the arrival of the German air force in the Middle East, favoured anything but minor operations to aid the Soviet ally.[108]

It is in this context that one can understand Churchill's suggestion to Sikorski that Polish units should replace Soviet ones in Iran, a proposal which did not come as a surprise to the Poles. On 24 October Churchill put to Sikorski a proposal couched as an intricate deal as a result of which Poland would support Britain in her dealings with the Soviet Union and in return Britain would defend Polish interests. Churchill's reasoning was complex. His objectives were clearly not those which he put to Sikorski. Churchill wanted the Soviet troops presently stationed in Iran to leave and return to the Soviet Union.[109] He appears to have decided to use the Poles as both an instrument of British policy and a smoke screen. Churchill proposed

> to General Sikorski to put in his conversations with Stalin and Molotov a firm request to the effect of transferring the Polish troops to the South, and to offer at that price to intercede with the British Government and support the Soviet request regarding the taking over of a sector of the Soviet front against the Germans by Britain.[110]

Churchill suggested that the withdrawal of Soviet troops from Iran would free the British troops occupied in preventing the Soviet troops from causing unrest. This in turn would free the overloaded rail links in that region for supplies to Russia. Stalin was to be told that he would thus be able to employ these troops more usefully in the defence of the Caucasus. Churchill offered a bait to the Polish Prime Minister. He admitted that 'the most appropriate thing from the British point of view would be to transfer these troops to Persia'. If the Russians opposed the transfer of Polish troops there, Churchill assured Sikorski that Britain would still supply the Poles, and in any case their moving to Astrakhan on the northern coast of the Caspian Sea would be in the long term a good idea.[111]

Nothing was quite as it appeared. The Poles had no political leverage in Moscow and the suggestion that they should put forward the British proposals there was most probably made because Churchill did not want to be seen by the Russians as mediating between them and the Poles to the strategic advantage of the British. The manpower issue was crucial. Churchill and the Middle East Command in particular needed Polish soldiers both in North Africa but also in Iran. The Poles were unlikely to want to stay in Russia, whereas the decision to include Soviet troops in the Iranian operation could have had long-term repercussions for British policies in that region.

The Poles in the Soviet Union were willing and were increasingly likely to end up fighting under British command. Britain had only recently been accused of fighting in the Middle East with Dominion troops.[112] On 16 September the Australians had decided to pull their units out of Tobruk. In the short term this raised serious doubts about the feasibility of launching the 'Crusader' operation in North Africa in November. In the long term it suggested that the Australians might dissociate themselves from the British war effort. Either way the event highlighted acute manpower shortages.[113]

The Poles were not fooled by Churchill's presentation of his request. British problems in Iran had been aired in the press and noted by the Polish Ministry for Foreign Affairs. A Polish military memorandum dealing with the army in Russia, written on 24 October, summarized the options available. It assumed that the Soviet government would insist on the creation of a small Polish army in Russia and therefore concluded that its evacuation was desirable. Britain was said to appreciate having the opportunity of using Polish soldiers both to continue the expansion of units in Scotland but also because they needed soldiers in the Near and Middle East.[114] General Wavell, it was believed, would soon need troops in Iran and possibly also in the near future in the Caucasus.

A similar memorandum prepared by the Polish government (undated, but clearly relating to problems which faced the Allies in October) dealt with the opportunities open to units which could be evacuated from Russia.[115] The author, basing himself on information gleaned from the British press, speculated on the possibility of Soviet troops being withdrawn from Iran to the Caucasus. The conclusion was that the vacuum thus created would be embarrassing to the British and would threaten them with loss of face. Thus the Poles could offer to step in and replace Soviet troops with their own soldiers. Soviet apprehensions about the concentration of excessive numbers of Polish soldiers east of the Volga could be soothed by suggesting that while one division go to Iran, another could remain in southern Russia.[116]

There can be little doubt that Churchill and Sikorski, for different reasons, felt that the evacuation of already trained Polish units out of Russia would be desirable. In October it was still felt that the mass transfer south of the army would serve two purposes: evacuation of already formed units to join General Wavell's command; and basing subsequently assembled units next to the Iranian border where they would be more easily supplied.

By November, the War Office, the Foreign Office and Churchill had all come to appreciate the need to clarify their thinking on supplies to the Soviet Union. Already in his conversations with Sikorski, Churchill had hinted heavily at his own willingness to offer the Soviet Union supplies. Now he became aware of the leverage which these assurances could give him in political talks with Stalin. The need to obtain Russian approval for the Polish move south was once more linked with the issue of supplies to the Soviet Union. This was broached by Harriman in a communication to Stalin on 11 November[117] and was one of the main issues discussed by Kot during a meeting with Stalin on 14 November.[118] The result was that Stalin accepted the Polish proposal for the creation of an army in excess of the existing limit of 30,000 men. He understood that supplying and equipping those troops became the responsibility of the British and the United States. At the same meeting Kot referred to the matter of the missing officers, which had apparently cast increasing doubts upon Soviet goodwill.

In principle the discussions that took place in the British military committees were intended to deal with evacuating the men necessary to build up Polish forces in the Middle East and Scotland and re-equipping the Poles in Russia, who would go to Iran temporarily and who were then supposed to return to Russia. In reality confusion seemed to have prevailed. The need to have the Polish soldiers in Iran in order to equip them and return them to the Soviet Union was referred to at the same time as calls were uttered for saving them from being wasted in Russia. On 10 November the Chiefs of Staff formally committed themselves to assisting the Poles by bringing them out to Iran and India.[119] Whereas the Chiefs of Staff officially referred to the need to re-equip and reorganize the Polish units, a few days later General Sir John Dill, the Chief of the Imperial General Staff, went further. Writing to Cadogan on 19 November to urge that the Foreign Office should assist in the process of removing the Poles from Russia, Dill started a paragraph of his letter:

> I should like to stress again the importance which I attach, for military reasons, to the evacuation of as many Poles as possible. We want 10,000 in this country and 2,000 in the Middle East to bring up to strength the Polish forces now in existence. The remainder – I believe that something like 150,000 are involved – would be a great contribution of good fighting men to our cause.[120]

Another paragraph of the same letter concluded: 'If they stay in Russia, not only will they never be equipped, but it seems likely that a large number may well starve to death.' At this stage the evacuation of the whole Polish army out of Russia was not the object of British endeavours. Nevertheless this removal became one of the unspoken assumptions of the British political and military leadership.

Further doubts about the likelihood of the Poles returning to Russia after recuperating and being equipped in Iran were raised by a frank admission by the War Office that neither Iran nor Iraq were appropriate places for training camps to be established. For this purpose India, Afghanistan or East Africa were considered better destinations.[121] Unless camps were opened in those areas, Poles coming out of Russia to Iran would be drafted directly into the British war effort in that region, where there was an acute shortage of military manpower.

On 31 October Sikorski, accompanied by Cazalet, left Britain to visit the Soviet Union. His trip was to take him to Egypt, Tobruk and a number of Polish camps in the Soviet Union. He returned to Britain in January 1942. The obvious purpose of Sikorski's visit to the Soviet Union was to ease difficulties which had arisen in Polish–Soviet relations. Of equal importance was the need to re-establish control over the Polish units in Russia, to remind Anders that he should follow instructions from London, and finally to consolidate his relations with British military leaders in the Middle East. This trip was also an attempt to establish direct contact with his soldiers and to stifle criticism of his policies.[122] Ending internal strife among the Polish émigrés was as important a goal as the need to gain allied approval and support.

The most important event of Sikorski's visit to the Soviet Union was his meeting with Stalin. This took place on 3 December. In spite of the friendly spirit in which the talks were conducted, the only subject on which the two leaders seemed to agree was an alleged lack of martial spirit among the Jews. Sikorski tried and failed to obtain Stalin's agreement to a withdrawal of Polish units to Iran for re-equipping. Stalin rejected personal assurances that the units would return to the Soviet Union and left Sikorski in no doubt that he believed the British were using the Poles to fight their battles. He sneered at Sikorski's insistence that the Poles were not subservient to the British and suggested that they were likely to end up fighting in Iran, Turkey and even Japan.[123] To recover his position Sikorski was forced to abandon the request for the temporary removal of the Poles from Russia and accept Stalin's assurance that all restrictions on recruitment to Polish units would be lifted and that they could be moved to southern Russia.[124] The final understanding was that Britain and the United States would supply equipment while food would be provided by the Russians. In his irritation Stalin made a comment to Sikorski which, in retrospect, was prophetic. Telling him that the Poles could take out all their troops, Stalin said: 'But we shall manage without you. We can hand over the lot. We'll shift for ourselves. We shall conquer Poland and then we'll give it to you.'[125]

Sikorski believed that his visit had been a success. He thought that the Poles had impressed Stalin. In a letter addressed to Raczkiewicz, written while still in the Soviet Union, Sikorski stated that it was essential to change earlier plans and not press for the evacuation of the two or three Polish divisions already assembled. He had noted Stalin's distrust of the British and concluded that the only way of removing the impression that he was no more than Churchill's puppet was to restate the Polish commitment to fighting in Russia.[126] Too visible collaboration with Britain would, according to Sikorski, be an obstacle to constructive Polish–Soviet relations.

During his stay in Cairo on the journey back to Britain, Sikorski confided to Sokolnicki, who had been summoned from Turkey, that he believed Poland's position in relation to the Soviet Union was strong. According to Sikorski this had been demonstrated by the Soviet authorities' agreement to create a large Polish army, as opposed to the previous agreement for the formation of two or three units only.[127] He did not propose to return the loan of 100 million roubles made by the Soviet government to the Polish government because he believed that it would be set against the reparations which Poland would receive from the Soviet Union after the war. Evidently Sikorski still believed that the war would strengthen Poland and weaken the Soviet Union.

Neither Cripps nor Cazalet, who travelled with Sikorski to Russia, were present at the talks between the Soviet leaders and the Poles. More importantly, Churchill tried to prevent Cazalet from joining Sikorski. When, at his own insistence, he was allowed to accompany Sikorski no instructions were given to him. Either no importance was attached to the meeting, or there was a deliberate attempt to distance Britain from Polish difficulties. Both explanations seem plausible. Cazalet was told by Eden that the visit was a 'military affair' and therefore presumably political guidelines were unnecessary.[128]

Sikorski's attempts to limit Anders' independence were not entirely successful. He himself was aware that if his plans were successful Anders was likely to end up commanding an army in the east numerically stronger than that being formed in the west. But for the present Sikorski confined his comments to restating the need to co-operate with the Soviet authorities.[129] Anders' aide-de-camp believed that his commander was satisfied with the outcome of the Sikorski–Stalin talks since the decision to move the Polish training camps south brought him closer to his ultimate objective of marching them out of the Soviet Union.[130]

While in the Middle East Sikorski visited the Polish Brigade in Tobruk and unnecessarily insulted Kopański by suggesting that he had not shown vigilance against Piłsudski loyalists.[131] The accusation was totally unfounded since Kopański, unlike Anders, distanced himself from political intrigues. In any case he and his soldiers had been directly involved in the defence of Tobruk and had had few opportunities for salon intrigues. On 10 December the siege of Tobruk was lifted and the Polish Brigade distinguished itself in the subsequent battles around Gazala. With Stalin's agreement to the removal of 30,000 soldiers from Russia to join units in the Middle East and Scotland, Sikorski was able to plan for an increased Polish contribution to the African campaign. The Independent Carpathian Brigade was to be expanded into a division and to continue fighting with the British Imperial Forces. After his Russian visit and these developments in the Middle East Sikorski's optimism appeared to be at its height. He was able to return to the subject of a Balkan front. On the assumption that Germany was likely to attack Turkey in the near future, Sokolnicki was again asked about the possibility of a Polish contribution to a Turkish–German war.[132] He was assured by the Ambassador that the preconditions for such co-operation did exist within Turkey.[133]

At the end of 1941 Sikorski's policies appeared to have resulted in Poland being placed in an extremely advantageous position. Poland's military contribution stood to be dramatically increased. While long-term Soviet objectives remained a source of anxiety, this was balanced by the apparently good relations between the Poles and the Russians. This sanguine view was belied even at this early stage of the war by the obvious lack of any political commitments to the Poles. The direct Polish contribution was to escalate but the basis for asserting and exercising political influence within the allied ranks had not been established. The opportunity for direct involvement in the liberation of Poland remained as hazy, if not more so, as before.

Foreign Office records contain evidence of an incident which throws an interesting light on this problem. At the beginning of December 1941 the War Office submitted to the Foreign Office a draft message for the Military Mission in Moscow concerning the substance of the Sikorski–Stalin arrangements for feeding and equipping the Polish army in Russia that was now to be expanded.[134] An unknown War Office civil servant mechanically restated the War Office's understanding of the new obligations. He minuted, 'all tonnage for Poles will necessarily be at direct expense of supplies for Russia and Sikorski will doubtless make this clear to Stalin'. Churchill noted the last point and furiously demanded to know who was the author of the letter. He minuted, 'We want the Poles armed as soon as possible. Why then should we tell the Russians that it will be at their expense?'[135] If nothing else, this exchange reveals the extent of the confusion prevailing on the subject of the Poles. No one in the Foreign Office was entirely clear whether to view Polish plans as directly relevant to the British war effort and therefore vital to British military plans. A constant anxiety also prevailed lest involvement with the Poles affect British relations with the Soviet Union. But this only raised the key question of what precisely was Britain's policy towards the Soviet Union.

5   1942, year of disappointments

On 26 May 1942 Britain and the Soviet Union signed a treaty. Though general in character, it was preceded by talks during which Britain to all purposes accepted the Soviet frontier adjustments that took place between September 1939 and June 1941. This meant that the incorporation of the Baltic states, Bessarabia and Bukovina, into Soviet territory was accepted as one of the war aims. The Polish frontier adjustments were included in these talks. Although their acceptance by Britain was not acknowledged, both Stalin and British politicians knew that, in the event of Poland being liberated by Soviet troops, Britain would not be able to reverse these earlier changes. British unwillingness to accept the frontier rectifications of September 1939 was the ostensible reason why both sides abandoned the text of the more detailed agreement discussed during the winter and spring of 1942. But the Soviet negotiators were left in no doubt that the Curzon Line would not be opposed by the British.[1]

The thorny question of war aims and post-war territorial settlements had been introduced into British–Soviet talks by Stalin's letter to Churchill of 8 November 1941.[2] In it the Soviet leader suggested that political talks had to precede any detailed agreements concerning joint strategy. Eden was forced to address himself to the issue in the full awareness that a failure to deal seriously with the Soviet request would heighten Soviet suspicions about British–American war objectives.[3] He argued that the Soviet Union feared that the two Allies would ignore Soviet interests. Eden's initial idea was to reassure the Soviet leadership that the Atlantic Charter created a sufficient basis for post-war territorial changes, and that once the war was finished they would be offered aid for reconstruction and economic recovery.[4] But Eden failed to divert Stalin from the topic of war aims. These became the main subject of discussions during Eden's visit to Moscow in December 1941. The British delegation found itself in a particularly difficult situation precisely because the aim of Eden's visit had been merely to reassure the Russians at a time when the British were finding it difficult to deliver promised supplies to the Soviet Union. In spite of their best intentions to deliver munitions and equipment to the Red Army, the Arctic Route was proving very wasteful and the Persian one was still very limited.[5] In these circumstances a refusal to discuss war aims would have been plainly imprudent.

Once in Moscow Eden found that the pace of debate was dictated by Stalin who was not impressed by the British Foreign Secretary's willingness to sign an agreement which referred only vaguely to military co-operation and principles laid down in the Atlantic Charter. He demanded that Britain accept the incorporation of the Baltic states into the Soviet Union. Furthermore Stalin insisted that Britain acknowledge the principle of the Soviet occupation of Bessarabia and Bukovina. In the case of Poland, Stalin made clear that he considered the Curzon Line, with a few adjustments, to be the only acceptable Soviet western frontier.[6] On hearing of these demands the War Cabinet implied that it could not accept the principle of Soviet territorial demands but acknowledged that at some time in the future it might be necessary to concede them. Clearly the next battle was going to be no longer over the principle of territorial adjustments, but over their details.[7]

When Eden returned from his trip to Moscow he championed Soviet demands. He was seriously perturbed by the possibility of events overtaking Britain. In particular he came to believe that the Soviet Union would emerge out of the war not weakened, but with enhanced prestige and militarily strong. In these circumstances it would be able to pursue policies independently of its wartime allies. He therefore concluded that the foundations for successful post-war co-operation should be built at a time of shared strife. Only then could Britain's prestige be established in Soviet eyes.[8]

In a memorandum entitled 'Policy Towards Russia', dated 28 January 1942, Eden discussed the complex issues.[9] As he pointed out, on the one hand there was the need to retain Soviet goodwill. On the other, he recognized the importance of retaining American help then and in the future. Eden was unwilling to deny that Britain was dependent on American aid. American policy on the subject of war aims was limited to the vague statements incorporated in the recently signed Atlantic Charter. Soviet demands and expectations were pulling Britain in the other direction, towards clear commitments in advance of a victory against Germany. Clearly compromises would have to be made somewhere. Eden was clear about a number of dilemmas. One was that Britain was not really opposed to conceding Soviet demands for territorial revision. Making outright concessions to the Soviet leadership was nevertheless considered an unwise move. Eden felt that a process of bargaining should be seen to be taking place. He thus wrote:

> It would not do to make this or, indeed, any concession to M. Stalin without requiring a suitable *quid pro quo*. He would, in his oriental mind, interpret such an omission as a sign of weakness. Besides, by insisting on our concessions being part of a bargain, we establish the rule that concessions must be mutual, and this will make it more difficult for the Soviet Government to press us subsequently to agree to yet further concessions, i.e., to push us on to the 'slippery slope'.[10]

Eden may have had some difficulty in finding suitable points which could be put to Stalin as viable bargaining issues. His counterproposals were rather general suggestions that the Soviet Union accept the establishment of British naval bases in Western Europe and subscribe to principles of no aggrandizement and support for confederations of smaller states.[11] Since none of these points were likely to elicit Soviet opposition, the hollowness of British bargaining with the Soviet Union could be easily exposed. Eden's own realistic assessment of Britain's influence over the position of the Soviet Union in Europe after the war was contained in a sentence: 'Our acquiescence or refusal cannot affect Russia's post-war frontiers one way or the other: if she is in occupation of the territory involved at the end of the war, neither we nor America will turn her out'.[12]

The Foreign Office too had a good idea of the problems which lay in store for British politicians once detailed negotiations on war aims were started with the Soviet Union. Its own analysis of diplomatic initiatives by a number of exile governments in Britain suggested that they would strongly oppose any pro-Soviet policy and were likely to form anti-Soviet alliances among themselves.[13] Nevertheless within the Foreign Office opinions were divided on the likely response to such a policy, and the relative importance of the response, by small Allies, the neutrals and not least of all the United States of America. There was fear and apprehension lest British actions and indecision alienate the Soviet leadership.[14]

Churchill strongly opposed Eden's suggestion that Britain should accept the Soviet demands. He adamantly stuck to the principle that territorial settlements should be agreed at a peace conference at the end of the war, and not earlier. The impasse was uneasily resolved by a joint decision to inform the American government of the substance of British–Soviet relations.[15] By then the question of whether to enter into closer agreements with the Soviet Union and whether to assist it more extensively had gone beyond the narrow confines of the government offices and had become a public issue.

The call for a second front in Europe to relieve the Soviet Union had been taken up by newspapers, trade unions and prominent individuals. In February 1942 the campaign became a particularly vociferous one in which support for the Soviet war effort became a rallying call for a variety of groups.[16] In the spring of 1942 Beaverbrook, who resigned from the Cabinet in February over the issue of aid to the Soviet Union, became a prominent figure in the campaign.[17] The result was that Churchill appeared to weaken in his resolve to oppose the conclusion of an agreement with the Soviet Union on the latter's terms. Public pressure and strong support for the idea from within the Foreign Office added to deep anxiety about the course of fighting in the Far East, where on 15 February Singapore surrendered. All this combined to make Churchill willing to reconsider the importance of the Soviet ally.[18]

By April 1942 the arguments for accepting the Soviet proposal for defining post-war boundaries became clearer. At the centre of all considerations lay the simple question of how much Britain needed the Soviet Union. In the spring the apparent answer to that question was simply that Britain needed the Soviet Union very much in order to continue fighting Nazi Germany and in order to be able to proceed with planning for the defeat of Japan.[19] From mid-April negotiations with the Soviet Union proceeded on the assumption that the incorporation of the Baltic states was a foregone conclusion.

On 20 April Molotov, the Soviet Minister for Foreign Affairs, arrived in London to conclude the talks for an agreement. The proposals which he brought with him exceeded even those to which the British had already expressed tacit agreement. Molotov now demanded a secret protocol specifying Soviet acquisitions. In addition Britain was effectively to dissociate herself from the course of Polish–Soviet exchanges.[20] The latter point proved a stumbling block. The British side was not prepared to dissociate itself from Poland. Molotov interpreted this as Britain taking Poland's side in the future conflict over the Soviet–Polish border. It has been suggested that Eden seized on this as an excuse to avoid an agreement which had in the meantime been aired publicly and as a result had caused deep offence to the smaller allied governments and threatened to create divisions within the government. He therefore suggested that the text of the agreement, which had been debated by the British and Soviet governments since January, be replaced by a simple treaty of mutual assistance without reference to war aims.[21] This was the treaty which was signed by both sides on 26 May 1942.

By that time the damage had been done. The course and substance of British–Soviet negotiations exposed the limits of American–British co-operation at the very time when it appeared that they were united in purpose. The Japanese attack on Pearl Harbor on 7 December and the resulting Japanese, German and Italian declarations of war against the United States and Britain ended a period during which the American administration had been pursuing different policies, reflecting the American government's ambivalent attitude towards the war. Bringing the United States now officially in as a wartime partner was a very welcome change for British politicians and military leaders. Nevertheless there were some disadvantages. The role of the Soviet Union in the war became a matter of direct concern to the Americans. The Soviet Union was an ally in the war against Germany but, more importantly, was also a prospective ally against Japan, even if in 1942 there was no likelihood of military action being taken by Soviet forces in Asia.[22] As a result American initiatives in relation to the Soviet Union became more overt and, therefore, pressure increased on Britain to fall in line with currently perceived United States priorities. This in turn affected British–American relations.

The first major disagreements between Britain and the United States emerged in December 1941 during Eden's visit to the Soviet Union. American State Department officials feared that he was unduly willing to accept Soviet demands for recognition of the June 1941 frontiers. Secretary of State Cordell Hull, supported by Roosevelt, strongly advised Eden against making any territorial commitments.[23] At the same time a policy of dissociation from British diplomacy towards the Soviet Union took shape. Hull firmly believed that when the time came to negotiate the peace treaty he would be able to drive a hard bargain. Prior commitments to any ally would therefore be imprudent.[24]

Throughout February 1942 America put pressure on Britain to prevent concessions being made to the Soviet Union. The State Department also disapproved of a British counterproposal to the Soviet Union, whereby the Soviet Union would commit itself not to interfere in territorial matters in Central Europe and the Balkan states in return for naval bases and a tacit acceptance of the inclusion of the

Baltic states, some Finnish territory, Bessarabia and Bukovina in the Soviet Union.[25] The ultimate threat used by Under-Secretary of State Sumner Welles was that the United States would dissociate itself from any Anglo-Soviet deal which was not based on the principles in the Atlantic Charter.[26] Eden and Churchill tried to resolve their own doubts and differences by deferring the whole matter until American approval was obtained. In this way they were swayed by Roosevelt's disapproval of their policies. Unable to obtain diplomatic co-operation and unwilling to defy American opinion, British politicians opted for a general treaty with the Soviet Union which did not address itself to territorial issues.[27]

Since the possibility of opening up a second front had receded, as well as hopes of increasing supplies to Russia, the weakness of the British negotiating position with the Soviet Union was that Britain had nothing to offer other than concessions on Soviet borders. In the spring of 1942 British policy-makers, notably Churchill, became anxious lest early Soviet victories cause Stalin to dissociate himself from the fate of Western Europe and concentrate on consolidating his victories in Eastern Europe.[28] Widely publicized rumours that the Soviet leaders were considering making peace with Germany were discounted at the Foreign Office. But they added to the air of tension and apprehension.[29] Eden felt hampered in his attempts to steer British negotiations with the Soviet Union, in the direction of accepting the 1941 frontiers, by Churchill's idiosyncratic leadership and a general lack of guidelines.[30]

Churchill's biographer has suggested a more complex reason for the lack of direction in the course of negotiations with the Soviet Union. According to Martin Gilbert, Churchill's interest in the Eastern front was reawakened in March 1942 by secret information which suggested that Germany would mount a major offensive in the near future.[31] But Churchill's decision to address himself to the question of Soviet demands was linked to the overall strategic situation in the Middle East and not merely the fate of the Eastern front. In view of British defeats in the Far East, and the renewed offensive by Rommel in North Africa, the Caucasus front became once more of key importance. Churchill drew Roosevelt's attention to this issue in a letter of 5 March. He wrote that the protection of the Levant–Caspian front depended 'entirely upon Russia, who will be formidably attacked in the spring'.[32] This led Churchill to put forward ideas which the British Chiefs of Staff did not like and which they did all in their power to sink. On the eve of Eden's December 1941 visit to Moscow, the Chiefs of Staff had been suddenly faced with Churchill's proposal to move troops from the Middle East to the Caucasus and a suggestion that British troops should be offered to Stalin to take part in the defence of that region. General Alan Brooke, who replaced Dill as Chief of the Imperial General Staff in November 1941, wrote in his diary that they were able to dissuade Churchill from making such an offer to Stalin.[33] As far as the British military leaders were concerned the reconquest of North Africa had to be followed by action in the Mediterranean and against Italy. There was no place in their plans for assistance to the Soviet Union in the Caucasus or elsewhere.[34] They, and ultimately also Churchill, preferred American assistance to go towards helping the British in the Far East. It was in these circumstances that both the Soviet and Polish leaders increasingly used Washington as a pretext in their negotiations with the British.

The Poles were well aware of their inherently weak bargaining position in relation to Britain and the Soviet Union. They therefore strove all the harder to prove Poland's worth and reliability as an ally. In the final analysis, the Polish government-in-exile had everything to gain from the alliance with Britain and not much, or so it was believed, from assuming an independent negotiating position in relation to the Soviet Union. The general assumption was that Britain and the United States would have a decisive say in post-war politics, and the Soviet Union, if it survived in its present shape and political profile, would be weakened and therefore unlikely to have a strong bargaining position.

On his return from his trip to Moscow and the Middle East in January 1942, Sikorski in the first place sought to reaffirm his commitment to Britain. An account of his visit to Russia was given to the British by Sikorski in a secret memorandum.[35] The Foreign Office was made aware that the Polish Prime Minister did not want his own government to know that he had informed the British in full about the course of Soviet–Polish talks.

On 19 January Sikorski had a meeting with Eden during which Sikorski explained that he had rejected Stalin's offer to discuss frontier agreements without reference to the British. Stalin had tried to dissuade the Polish Prime Minister from thinking in terms of three-power co-operation. He sought to assure Sikorski that all difficulties between the two states could be resolved without reference to Britain. It would appear that Stalin was prepared to accept the Polish government's key demands, notably the restoration of the eastern regions about which Stalin promised he 'would not be difficult'. He was willing to see the town of Lvov go to Poland. In addition he stated that East Prussia

should be Polish. Most notable was Stalin's attempt to persuade
Sikorski that agreements should be made between the two governments 'in advance of the peace settlement without reference to His
Majesty's Government'.[36] Sikorski loyally reported to Eden that 'his
answer to Stalin's approach had been that he could not discuss these
territorial matters at present and that he must continue to collaborate
with His Majesty's Government who had been entirely loyal to the
Polish Government'.

Sikorski's decision to reject Stalin's overtures and not to negotiate
with the Soviet Union on a bilateral basis was based on an excessively
optimistic evaluation of the future course of Polish–British relations.
The Polish government appeared to believe that the military units
under their command would continue to expand. Furthermore they
were convinced that joint military action in the Middle East and Africa
would increase the government's standing in British eyes. The proposed removal of some of the troops from the Soviet Union and the
apparent British need for the build-up of the army in the Middle East
and North Africa seemed to suggest that Polish–British unity would
soon be consummated and that political co-operation would be the
natural fruit of such an alliance. Nevertheless Sikorski, as much as any
of his Polish opponents, was wary lest the proposed marriage should
be found upon closer inspection to be mere concubinage. He intended
to see that the British made commitments before troops were handed
over to them. But the exile government's rejection of Soviet overtures
meant that, if the British showed themselves unwilling to make any
political commitments, the Poles would still have no choice but to fight
in the west. Were the Poles to withdraw from military co-operation
with Britain then this would amount to relegating Poland to the status
of an object of other powers' diplomatic and military decisions. Political unity had to be achieved simultaneously with joint military action
if the Poles were to achieve their objectives.

Therefore in order to reinforce in British minds the Polish
government-in-exile's commitment to its British ally in shouldering
the burden of fighting, Sikorski used his meeting with Eden on 19
January 1942 to remind him of the need to start making joint plans for
the future.[37] The full extent of Polish aspirations was laid in front of
the British Foreign Secretary. Post-war Poland, according to Sikorski,
would be restored to pre-war borders and being 'more closely connected with Great Britain, [Poland] ought to play a cardinal part in Central
Eastern Europe'.[38] Sikorski drew parallels between the stability of
Europe and that of Poland:

> The security of Poland is identical with the security of Europe. That is proved by various events of the war which is now going on. In order to guarantee Polish security we must win for ourselves the frontiers which correspond to our own most modest strategic requirements.

One of those requirements was the creation of a Polish–Lithuanian Federation. That the Lithuanian side did not show enthusiasm for the proposal was noted by Eden, but did not stop Sikorski from dwelling on the hope that the Polish–Lithuanian unity, which had been the strength of the Polish crown in the fifteenth century, could once more be established to Poland's advantage. He confided to Eden the Polish hope that an English prince would be permitted to become the monarch of a restored Poland. Before departing Sikorski broached a subject dear to the hearts of many pre-war Polish politicians, the removal of Polish Jews from Poland. Clearly suggesting that they could not be considered to be a Polish responsibility Sikorski stated: 'It is quite impossible ... for Poland to continue to maintain 3.5 million Jews after the war. Room must be found for them elsewhere. If Palestine could be highly industrialized, there might be room for them there'.[39]

The vision of a Greater Poland, the bulwark of Christianity in the east, with a monarchy which had been seeded from an imported British prince, *Judenfrei* since its Jewish citizens would have become the responsibility of the British in Palestine, contained no element which could have appealed to the British Foreign Secretary.

The Poles did not depend merely on persuasion to obtain British support for their post-war aspirations. By the beginning of 1942 the government-in-exile consciously embarked upon a policy of wrecking allied unity with the Soviet Union.[40] Sikorski's submission to Eden was the opening salvo of that programme. Another element in that programme was an attempt by the Poles to start a propaganda campaign in the United States aimed at obtaining direct United States commitments to the Polish government and to seek Roosevelt's support in persuading the British against signing agreements with the Soviet Union.[41]

In December 1941 the Polish Ambassador in Washington, Jan Ciechanowski, sought to persuade the State Department that there was a need to be vigilant when dealing with the Soviet Union since it was harbouring hidden territorial aims in Europe. Neither he nor Raczyński, who arrived in the United States in February 1942 with a similar message, were successful.[42] Roosevelt refused to consider signing a separate treaty with the Polish government-in-exile and Welles warned Raczyński that, even though territorial adjustments had not been discussed by the American and Soviet governments, the State Department felt that the Soviet Union would be entitled to borders which took into account its security needs.[43] Even though the State Department had decided to recommend that post-war territorial adjustments and American war aims be discussed by a commission specially set up for that purpose, the Poles were not informed of its deliberations.[44]

Sikorski's second visit to the United States took place between 24 and 30 March. Prior to his arrival there a decision had been made by American politicians not to encourage him in his plans for a Central European Federation. There was also strong opposition within the State Department to Sikorski's attempts to mobilize the Polish community. It was felt that it would interfere with the stated objective of emphasizing the Soviet Union's role as an ally.[45] Not surprisingly therefore, in spite of having two meetings with Roosevelt, Sikorski failed to obtain American support. Roosevelt let it be known that he did not support British attempts to sign an alliance with the Soviet Union. Nevertheless his reaffirmation of the Atlantic Charter, accompanied by a statement that questions relating to territorial adjustment should be settled after the war, rendered Sikorski's trip futile.[46] During the critical March days when the extent of British and American dissociation from Polish–Soviet relations was finally impressed upon him, Sikorski may have seriously considered abandoning his commitment to Poland's western partners and allying himself directly with the Soviet Union.[47] Sikorski's communications with the Allies and the Soviet Union reveal little to substantiate this.

Polish attempts to gain support in Washington and efforts to undermine the British–Soviet negotiations caused fury in the Foreign Office. The Poles' public pronouncements suggesting that Britain was not in favour of the Curzon Line and that Polish aspirations towards Lithuania were viewed favourably by Britain, had the opposite effect to the one sought by the Poles. Forced to re-examine commitments made to the Poles, Foreign Office civil servants were able to consider anew the history of Polish–British relations and thus remind themselves of how little in fact united the two nations. Eden now justified his personal preference for negotiating with the Soviet Union by contrasting the British need for the Soviet ally with the rather tenuous recent links with Poland. Commenting upon a record of a conversation between Ambassador Kot and Lacy Baggallay, the British Counsellor in

Moscow, from which it appeared as if the Pole tried to provoke a negative British reaction to Stalin's demands, Eden furiously minuted his doubts about the Polish cause.[48] He demanded to know whether there existed any statements by British officials repudiating the Curzon Line principle. He also reminded the Foreign Office that 'Poland attacked Lithuania and robbed her of Vilna after the last war'. Already in January the mood within the Foreign Office was hardening against the Poles. Decisions were made to end Polish interference in British policies. On 26 January Eden saw Raczyński to dissuade the Poles from using the term 'territory of the Polish Republic' in relation to areas incorporated into the Soviet Union in 1940. Among a number of Foreign Office minutes, that written by the Deputy Under-Secretary Orme Sargent contained the frankest statement of the British position:

> I am inclined to think that we ought to take this opportunity to make it quite clear to the Polish Government that we cannot allow them to complicate an already delicate situation by putting forward suddenly a quite unwarranted claim in regard to Lithuania ... they have no case whatever on legal grounds such as exist in the case of Lvov for putting forward a claim to treating Lithuania as within Poland's sphere of influence. But after all, it is not our concern. What is our concern is that we do not choose to have our relations with the Soviet Government complicated by the Polish Government butting in quite irresponsibly with this untenable claim.[49]

According to Armine Dew of the Northern Department, although the future of Poland depended on the three big Allies, the Soviet Union would inevitably have the biggest say on developments in Central and Eastern Europe after the war. If the Poles failed to understand this they would, according to Dew, 'suffer the same fate as the Bourbons whom they appear closely to resemble'.[50]

On 27 March Eden informed Cecil Dormer, the British Ambassador to the Polish government-in-exile, of an interview which Cadogan had had with Władysław Kulski, the Polish Chargé d'affaires. The purpose of the interview was plainly to reprimand the Poles for their public expression of disaffection with British policies. Cadogan had told Kulski, 'The Soviet Union were at the moment heavily engaged in fighting our common enemy, and would shortly be called upon to resist a further powerful thrust. All our fortunes were bound up to a considerable extent with the success of the Soviet effort'.[51] Writing to Raczyński on 17 April, Eden re-emphasized this point by stating that the goodwill and collaboration of the Soviet Union were vital, both in order to defeat Germany and in order to implement post-war settlements. With their contribution to the war being so important, the Soviet Union could not be denied either then or in the future a say commensurate with that contribution.[52]

Polish expectations that the defeat of Germany would automatically bestow territorial benefits on Poland posed a problem in the Foreign Office. In spite of persistent denials to the contrary, the Poles chose to believe that British–Soviet discussions were in essence a debate over spheres of influence in post-war Europe. The Polish government therefore expected their claims to be considered and discussed too. In addition to hopes that Lithuania would be recognized as being in the Polish sphere of influence, they let it be known that they expected to receive East Prussia. After all Stalin had supported this claim during Sikorski's Moscow visit. The Foreign Office always opposed the ideas mainly because publicizing prior claims to German territory would make it difficult, when the time came, to reach a negotiated peace with a post-war German government. Writing on 16 April Sargent noted that British support for a Polish claim on East Prussia would be disastrous since 'such a declaration would rally German public opinion in defence of German territory, especially of a territory which stands for so much in German history as does Eastern Prussia'.[53] Eden concurred with this view. Sargent's suggestion that, instead of Britain making a public declaration that Poland would receive East Prussia, the Russians should be induced to make such a statement, was not proceeded with.

While the government-in-exile concentrated its diplomatic efforts on persuading the British government to abandon its proposed alliance with the Soviet Union and on obtaining American assistance, the biggest threat to Sikorski's vision of a strong independent Polish role within the allied ranks came from the Polish military leadership. Anders' removal of the whole army from the Soviet Union to Iran probably lost the Poles any chance of exercising an independent policy in relation to the Soviet Union and Britain. By the end of 1942 the departure for Iran of all Anders' troops placed all Polish fighting units abroad under direct British command without any prior British reciprocal commitment to safeguard Polish political interests.

Equally damaging to Sikorski's vision was the fact that, outside Russia, Anders' units could no longer participate directly in the liberation of Poland. According to Anders, their role was to go into battle together with the British. By the end of 1942 the Balkan front was no longer a priority whereas the Mediterranean and North Africa, and after that Italy, came to dominate British military debates. Thus

Anders' actions spelt an end to the hope that soldiers of the government-in-exile would liberate Poland. As it turned out that would only be possible from the east, where no units loyal to London remained.

The decision to get Polish soldiers out of the Soviet Union was made in a piecemeal way and was the outcome of various circumstances. By limiting the army's expansion, the Soviet leadership let it be known that they wanted the Poles to leave. Anders had long been conducting a campaign of disobedience and Sikorski had little control over his actions. Finally the British military authorities in the Middle East were very helpful since they were in dire need. The link between Poland's political aspirations and her military contribution had always been more of a hope than a reality. Sikorski could not realize those aspirations even when asked to make the ultimate contribution of all the soldiers under his command. By the end of 1942 all Polish units came under British direct or indirect command.

The removal of the Polish units and civilian dependants to Persia remains an intriguing and not entirely clearly documented episode in the history of the Second World War. The degree of Soviet complicity is uncertain. So too is the role of the British military command in the Middle East. Clearly Anders and the bulk of his officers and men did not want to stay and fight in the Soviet Union. It is also apparent that no political concessions were made by the British in the wake of the Poles joining their hard-pressed troops in the Middle East.

The events which precipitated the Polish evacuation from the Soviet Union most probably started with an interview on 2 January 1942 between General Georgi Zhukov, the Soviet liaison officer with the Polish army, and General Anders. The purpose of the meeting was to ask officially when the Polish troops would be ready to go into battle.[54] Anders refused to give a binding answer, pointing out that neither food, clothing nor equipment had been available, thus delaying the preparedness of the Polish soldiers. He refused to accept Zhukov's suggestion that the participation of the Polish units in the Soviet war effort would have important political implications.[55] The Soviet commander was not convinced by Anders' arguments that individual units could not go to the front. He pointed out that the use of Polish troops as a whole rather than individual units had not been a precondition for Polish action with the British in Tobruk.[56]

Sikorski approved Anders' reply to the Soviet authorities in a message which he sent to Anders on 7 February.[57] He furthermore authorized Anders to inform the Soviet leaders that he (Sikorski) remained committed to military co-operation but 'could not agree to their neglect of that enormous allied trump card, which the use of the whole of the Polish army would be'.

This agreement between Sikorski and Anders was deceptive. Both leaders were aware of the British need for troops in the Middle East. In his memoirs Anders made an oblique allusion to the possibility of Sikorski weakening and succumbing to Soviet demands to send individual Polish divisions to the front. Writing how he informed Sikorski about the substance of Zhukov's communication he stated, 'I had my doubts, because I knew that General Sikorski had earlier ... put forward an idea that two divisions, even if unarmed, should go to the Caucasus, in order to defend the oil-fields'.[58] For his part, Sikorski felt that he was likely to lose control over developments so far away from London, in particular because he was *en route* to the United States and would be unable to supervise closely the crisis unfolding in the Soviet Union. This is apparent from a telegram he sent to the Polish Ministry for Foreign Affairs on 10 February in which he referred to rumours that British and Soviet military and political authorities had held a conference about the evacuation of 25,000 Poles from the Soviet Union.[59] Rather touchily, Sikorski pointed out that appropriate decisions had been made as a result of Polish–Soviet talks and not British–Soviet talks.

On 23 February Anders informed the Polish government in London of an increasing feeling that the Soviet authorities were becoming suspicious of Polish unwillingness to go into battle. In response to an enquiry he also reported that rumours about the formation of another Polish army in Siberia had not been confirmed.[60]

The British desire to receive Polish soldiers in the Middle East in order to reinforce troops there coincided with Anders' determination to depart from the Soviet Union. The idea that Poles from the Soviet Union might reinforce British units in the Middle East had been extensively aired by Sikorski and in principle he supported the idea. There was nevertheless a crucial difference between his view and that of Anders. While Sikorski wanted the restructuring of units which had already fought with the British in North Africa and the replenishing of the army being trained in Scotland, he also wanted the Polish military presence in the Soviet Union to continue.

The decisive factor which precipitated the decision to leave was the Soviet authorities' resolution to reduce food supplies to the Polish units. In a communication on 10 March Stalin confirmed the earlier instructions of his quartermaster-general to reduce rations to the

Polish army to feed only 30,000 men. This move was justified by the apparent inability of the British and the Americans to supply the Russians with food. Stalin's communiqué stated that: 'In view of the above we had to reconsider the maintenance plan of the Army favouring the actually fighting divisions at the expense of non fighting divisions'.[61] Stalin's message ended with an invitation to Anders to go to Moscow to discuss the matter directly with him. Anders availed himself of the opportunity thus offered and the two men met on 18 March.[62]

Stalin evidently wanted the number of Polish troops in the Soviet Union reduced. It is possible that he had already decided to end his agreement with Sikorski. Anders, on the other hand, wanted to join the British. The two men had no difficulty in agreeing that, while a force of 44,000 men should remain in the Soviet Union, the remainder, approximately 40,000 men, should swiftly depart for Iran. The tone of the conversation was intimate. Anders spoke fluent Russian, so they met without an interpreter. Stalin was keen to stress the common aim of fighting the war. He digressed frequently to emphasize that he was aware of the small inconveniences experienced by the Poles. For his part, Anders was agreeable and accommodating. The key decision concerning the departure of Poles for Iran was made within a minute. The conversation moved as follows:

> STALIN: ... I am not pressing for you [the Poles] to go to the front. I understand, that it will be better for you to go to the front, when we come nearer to the Polish border. You should have this honour, of being the first to enter on Polish soil.
> ANDERS: Well, if there is no other way, the rest (surplus to the approved 44,000) should be sent to Persia.
> STALIN: Agreed. 44,000 of your soldiers will remain with us, the rest will be evacuated. There is no other way.[63]

Decisions made at this meeting were quite specific. It was agreed that the point of evacuation should be Krasnovodsk, a port on the south-eastern coast of the Caspian Sea. The troops would be shipped to the Iranian port of Pahlevi on the south-western coast where, according to Anders, the British had already prepared reception points for approximately 25,000 Polish servicemen. These were in addition to pilots and sailors who were to be evacuated under earlier agreements. Anders was convinced that the British would be helpful and that ammunition would be made available from British and confiscated Iranian stores. Stalin also agreed to give Anders an aeroplane so that he could go to Cairo and from there to London. A renewed attempt by

Anders to ascertain the fate of Polish officers from the camps of
Starobielsk, Kozielsk and Ostaszków was unsuccessful.[64]

The decision to evacuate the troops was unexpected and was
received with surprise in London. On 24 March Ambassador Kot had
an interview with Andrei Vyshinsky, Deputy Foreign Minister, in
which he tried to reverse the agreement made between Anders and
Stalin. While there is no evidence that he was acting under instruction
from Sikorski, who was in Washington, Kot nevertheless spoke in his
own and the government's name. He reminded Vyshinsky that
Sikorski and his government were committed to maintaining a Polish
army in the Soviet Union. Neither Kot nor the Polish government
were able to get in touch with Sikorski and were forced to confine
themselves to expressing regret at the Soviet government's decision to
limit the Polish troops in the Soviet Union to 44,000.[65] Kot had the
reputation of an inveterate intriguer, but he was known to be
Sikorski's confidant. It is therefore safe to assume that his comments to
Vyshinsky reflected Sikorski's feelings. Kot's attempt to reverse the
agreement made with Anders was unsuccessful. Vyshinsky reaffirmed
the Soviet leadership's determination to proceed with the evacuation
to Iran of the Polish troops in excess of the permitted 44,000.

Evidence available does not suggest that Stalin, or any other of the
Soviet leaders, at this stage at least considered entirely abandoning the
agreements made with the London Poles. General Zygmunt Berling,
who subsequently became the Commander of the Polish Kościuszko
Division formed in the Soviet Union after the diplomatic break
between the Polish government-in-exile and Moscow in 1943, wrote
that prior to Anders' departure for Iran the Soviet authorities were
unwilling to give approval for the creation of Polish units within the
Red Army. They considered that the army which was being formed by
Anders reflected the spirit of the Soviet–Polish agreement.[66] Further
evidence concerning Soviet objectives is available from Wanda
Wasilewska, an ex-member of the Polish Socialist Party who had
become notorious among her compatriots for sitting as a Supreme
Soviet deputy for the occupied region of Western Ukraine, thus legiti-
mizing the Soviet occupation of Poland's eastern territories. In her
recollections she states clearly that Stalin did not answer her earlier
letter, written in the autumn of 1941, in which she had asked that Poles
should be accepted directly into the Red Army. She believed that his
unusual reluctance to answer her could only be explained by Stalin's
feeling bound by the agreement with Sikorski, which stated that Poles
in the Soviet Union should be sent to the Polish units formed under

Anders' command.[67] Although the Soviet authorities did try to set up a pro-Soviet organization in occupied Poland, agents were not parachuted into Poland until December 1941.[68] First contacts between the Soviet authorities and the scattered and disorganized groups of Communists in Poland which were to form the Polish Workers Party were not established until approximately May 1942 when regular radio contact became possible.[69] During 1941 and the first months of 1942 Sikorski believed that the Soviet government did abide by the terms of the Sikorski–Maisky agreement. For reasons which were not entirely understood in London, this changed in the spring of 1942 to obstructiveness and a determination to limit the size of the Polish army. Military difficulties and supply shortages were considered to be the most obvious explanations of this change. Nevertheless Sikorski did not believe that these were being used to force Polish government representatives to stop recruitment and leave the Soviet Union.

Once Anders and Stalin had agreed to the evacuation of some of the Polish troops to Iran, the operation was started and completed by 3 April. Since the British authorities had already prepared facilities to receive 27,000 men in Pahlevi, and their Middle East Command undoubtedly wanted the Polish soldiers, neither the Polish nor British authorities in London were able to control the unexpected developments. Instructions from London tended to follow in the wake of already resolved local problems. On 19 March the Polish authorities in London were informed of the War Office's decision to receive 27,000 men from Krasnovodsk. According to previous agreements made by Churchill and Sikorski 15,000 men were to stay in the Middle East and the remainder were to join Polish formations in Britain. That same day Sikorski's assent to this was received.[70] But on 22 March the War Office received a request from the Commander-in-Chief Middle East that all Poles from Russia be retained in the Middle East rather than despatched to Britain.[71]

Churchill agreed with this proposal. On 29 March he telegraphed Sikorski suggesting that instead of the Polish soldiers coming to Britain they should all be deployed in the Middle East.[72] Sikorski's answer clearly showed an attempt to make a virtue of an unexpected situation over which he had little control. In his response he implied that his analysis of military developments had led him to conclude that there was a need to create a strong army in the Middle East.[73] He agreed that the main area of concentration of the Polish army should henceforth be the Middle East. Nevertheless he still wanted airmen and sailors to be brought to Britain, together with personnel for the formation of an armoured division and a paratroop brigade. But Sikorski was still not thinking in terms of reducing the army in the Soviet Union. In the same message to Churchill he requested that Britain put pressure on the Soviet authorities to maintain the recruitment programme of Poles, so that it should continue without any ceiling on the numbers under Anders' command. As he pointed out, Polish soldiers in excess of those required in Russia would in any case be evacuated to the Middle East.[74]

The latter point caused a flurry of discussion within the Foreign Office. Roger Makins, head of Central Department, drew up a memorandum which captures the disdain with which British officials came to treat Polish requests and with which Eden concurred. Having acknowledged that Britain was to receive a reinforcement of 35,000 fighting men in the Middle East, Makins wrote: 'In any case, the question of drafts for the Polish divisions in the USSR is one which the Poles and the Russians ought to be able to settle between themselves'.[75] Oblivious to any suggestion that Britain was now benefiting from the recruitment of those Polish divisions in the Soviet Union, and untroubled by pangs of gratitude, Eden agreed with Makins' analysis. Both Cadogan and Oliver Harvey confined the comments in their respective diaries to irritation at Polish intrigues against the British–Soviet treaty, with Harvey writing on 12 April: 'They have drawn heavily on their credit with A. E[den]'.[76] The manpower contribution made by the Poles to the British war effort in North Africa was evidently not credited to their political account.

As on so many occasions, the Poles proved to be their own worst enemies: at least in this case Anders proved to be Sikorski's key antagonist. Through Colonel Hulls, the British liaison officer with the Polish forces in the Soviet Union, Anders had already established direct contact with Middle East Command and proceeded to negotiate with it. Sikorski's policy objectives were seen increasingly as obstacles not merely to Anders' endeavours but also to the needs and plans of the British Commander-in-Chief in the Middle East.

Anders' decision that civilian Poles who had made their way to the Polish camps should not be abandoned but evacuated with the troops was as unexpected to the British authorities in Iran as it was to the Poles in London. But Anders refused to change his mind. He had always viewed his mission as broader than merely organizing Polish military units. He saw himself as creating havens of safety for Polish people in the Soviet Union, asserting that if left unprotected, those dependants would most probably die. Poles frequently arrived at army recruitment points together with families who had suffered deportation with their menfolk. Even those who were unlikely to be recruited into the army gravitated to the Polish recruitment centres seeking protection. All of them were invariably in need of assistance. This reinforced the determination of the army recruitment officers to extend protection to civilians. These circumstances contributed further to the bond of loyalty which united the people who had left the Soviet Union with Anders. Neither Kot's disapproving message to London[77] nor the ensuing rebuke addressed to Anders by Sikorski[78] had any effect on the situation. As a result of Anders' insistence that civilians leave with the army, the first evacuation from the Soviet Union consisted of 33,000 military personnel and approximately 11,000 civilians.

As the Polish troops prepared to depart, the Soviet authorities insisted that Polish citizens who were Jews, Ukrainians and Byelorussians should not be allowed to join the transports. The Soviet authorities had earlier made it difficult for Kot to represent the interests of Polish Jews.[79] After the first evacuation had been completed representatives of the Polish authorities in Russia came under strong attack for their failure to include Jews in the transports to Pahlevi. According to Kot and reports filed after the first evacuation had been completed, Soviet officers rigorously inspected the operation and weeded out all those whom they suspected of being Jewish.[80]

The determination of the Soviet authorities not to allow Polish Jews to leave with the army was not the only reason why a high proportion of Polish Jews were left behind. A study of numerous personal accounts deposited in the Sikorski Institute in London by Poles who had participated in the evacuation of troops from the Soviet Union in 1942 reveals a very complex and mixed picture. While the Soviet authorities made a legal distinction between Poles of Polish nationality and Polish Jews, whom they treated as non-Polish nationals and since December 1942 as Soviet citizens, the Polish authorities were guided by crude nationalist and anti-Semitic prejudices. This meant that local recruiting agents, who had total freedom to decide who was allowed to join the army in the Soviet Union, could determine whether Polish Jews were eligible to join the army. In a lot of cases, reflecting the prevailing prejudices of their community, they refused to accept them. General Anders' aide-de-camp Klimkowski claimed that in January 1942 Anders asked the Red Army liaison officer Colonel Yevsiegnieyev to tell the Soviet authorities to stop directing non-Polish nationals, in particular Jews, to the recruitment centres.[81] According to Klimkowski Anders consistently aimed at creating a national Polish army, a process in which the Soviet authorities assisted him, albeit for different reasons.

During his meeting with Stalin on 18 March Anders had requested permission to go to London. This he did in April, travelling first to Cairo then through Nigeria, Lisbon, Ireland and finally from Bristol to London. General Kopański followed in his footsteps on his way to Britain after ten months' active service as Commander of the Polish Independent Carpathian Brigade with the 8th Army in North Africa. On arrival in Bristol Anders, with Hulls and his aide-de-camp, was flown to London while Kopański had to make his way there by train.[82] The impression created was that Anders was being lionized by the British.

Although the official purpose of his visit to London was to report to and obtain further orders from Sikorski, he in fact took advantage of his stop-over in Cairo to seek Auchinleck's approval for the removal of the remainder of the Polish forces from the Soviet Union to the Middle East.[83] According to Klimkowski, Auchinleck was persuaded to support Anders' plan. Anders assured him that the units still in the Soviet Union were in better physical condition than those just arriving in Iran, and that they were ready for military action.[84] Klimkowski believed that Anders, with support from Hulls and Auchinleck, decided then that his plan for getting the whole Polish army out of Russia was likely to succeed. While details of these exchanges cannot be verified, Anders undoubtedly made a very good impression on the Middle East Command. On 4 April Middle East Command sent a message to the War Office requesting support for Anders' case.[85]

While Auchinleck's enthusiasm for the idea of receiving six Polish divisions is understandable, his willingness to support Anders' political strategy is less obvious. The message to the War Office contained an argument which must have been put forward by the Poles, namely that 'Stalin favoured concentration of all Poles in the Middle East and if he heard they were going elsewhere he might close doors on further evacuation'. This argument was used on 22 April by the Defence Committee and the Chiefs of Staff to support the proposal to get all Polish troops out of Russia and into the Middle East.[86] The British government had other reasons to support Anders against the Polish authorities in London. His willingness to place himself unconditionally under British command contrasted with the exile government's attempt to barter and wheedle political support in return for military co-operation. Within the British military leadership the debate was concluded in the last week of April when discussions took place within the Chief of Staff Committee. The War Office bowed to pressure from the Middle East Command and requested that all Poles evacuated from the Soviet Union be concentrated in the Middle East.[87] One small obstacle remained: Sikorski's opposition to this strategy.[88] But by 29 April the Chiefs of Staff were told that Sikorski had expressed his agreement to their proposals.[89]

If one is to judge Anders' visit to London by his contacts and negotiations with British military and political leaders, it had been a success. At the time, some even felt that he had become intoxicated with attention accorded him by the British in the Middle East and in London.[90] By contrast his relations with the Polish government were neither smooth nor easy. Anders had come to London with the express intention of persuading Sikorski to accept a proposal to abandon the Polish–Soviet agreement, although it has also been suggested that he wanted to establish contacts with Sikorski's political opponents.[91] During briefings of the Chiefs of Staff of the Polish Armed Forces Abroad on 23, 25 and 27 April, in which Anders participated, two different strategic views were discussed, reflecting the different political and military perspectives of their respective proponents, Sikorski and Anders.

Anders remained convinced that the Soviet Union's military effort would collapse and that the main German thrust would be towards the Middle East. Since he believed that the second front would not be opened in the near future he considered that all Polish forces should be concentrated in the Middle East. This would enable them to enter Poland from the south or south-east. According to him Polish troops had to reach Poland before the 'Bolsheviks'. Anders further suggested that Stalin would welcome his proposal to move all Poles out of Russia and concentrate them in the Middle East, in preference to proposals to send Polish soldiers to Britain. He argued that Stalin wanted to see the British war effort in that region reinforced.[92] Anders had apparently presented this thesis to President Raczkiewicz and obtained his support.[93]

Sikorski, supported by the Minister for National Defence, General Marian Kukiel, opposed both Anders' analysis and his conclusions. He insisted that Polish troops should participate in allied military action on the Continent of Europe and not in the Middle East. He and Kukiel did not discount the possibility of a second front being opened in the west in 1942. Accordingly an army of 44,000 should remain in the Soviet Union with the explicit aim of co-operating and entering into Poland with Soviet troops. Sikorski opposed the idea of concentrating all Polish exile forces in the Middle East to satisfy Auchinleck's self-interest.[94] Political commitments would be obtained from the Allies in return for Poland's military contribution to the war. Anders did not agree.

By the final meeting of the Polish Chiefs of Staff, on 27 April, Sikorski had been clearly forced to accept Anders' points. The reasons for his failure to defend his own policy are not entirely clear. There is no doubt that he was forced to bow to pressure from within the Polish exile community and from the British. Anders' political influence in Britain is difficult to assess. It may be that his ideas merely coincided with those of the British military leadership. That much can be concluded from the interview he had with General Alan Brooke on 24 April, when Anders assured him that not only Sikorski but also Stalin were in agreement with his proposal to concentrate Polish forces in the Middle East.[95] Needless to say Brooke was delighted to hear of the decision to retain the bulk of the Polish army in the Middle East since Syrian deployments needed reinforcement.[96] When Sikorski informed Churchill of the decision to leave the troops evacuated from Russia in the Middle East, he made the proviso that 1,200 men be brought to Britain to join the Polish navy and 1,500 to join the air force.[97]

Anders had moved a step further towards ending the Polish military presence in the Soviet Union. He himself admitted that throughout he had thought in terms of evacuating the remainder of the Polish troops out of the Soviet Union.[98] He was convinced that Churchill supported him. During his meeting with Anders Churchill had apparently expressed interest in the soldiers still on Soviet territory.[99] Anders took this to be a discreet hint that the British could make use of those men too. Sikorski was the main obstacle since he persisted in his policy of keeping some Polish units in the Soviet Union even after being forced to accept the concentration of Anders' Polish army corps in the Middle East. This he hoped would form the nucleus of a larger Polish army in the Middle East. Ever anxious to be seen exercising influence over strategic matters, Sikorski at the time suggested to Brooke that a number of Polish officers could be available 'for consultation in operations for the development of a second front'.[100]

When Anders went back to the Soviet Union he knew that he could defy Sikorski's instructions with impunity since he would be supported by the British military authorities. Anders was right in one respect. His belief that the second front was not going to be opened in 1942 proved correct. Nevertheless his London visit marked the end of Sikorski's policy of staking out for Poland a role as an ally in a joint war effort, rather than narrowing Poland's options down entirely to one of supporting Britain. Arguably by the spring of 1942 the Polish government-in-exile had no political influence. But Sikorski never lost sight of the political potential of any military contribution that the Poles either offered or were asked to make to the war. Anders' actions weakened his bargaining position by committing all the manpower resources of the Polish government-in-exile to one ally, who was already showing signs of weariness with the Poles. From this point onwards the Poles would have no alternative but to continue pledging further resources to the British cause. They had lost the freedom to decide in which theatre of war they made their military contribution. By having effectively handed over their main manpower resources to the British Middle East and African command, the Poles were not able again to influence their troops' disposition. Like the British, they knew that they would not be able to withdraw from joint military action: that would have amounted to abandoning any direct contribution to the war. The *raison d'être* of the Polish government-in-exile had been to assert Polish influence by making a direct contribution to the war. Neither Sikorski nor Anders could now qualify their commitment to the British without appearing reluctant to fight for the common cause. The little influence that Sikorski might have tried to assert in the spring and summer of 1942, when the British were in particular difficulties, had been undermined by this total pledging of Polish resources to Britain.

These were much needed by the British. Even though the entry of the United States into the war was a source of great comfort to Churchill, in April 1942 he had to admit that British losses since December dramatically exceeded those of the period before Pearl Harbor.[101] While the Japanese threat to Australia had to be taken very seriously, Churchill had decided to concentrate resources on the North African and Caucasus fronts. On 26 May General Rommel attacked British positions on the Western front. British difficulties were compounded by the bombing of Malta and an enemy attack on Madagascar exposing weaknesses in British communication links.[102] The fear that the Red Army counterattack in the south might not be successful preoccupied Churchill just as much as his difficulties in North Africa. He was therefore determined to aid the Soviet Union with as much equipment as could be sent there. Unfortunately shipping losses in May had been heavy. Churchill even considered military action against Norway in order to safeguard supplies to Archangel. British anxiety about the Caucasus continued to be so serious that, even though Polish co-operation was much appreciated, it could not divert Churchill from a stronger commitment to the Soviet Union.[103]

Sikorski was never free from petty intrigues and attacks from within his own government. At the beginning of 1942 problems within the ranks of the Polish community increased. As long as the opposition was disunited and confined only to political groups established in London, Sikorski's situation was difficult but not entirely perilous. But during 1942, opposition to him became more vocal and better organized. Attacks on Sikorski focused on the question of co-operation with the Soviet Union.[104] But in practice criticism of Sikorski's holding of the position of Prime Minister and Commander-in-Chief came to challenge the way in which Sikorski ruled. In the autumn of 1942, Sikorski defeated an attempt led by Marian Seyda, leader of the National Democrats, to restructure the government. Criticism of Sikorski was not limited to the Sanacja followers of Piłsudski and the extreme right. Adam Pragier, the leader of the Polish Socialist group in exile, bitterly castigated Sikorski for having put Poland in the role of a British satellite. He distrusted Sikorski's Soviet policy and felt that Sikorski should have demanded from the British a stronger commitment to the Polish cause.[105] The parliament-in-exile, the National Council, also felt increasingly irritated at being rarely consulted. Its members felt that Sikorski kept them in the dark, most notably on the subject of Polish–Soviet relations.[106] The appearance of leaks of secret documents relating to difficult and contentious diplomatic issues, in the Polish anti-government publications of a leading supporter of the Sanacja regime, Stanisław Mackiewicz, was embarrassing to Sikorski personally and irritated the British.[107] Several official enquiries suggested that these leaks had been made by either the President or General Sosnkowski with the explicit aim of discrediting Sikorski.[108] Sikorski's aide-de-camp suggested that they fought not for a new orientation in the exile government's foreign policy but for power.[109]

More painful to Sikorski were signs of disaffection within the ranks of soldiers in Scotland. They had been inactive since coming to Britain from France. Their only task was to prepare for action on the Continent of Europe. As plans for a second front were delayed, boredom and frustration fuelled the intrigues of the disproportionate number of officers imbued with the elitism and political ideas of the old regime. (Sikorski's attempts to weed out obvious opponents from his civil service and army were never very successful.) Increased political activity and the consolidation of disparate right-wing political groups in the summer and early autumn of 1942 increased their influence in military units and their attempts to draw soldiers into political debates. Mackiewicz's pamphlets called for the Polish units in Russia to be pulled out and placed as near as possible to the British operational zone.[110] In one pamphlet he argued that the army should be concentrated in the Middle East under one command.[111] This implied that Anders should take over control of all Polish troops abroad. Mackiewicz's publications were taken very seriously by Sikorski. Other anti-Semitic and anti-government leaflets were circulated widely in Scotland.

Sikorski could not ignore these challenges to his authority. Throughout the period 1939–1941 he had had to contend with attacks from the Sanacja politicians and military men. At the end of 1942 these appeared to be considerably more serious because they constituted a challenge to his political and military strategy as a whole. Anxiety about Anders' disloyalty combined with disaffection in Scotland threatened to undermine his policy of claiming for the exile government a say in post-war decision-making by making deliberate and carefully thought-out contributions to the allied war effort. As Polish–Soviet difficulties increased, Sikorski more than ever needed to be able to decide what that military contribution was going to be. The demands of the National Council for increased consultation was discrediting the Poles by showing the degree of their disunity. Calls for closer co-operation with Britain, when Sikorski knew that neither of the two western Allies was prepared to champion unreservedly the Polish cause, seemed to him inappropriate. If he lost control of his own men it might only be a question of time before the Allies too considered him superfluous.

6   The illusion of an alliance ends

On 28 June 1942 German troops in Russia started Operation 'Blau', the aim of which was to destroy the Bryansk front and to break through the South East front. By 12 July both had been breached and German troops advanced south-east, threatening Soviet communication lines with the east and the key oil supply route.[1] Throughout the summer it appeared that nothing could stop the relentless German progress. On 23 July Rostov fell. At this point the German army divided in order to proceed in two different directions: one towards the Don where it got bogged down at Stalingrad and the other, Army Group A, south-east towards the oilfields of Batum.[2] The latter move was particularly successful. By August it reached the coast of the Black Sea and looked likely to succeed in capturing the Baku oilfields and destroying the Russian North Caucasian front.[3] By September German troops were moving south along the Black Sea coast towards the strategic bases of Temryuk and Novorossijsk.[4] In the meantime Stalin himself had decided that a stand had to be made in Stalingrad. Key German units in the south were in due course diverted away from the successful drive to the south-east and into the stalemate which developed around Stalingrad.

In spite of this loss of momentum the allied strategists feared that the German progress to the south-east would have very serious diplomatic repercussions. Added to anxiety about the loyalty of the tribes living in the Caucasus was a worry lest Turkey's commitment to neutrality be put to the test. In the Soviet Union and in Britain apprehension was expressed about the very real possibility that German entry into the Caucasus would encourage Turkey to commit herself to Germany.

These events were the background to Soviet recriminations about the second front and British supplies to Russia. The uncompromising attitude of the Soviet leadership was also evident in negotiations concerning post-war settlements. Britain and her smaller Allies were at a disadvantage because, in the summer of 1942 when the hardest battles in the war against Germany were on the Russian front, there was little that could be offered to the Soviet Union as proof of British support. The June supply convoy from Britain to Murmansk had experienced heavy losses which led to the temporary postponement of further northern convoys.[5] At the beginning of July Churchill agreed with the Chiefs of Staff that the second front could not be opened in 1942.[6] Churchill had concluded that Britain was not in a position to build a strong enough front in the west to cause the Germans to move appreciable numbers of troops from the east. Instead he chose to push for British–American action in North Africa. During a joint meeting with American military leaders it was agreed to put off temporarily plans for a cross-Channel invasion and instead to concentrate on the North African campaign, now codenamed 'Torch'.[7] Inevitably this promised serious problems with the Russians, in particular because Roosevelt, as recently as 11 June, had made a commitment to Molotov that a second front would be opened in 1942.[8] None of the smaller Allies were able to accept that Britain's influence in Moscow was diminished by these strategic moves. Their anxieties and ensuing diplomatic manoeuvres to persuade the British and the Americans to guarantee their aspirations were liable to be a source of embarrassment and difficulty, adding further to the strains in Britain's relations with the Soviet Union.

In order to avoid diplomatic problems with the exile governments in Britain, the Foreign Office was forced to monitor their activities and intrigues. On the whole the British authorities had no problems in finding out what was taking place within the community of foreign governments and authorities stranded in London for the duration of the war. Furthermore there was no difficulty in preventing the formation of inconvenient blocs. The lack of any unity between the various exile governments and their keenness to ingratiate themselves with their hosts made the Foreign Office's task so much easier. On 21 January 1942 the Poles approached the Yugoslav government-in-exile with a view to signing a military alliance. It was the Yugoslav Minister for Foreign Affairs, Nintchitch, who informed the British Ambassador of the initiative and of his government's unwillingness to proceed with agreements which could provoke Russia.[9] Likewise when Sikorski spoke frankly to the Greek Prime Minister, Emmanuel Tsouderos, about establishing a bloc 'comprising peoples of the Balkans and Central Europe as a counterweight to the USSR', that information was conveyed immediately to Eden. Tsouderos let Eden know not only that he felt slighted at Poland assuming a leading role in the proposal but also that he 'deprecated any arrangements obviously aimed against Russia'. The Greek Prime Minister's motives had little to do with loyalty. He, like all exile leaders, looked to Britain assuming a more active role in plans for post-war Europe. He therefore told Eden that 'unless HMG took some such lead there was a danger of other nations attempting to summon the refugee Governments themselves, and thus creating an impression that an opposition to the policy of HMG existed'.[10] This warning was taken very seriously by the British authorities.

The Poles themselves used the initiatives of other small allied governments and authorities to ingratiate themselves with the British. When Maurice Dejean, de Gaulle's Commissioner for Foreign Affairs, approached the Polish government with a view to exchanging representatives, this information was maliciously leaked to the Foreign Office.[11] Sikorski did not want to grant de Gaulle recognition in excess of that accorded by the British. Only in the autumn of 1942, when the bulk of the Polish infantry was assembled in the Middle East, did the Polish government think that establishing relations with the Free French might be of advantage to them. On 29 November Sikorski urged Anders to exchange liaison officers with General Georges Catroux, the Free French representative in Egypt.[12] On 4 December an announcement was made that the 'Polish National Council had confirmed the friendship which unites the Polish nation with the French nation'.[13] Notwithstanding the friendship uniting the two nations, anxiety about British disapproval and doubts about the extent of de Gaulle's authority made the Poles confine themselves to general affirmations of unity.

The Polish government-in-exile wanted to see the security of post-war Poland based on some form of Central European co-operation. The acquiescence of the major Allies to these plans was an obvious precondition if such plans were not to be the cause of disharmony between them. It was generally appreciated by British politicians that the exile governments would try to exploit conflicts and divisions between the three most powerful Allies. But any common approach by the big three gave rise to suspicions among the minor Allies that decisions would be made about the future of Europe without their consent. This too caused the small Allies to think of means to upset any such big power consensus. When a deterioration in Polish–Soviet relations in the second half of 1942 coincided with apparent strains in Sikorski's dealings with the British government, projects for Central European federations were pursued by the Poles with increased vigour. Relations with Czechoslovakia and plans for a Polish–Czechoslovak federation were the most important initiatives pursued by the Poles in relation to allied governments.[14]

Talks between Sikorski and Eduard Beneš, the ex-President of the Czechoslovak republic, aimed at creating a Polish–Czechoslovak federation had already been initiated in France.[15] From the beginning a major obstacle was the Trans-Olza region which Poland had occupied in the wake of the Munich conference. Sikorski disclaimed responsibility for the previous regime's policies. But his unwillingness to consider the revision of the Polish border of September 1939 suggested that the post-war Polish government would not return to Czechoslovakia territories which had been occupied as a result of Polish–German co-operation in 1938. Beneš was adamant that these should be returned. The issue remained unresolved, and further attempts to proceed with plans for a federation during the first two years of the war were delayed by further serious differences between the two governments. The Czechoslovak–Polish Co-ordinating Committee, which was established to discuss and direct the process of negotiations, had its first meeting in January 1941. The Polish proposal contained a suggestion that the foreign and economic policies of both states should be co-ordinated.[16] It envisaged total economic integration, which the Czechoslovaks found unsatisfactory because they felt that this would restrict their economic development which was more advanced than Poland's.[17]

British–Soviet co-operation also had very serious repercussions on Polish–Czechoslovak relations. While Polish politicians tried to present their plans for European federations as no more than attempts to prevent a resurgence of German power, no one was convinced that this was their sole objective, not least because the Poles frequently departed from their stated aims to voice strong anti-Soviet sentiments. The Polish government's objective was to see the establishment of two federations. The Central European one was to include Lithuania, Poland, Czechoslovakia, Hungary and Romania. The second was to consist of Yugoslavia, Albania, Bulgaria and Greece. These political federations would be united by the objective of opposing Soviet economic domination of the region.[18]

Inevitably the British Foreign Office queried the significance of these initiatives for the Soviet Union. Władysław Kulski, the Polish Chargé d'affaires, told Strang on 9 February 1942 that the aim was for the eight smaller European powers to assert 'their intention to maintain community of outlook after the war on political, economic and possibly on military matters'.[19] Eden was not fooled. His minute, written after reading Strang's memorandum, suggests that he perceived the very real danger of the Poles and the other exile authorities arriving at a policy towards the Soviet Union which the British considered undesirable.

Beneš' attitude towards the Soviet Union was radically different from that of the Polish leadership. The Poles were most worried by Beneš' renewed demand, immediately after the Soviet entry into the war, for the return of Trans-Olza to Czechoslovakia.[20] The Czechoslovak leader made clear to the Foreign Office his belief that Soviet approval for the proposed federation was a precondition for its establishment.[21] Raczyński sourly commented that the Czechs had been given a bribe by the Soviet Union in the form of the Soviet recognition of their pre-Munich frontiers.[22] Beneš had obtained this assurance during Molotov's visit to London in May 1942. Thereafter Polish–Czechoslovak talks were pursued by both sides without conviction.

The Poles returned to their federation idea with renewed vigour in the autumn of 1942. A deterioration in Polish–Soviet relations, compounded by the lack of British support for Polish territorial demands, caused the government-in-exile to renew their interest in European unity. This time a planning Committee of Foreign Ministers of the Governments established in London was formed. Raczyński became Chairman, with Kulski and Józef Retinger, Sikorski's friend and advisor, acting as Secretaries. Meetings of the Committee took place at Sikorski's residence in Kensington.[23] This was an entirely Polish-led initiative, whose tacit aim was to encourage anti-Soviet unity. Other exile governments were prepared to go along with the Poles if only to signal to the British their disquiet about the lack of British commitment to post-war spheres of influence in Europe.[24]

The British attitude towards these policy initiatives was always hostile. The Foreign Office worried that they could affect their relations with the Soviet Union. It also feared that 'the main danger ... would be the formulation of a bloc with aims divergent from our own after the war'.[25] The fact that the United States government was still unwilling to address itself to the complexities of planning for post-war Europe was seen as a further constraint on British policy-making. As a result no encouragement was given to the exile governments. Instead a wary eye was kept on their efforts to mobilize public opinion. Sikorski's attempts to publicize his ideas on European confederations were discouraged by the Foreign Office.[26] Responding to an enquiry by the Foreign Minister of the Netherlands exile government about British views on the future balance of power in Europe, Frank Roberts debated the issue in a Foreign Office minute dated 23 October 1942.[27] He was forced to admit that while public statements had been uttered in support of the Polish–Czechoslovak declaration of 1940, the Greek–Yugoslav agreement and in favour of 'smaller states weld[ing] themselves into larger though not exclusive groupings', in reality there was no policy on the matter.[28] There were many reasons for this:

(a) we have asked the Americans on what post war problems they would like preliminary discussions with us and in what order: they have replied that they hope to let us have an answer and make suggestions after the New Year

(b) at some point we shall presumably have to address a somewhat similar enquiry to the Russians. Possibly the best moment to do this would be when we offer to talk *à deux* with them about reparations if we do decide to do this ... But the Malkin Committee on Reparations has not yet met and we are a long way off seeing what if anything we are likely to want to say to the Russians and anyone else.
...

(f) as regards politico-strategic matters we have only now decided to make a start 'under our own roof' on arranging our thoughts through the agency of the proposed Committee under Mr Law

(g) when that Committee had made some progress, we shall have to consider starting informal talks with the Allies under the aegis of the Foreign Office on the model of the talks sponsored by the Treasury and Board of Trade, subject of course to any view which may by then have been expressed by the Americans and the Russians.[29]

While this way of proceeding might have been the most obvious one in view of the government's preoccupation with much weightier matters in the conduct of the war, it nevertheless caused discontent among the London based governments-in-exile and inflamed their already visible and profound distrust of British motives towards the Soviet Union. Compared with other exile governments, the Polish government-in-exile expected more than any other, not least because it had pledged most in relation to its possibilities. At the same time, among those governments, it was the most in need of diplomatic, if not outright military support, if its minimum territorial demands were to be realized at the end of the war.

One of the factors influencing Polish–British relations in the second half of 1942 was an increase in military collaboration between the two governments. With the incorporation of the troops from the Soviet Union into the British Middle Eastern Forces, Polish frustration with

Britain's reluctance to draw the Poles into political and military planning also increased. Oblivious to Sikorski's frustrations, Anders continued to press for the speedy evacuation of the remaining Polish troops from the Soviet Union in order to reinforce the British strategy in the Middle East. The fate of Polish troops left in the Soviet Union continued to be the object of complex, behind the scenes intrigues. Anders had the most consistent commitment to removing as many Poles out of the Soviet Union as possible. This was opposed by Sikorski who wanted the recruitment of Polish soldiers there to continue but insisted that the new formations should remain in the Soviet Union. The British authorities, in particular Churchill, had come to view British requirements for manpower in the Middle East as more urgent. As the likelihood of German success in the Caucasus decreased, Churchill once more contemplated the Middle East as a British priority. The British therefore were willing to facilitate Anders' plans. Of all the protagonists Sikorski undisputedly was least able to ensure that his wishes were heeded.

In the spring of 1942 the conflict between Sikorski and Anders, which had so far manifested itself only in minor acts of insubordination on Anders' part, flared up. The tacit British and Soviet support that Anders was able to obtain for his plans marginalized Sikorski. What ensued was a battle between Sikorski and Anders for control over military decisions concerning Polish troops in the Soviet Union and the Middle East. On 1 May Sikorski wrote to Anders in an attempt to impress upon him the need to abide by the decisions of the Council of Ministers.[30] Sikorski pointed out that the key question of what was the shortest route back to Poland could not then be answered. The military situation was still unclear and this necessitated the distribution of manpower in such a way that Poles would be able to respond to any of a number of possible developments. In Britain Sikorski wanted the gradual formation of an armoured corps which would include a parachute brigade. This would be used as an advance guard destined to be dropped into Poland at the critical moment of liberation.[31] The air force was to remain in Britain. In the Soviet Union and the Middle East, army corps, numbering approximately three divisions each, were to be formed. These two were not to be brought together and the only circumstances in which Sikorski considered this to be desirable would be in the event of the collapse of the Soviet Union. Likewise Sikorski emphatically forbade Anders to plan for a possible single command for Polish units in the Middle East and the Soviet Union. In the Middle East Polish troops came under British operational command while those in the Soviet Union came under Soviet command.[32] Sikorski emphasized that not all Polish military potential should be concentrated in one theatre of war since he feared that this would entail a risk of that potential being partly or completely 'used up' before Poland was liberated. He reinforced his message by instructing Kot to press the Soviet authorities to allow the resumption of recruitment to the Polish army, in accordance with the earlier Stalin–Anders agreement.[33]

Anders nevertheless pursued his own strategy encouraged, as some believed at the time, by commitments obtained from the British when he stopped in the Middle East on his way back from visiting Sikorski in London. Richard Casey, the British Minister of State in Cairo, and Auchinleck are credited with having given Anders assurances that all assistance would be given to get the remainder of the Polish army out of the Soviet Union.[34] His communications with the Soviet authorities and telegrams back to London reveal that he continued to aim for the army's wholesale departure from the Soviet Union, irrespective of decisions made by the exile government during meetings which he had attended. Reporting a conversation with Auchinleck, Anders informed Sikorski that he had discussed the ultimate removal of 'my army' to the Middle East.[35] Writing on 22 June General Bronisław Regulski, the Polish military attaché in London, stated that he was under constant pressure from the War Office about the fate of the Polish soldiers still in the Soviet Union.[36] He believed that the British authorities wanted their evacuation to the Middle East to continue and even to be accelerated.

In June Anders unsuccessfully sought an interview with Stalin. During preliminary talks with NKVD Colonel Tishkov about the agenda for the meeting, Anders stated that, in addition to the resumption of Polish recruitment, he wanted to discuss the possibility of moving the whole army to the Middle East.[37] He argued that this was needed to unite the whole army. He also alluded to the possibility that all troops in the militarily most vulnerable areas, notably the Middle East, might need to be concentrated. Shortages in the Soviet Union were given as another reason for leaving Soviet territory.[38]

As well as dealing with Stalin, Anders had to overcome Sikorski's resolve not to allow the whole army to leave the Soviet Union. In a telegram to Sikorski, dated 7 June, Anders explained his case.[39] Claiming that it was the Russian side that wanted the Poles to go to Syria, he pressed Sikorski for permission to take the troops there. The other alternative, according to Anders, was for the troops to go into battle on the Russian front. In those circumstances they would only receive arms on arrival in their battle-zone, as was the Russian practice. That possibility and a general decrease of supplies was apparently causing the collapse of morale which could only be revived by departure from the Soviet Union.[40]

Sikorski's answer, dated 11 June, was a last attempt to bring Anders to heel.[41] He did not believe that the Russians really wanted the Poles to go to Syria. He rejected all arguments presented by Anders, notably suggestions that further recruitment could only take place if the present army left. Appealing to the soldiers to maintain discipline and be patriotic, Sikorski instructed Anders to ensure that government orders were obeyed. Since Sikorski would not approve Anders' plans the latter proceeded without further reference to London. Assisted by the British authorities in the Middle East, and facilitated by the Soviet decision to get rid of the Polish army and recruitment centres, Anders defied orders.

The decision to allow the three remaining partly-armed Polish divisions to leave Soviet territory was in the end made by Stalin on 30 June.[42] It is not clear why, and what pressures were on him to do so. With the signal exception of Sikorski, few in the Polish government and army did not welcome this move. The Soviet authorities attempted to present the decision as a gift to Churchill.[43] In retrospect Sikorski appeared to claim that the whole idea had been started by him when he suggested to the British that they take up the matter of Polish units in the Soviet Union with Stalin. As a result Stalin instructed Molotov to make an offer of the Polish troops to the British.[44] Anders, who was in Kuibyshev awaiting his interview with Stalin, was delighted. The British Ambassador in Moscow, Clark Kerr, was left somewhat bewildered by the speed of events but happy to be able to inform Anders that the British authorities were going to accept women and children in addition to soldiers.[45]

This time the Polish government tried to obtain more tangible benefits from handing their troops over to Auchinleck when it was well known that they were much needed. In a communication to the Foreign Office dated 4 July the Polish government tried to link the recent developments with outstanding problems in Polish–Russian relations.[46] In particular the Poles hoped to secure the continuing recruitment of men into Polish units in the Soviet Union and 'the collaboration of HMG in the further search for Polish officers missing in Russia'.

The weakness of the Polish negotiating position, and their inability to link political concessions to military contributions, was shown by Churchill's minute on the memorandum. In this he wrote to Eden, 'The above leave me in doubt whether you want the 3 Polish Divisions or not if you have to take with them this mass of women and children ...'.[47] In any case, as it turned out, the Soviet authorities rejected British representations on behalf of the Poles.[48] Vyshinsky was not prepared to haggle over the Soviet decision to allow the departure of Polish troops, while the British Prime Minister did not want to assume responsibility for civilians whose departure from Soviet territory the Poles considered vital. As a result the Foreign Office suggested that 'General Sikorski might be urged to press the Polish Cabinet to show a rather more accommodating attitude on this question'.[49] Churchill finally agreed to support the request for the evacuation of civilians but did not raise the issues of further recruitment or the missing officers.[50] On 26 July Anders received Soviet permission to evacuate the whole army. Once more the route taken was from Krasnovodsk to Pahlevi. 70,000 people, including 25,500 civilians, were taken out of the Soviet Union.[51]

On 31 October Alexander Bogomolov, the Soviet Ambassador to the Polish government-in-exile, handed Raczyński a note in which the Soviet authorities explained the reasons for ending all recruitment of Poles on Soviet territory.[52] This gave Anders the opportunity to accuse Sikorski of pursuing a policy damaging to Polish interests. Since Anders' aim was Sikorski's removal he challenged Sikorski to resign in order that this act alert world opinion to Soviet duplicity.[53] At the same time he wrote to President Raczkiewicz a letter confidently addressed to someone who shared his views. Anders explicitly blamed the Polish government and its leadership for all its failures in relation to the Soviet Union. He recommended that the Poles should expose the Soviet Union and that the world should be made aware of its duplicity and long-term objectives in Europe. Since the present government could not and would not do this the, according to Anders, new people should be given the opportunity to assume control.[54]

Anders' denunciation constituted a serious challenge to Sikorski's authority at a time when the Polish Prime Minister was in a particularly vulnerable position. Anders had ceased being merely the leader of one of the sections of the Polish armed forces abroad and presently commanded the biggest group of Polish soldiers outside Poland. Between Anders and his soldiers and officers there existed a strong bond of personal loyalty. He also seemed to be the darling of the British Command in the Middle East at a time when the British government appeared to be distancing itself from Polish issues. All this combined to weaken Sikorski's authority. It was rumoured that Anders' actions had been directed by the British authorities because they now found Sikorski expendable. These rumours were traced back to Anders' aide-de-camp. He in turn wrote in his memoirs that Hulls had virtually dictated Anders' letter to Sikorski.[55] Anders would not easily have allowed anyone to dictate anything to him. It is very likely that he felt encouraged to express his political ideas by the warm appreciation for his willingness to place his men under British command that was expressed by British officers in the Middle East.

Sikorski dealt with Anders after he had returned from his visit to Washington. He addressed two letters to Anders, the first dated 15 March and the second, which was meant to be a personal one, dated 17 March 1943. Sikorski explained to Anders the reasoning behind his policy of *rapprochement* with the Soviet Union and begged him to think of the consequences of his actions.[56] It is clear from the contents of these two communications that, in spite of setbacks, Sikorski still believed that Polish interests could best be served by continued adherence to agreements concluded by the wartime Allies. Notwithstanding difficulties in Polish–Soviet relations, Sikorski still felt that allied diplomatic support would help to resolve them in the end. In the meantime, he reminded Anders, intrigues, disunity and instability within the exile government would only alienate allied governments.

In his attempt to retain some clarity of purpose and commitment to the allied cause, Sikorski had to contend with the hostile atmosphere towards his policies which prevailed within his own government. During the first months of 1942 Sikorski's enemies in Britain seemed disunited and, although vocal, still badly organized. But in the Middle East, notably in Palestine, Sikorski's opponents formed an influential Democratic Club and some of them remained in close contact with the last foreign minister of the pre-war Sanacja government, Colonel Józef Beck, who was interned in Romania.[57] The arrival in the Middle East of troops from the Soviet Union strengthened these groups. Polish consulates regularly informed Sikorski of contacts between the Democratic Club and the violently anti-Soviet Polish officers and men newly arrived in the Middle East.[58] Kot, who left the Soviet Union and was now posted to the Middle East, warned about major intrigues and conflicts among the Anders' senior officers and between them and junior officers. Anders' aide-de-camp Klimkowski was now associated with them to such an extent that the word 'klimkowszczyzna' was coined to describe the political challenge of the junior officers.[59]

Sikorski's Chief of Staff, General Tadeusz Klimecki, was dispatched to the Middle East to discuss the reorganization of units in the Middle East but primarily to enforce discipline and to reinforce Sikorski's authority.

Sikorski's anxiety that the Anders' evacuation would spell the end of co-operation between the Soviet government and the Polish government-in-exile was fully justified. At this stage, at least, the Polish government-in-exile tried to continue as before, but it had lost avenues of contacts as well as matters for direct communication with the Soviet authorities. Sikorski, in common with most Polish politicians in exile, jealously guarded the exile government's prerogatives, in particular that of an independent foreign policy. The absence of opportunities for low level diplomatic contacts between the Poles and Soviet representatives meant that British politicians had become spokesmen on Polish matters in their dealings with the Soviet Allies. Nevertheless, as has been shown, British politicians' feeling of obligation to the exile government was, at best, dubious. Thus Sikorski's government was losing control over matters relating to the future of Poland and Poland was increasingly likely to become an object of other powers' negotiations. If the Soviet Union could not be trusted, neither could the British be relied upon to defend Polish interests.

The signing of the British–Soviet agreement in May 1942 had only been possible because of a joint British and Soviet decision to avoid the contentious issues of the Polish eastern frontier and the second front. These matters would still have to be addressed, even if they could not then be resolved. Churchill's visit to Moscow in August 1942 was intended to underline the newly confirmed understanding between the two statesmen. The postponement of the second front required very careful handling indeed. This issue probably more than any other was the cause of Churchill's decision to seek a meeting with Stalin. There was also the question of the Soviet ability to defend the Caucasus and the Black Sea.[60] Churchill believed that the delicate problem of explaining to Stalin why Britain had decided to postpone the second front could best be done in a direct meeting between Churchill and Stalin. On the positive side Churchill hoped to be able to explore the possibility of British and American air forces assisting the Soviet Union in the Caucasus region.[61]

It was inevitable that the British Prime Minister's visit to Moscow would antagonize the Poles. Little was done to reassure them that the British would concern themselves with Polish interests. The worst Polish suspicions were confirmed when Churchill failed to consult them before his departure. No attempt had been made to co-ordinate British policies towards the Soviet Union with Polish objectives. That was probably due to the need to concentrate on more pressing military priorities with the result that long-term foreign policy aims were temporarily set aside.

Churchill travelled to Cairo, then on 12 August to the Soviet Union and then back to Cairo. Anders, to Sikorski's fury, was first invited to dine with Churchill in Moscow on 15 August, and then got swept up into Churchill's entourage and briefly became one of the Prime Minister's travelling companions.[62]

By all accounts, the British Prime Minister's idiosyncratic behaviour, as much as his unwillingness to accept guidance from British officials in the Soviet Union, and the lack of any benefits that Britain could offer the Soviet leader at the time, made it obvious that the visit would yield few tangible results.[63] The British refusal to plan for the opening of the second front in 1942 and difficulties in supplying the Soviet Union with arms and equipment placed Churchill in a position in which he could neither ask nor demand favours from Stalin. Churchill's offer of aerial assistance to the Caucasus front carried little weight with the Russians. Neither the British nor the American Chiefs of Staff liked the proposal. During direct talks in November between Soviet and allied representatives, the Soviet commanders demanded that they retain operational control over allied planes sent to assist them. By December the subject was dropped at Soviet insistence.[64]

Churchill's failure to take up with Stalin any Polish grievances was seen by the Polish government-in-exile as a major development contributing to the loss of Polish influence in Russia. Churchill did not decide to leave Polish demands off the list of points put to Stalin. The more likely explanation was that he simply did not think of them at a time when more urgent problems of British–Soviet co-operation were raised. Polish co-operation did not naturally present itself as a counterweight to what was at the time a desperate need to appease and court the Soviet ally. Churchill had invited Anders to present his case, nevertheless Stalin's belligerence towards Churchill had nearly caused a premature end to the visit. Anders had therefore no opportunity to speak to Churchill and was instead invited to join him in Cairo.[65]

Within the Polish community Churchill's actions acquired a totally different meaning. Not only did they fuel the rivalry already existing between Anders and Sikorski but they also cast further doubts on Britain's commitment to Poland. Sikorski found out from a message dated 17 August about the failure of the Polish representatives in Russia to place Polish issues on the agenda of the Churchill–Stalin meetings.[66] The Polish Chargé d'affaires in Kuibyshev, Henryk Sokolnicki, reported that, although Anders had a meeting with Churchill, the latter claimed not to have any knowledge of the problems and confined himself to questioning Anders about Soviet internal and military problems.[67] Harriman, who accompanied Churchill, had also been informed of Polish grievances in relation to the Soviet authorities. But when asked by Anders whether he had taken up any of these issues in his contacts with the Soviet officials, Harriman confined himself to a statement that 'he had not had the opportunity to speak about our matters'.[68] It later turned out that Harriman had been given no instructions by his government to speak on behalf of the Poles.

Sikorski reacted very strongly to news that Anders had a meeting with Churchill in Moscow. He detected signs of insubordination in Anders' contacts with Churchill, Auchinleck and Alexander. On 18 August, in a strongly worded message to Anders, he forbade him to make any representations to the British concerning the organization of troops in the Middle East.[69] He also instructed him to cancel his trip to Cairo. Organizational matters relating to the Polish army were to be discussed by General Klimecki, the Polish Chief of Staff, who was leaving for Cairo.[70] In a desperate bid to prevent the British and Anders from keeping his whole army in the Middle East, Sikorski also wrote to Generals Auchinleck and Alexander informing them of Klimecki's mission. The build-up of Polish units in Scotland was being pursued with the aim of preparing them for liberating Polish territory. Sikorski wrote with deep emotion to both generals:

> Attaching as I do, a great importance to the development of the armed forces in the Middle East, I must nevertheless take into account the necessity of coming to the help of the Polish Nation in the fight it will take up against the occupants at the moment when the ultimate outcome of the war will be in the balance, so as to hasten its liberation and to co-operate directly in the allied operation in the continent.[71]

The truth of the matter was that Sikorski was not merely fighting for the leadership of the exile government but more importantly for his policy of an independent Polish contribution to the war. The liberation of Poland was the most important objective of the military forces. Anders' actions threatened to reduce the capacity of the government to act independently and to reduce it to a supporting role in a British war. This in turn exposed the Polish government's failure to obtain a British commitment to the restoration of Poland in pre-war borders.

The placing under British command of all manpower resources created a situation in which Sikorski felt obliged to show that he was securing some commitments from Britain. The failure of British and American politicians to defend Polish interests undermined his policy and his defence of it.[72] This very point was made by Kot on 21 August.[73] Kot had left the Soviet Union and, as special representative of the Polish government, was in the Middle East from where he continued sending messages full of innuendos and malice. He wrote to Sikorski that he had received information from Moscow that 'Churchill and Harriman's failure to raise our cause even in passing was immediately sensed by the Soviets as a repudiation of ourselves by the Anglo-Saxons'.[74] According to Kot, no assurances, which Churchill might subsequently give Sikorski, could alter the impression given that the British and Americans were backing out of assisting the Poles. For good measure, Kot added that Polish troops in the Middle East had been billeted in desert malarial areas which were considered unfit for British troops. Nevertheless, Sikorski chose to believe the argument put to him by Eden that Britain's failure to support Poland was due to a militarily inauspicious time being experienced by the British.[75]

Undeterred by his neglect of the Polish case in his conversations with Stalin, Churchill felt free to enquire how best Polish soldiers could be utilized in the British war effort in the Middle East. In Cairo, at a conference attended by Churchill, Anders and General Maitland Wilson, who was soon to assume responsibility for the Persia–Iraq Command, the Prime Minister stressed the need for Polish manpower.[76] Discussing Anders' request that pressure be put on the Soviet authorities to obtain the release of an additional 60,000 men trapped in work battalions, Churchill reaffirmed that he would like to see as many men as possible from the Soviet Union added to the Polish formations in the Middle East. He nevertheless reserved for himself the choice of the moment to put pressure on Stalin.[77] He was aware that it would be some time before Britain would be in a position to request favours from the Soviet Union and told Anders, 'The Russians have an entirely justified impression that we are being idle'.[78]

On 20 August Sikorski had a meeting with Churchill at Chequers to discuss the latter's visit to Moscow. Churchill's handling of Sikorski was a mixture of bluster and crass insensitivity. Neither was likely to impress or placate Sikorski who wanted to talk about the Poles still in the Soviet Union and the need to put pressure on the Soviet authorities to allow their recruitment into Polish units. Initially Churchill tried to explain to Sikorski why he was not in a position to make any demands of the Soviet Union.[79] He pointed out that on the one hand he had no victories to show and, on the other, he was not able to promise the Russians any assistance, not even in the form of supplies. He tried to assure Sikorski that as soon as the British military situation was improved he would put pressure on the Soviet authorities to satisfy all Polish demands. Sikorski disagreed with Churchill's claim that he had nothing to show. He claimed that British participation in the war was of key importance as a moral factor. By underestimating it the British denied themselves an opportunity to put pressure on Stalin. It was unfortunate that, at the end, Churchill with remarkable insensitivity advised Sikorski to go and visit Stalin once more. Churchill's jocular statement that Sikorski and Stalin were men of very similar temperament was unlikely to be taken as a compliment by the Polish leader. Nor was his encouragement to Sikorski to visit Roosevelt couched in more tactful terms. Churchill pointed out that the main benefit to be derived from such a visit would be the support Sikorski could give the President in his campaign for re-election.[80] Churchill's sweeping commitment to support all Polish demands at the eventual peace conference did little to improve the intimacy of the occasion. The British Prime Minister seemed oblivious to the annoyance felt by the Poles, in common with other exile governments, at British unwillingness to get down to planning for the forthcoming victory.

In the meantime the Poles persisted in the belief that plans for the liberation of Poland could now be developed and co-ordinated. The second front had been widely discussed in the course of 1942. They had always planned for military action in Poland to coincide with the invasion of Europe. Unfortunately, the tenuous nature of communications between the Home Army in Poland and the exile government in London meant that details of joint action could never be fully co-ordinated with the operational head of the Home Army, General Stefan Grot-Rowecki. The strategy of the Home Army leadership was based on the assumption that the defeat of the Germans by Anglo-American forces would lead to the emergence of a power vacuum. This would give the Home Army an opportunity to establish control over Polish territory. In the event that the Soviet Union played a decisive role in the defeat of Germany in the east, the Home Army planned to 'conserve its resources' in order to take action subsequently against Soviet troops.[81] In March 1942 Sikorski defined the role of the Home Army more narrowly, in particular forbidding it to take action against the Russians.[82] Disagreement between the Home Commander and Sikorski rumbled on through 1942.

In addition Sikorski tried to co-ordinate the objectives of the Home Army with allied Chiefs of Staff rather than just the Special Operations Executive (SOE). This suggests a certain lack of faith in the SOE, who were commissioned by the British government to liaise with European resistance movements. Moreover, among the British and allied leaders, the idea of national resistance movements assuming a key role in the liberation of Europe had, by the end of 1941, given way to plans for a large-scale invasion of Europe.[83] The reasons for the SOE's failure to establish its authority with the Polish government-in-exile were obvious. Once British and United States planners had decided on a European invasion in 1943, supplies to the SOE were limited. In August 1942 the SOE decided to stop supplying equipment to the Polish and Czechoslovak secret armies.[84]

Sikorski's distrust of the SOE had crystallized when, in April 1942, he had proposed the creation of an Allied General Staff, whose aim would have been to co-ordinate plans for the invasion of the Continent with insurrections in the occupied territories.[85] In his reply to Sikorski dated 6 May General Brooke suggested that there was no need for an Allied General Staff and reiterated previous arguments that airborne action from Britain over Central Europe was impossible without diverting resources from Bomber Command and developing bases in Soviet territory. Since neither was possible at the time, British aerial action over Poland could not be considered seriously.[86] There were other reasons for the Chiefs of Staff refusal to be drawn into Sikorski's disagreements with the SOE. Their own reluctance to bypass the SOE was mingled with an anxiety lest the Polish government-in-exile dominate any association of small allied states.[87] In May 1942 a British government enquiry resulted in the SOE being given clearer guidelines for future action. These went counter to the terms of reference sought by Sikorski which would have given the Home Army a central role in planning for the liberation of Poland. New directives issued to the SOE on 12 May specified clearly that henceforth the SOE was responsible for liaising and co-ordinating resistance action on the Continent.[88]

During the summer of 1942 Sikorski concentrated on what had by then become the key strategic issue of trying to ascertain the role assigned to Polish forces in British and American plans for the forthcoming invasion of Europe. All Polish military planning since October 1939, when it had been decided to establish troops outside occupied Poland, had hinged on the premise that Poland would be liberated by military units coming back to Poland. The success of this plan depended on allied co-operation. It was always realized that Polish forces abroad, even in co-operation with the Home Army in Poland, would not be strong enough to defeat the enemy unaided. In 1942, when the Poles became aware of joint Anglo-American strategies for the invasion of Italy and discussions with Stalin about plans for the second front, they became impatient to find out when and how the Allies proposed to liberate Poland.

Sikorski assumed the initiative in relation to the British Chiefs of Staff in August 1942. Writing on 26 August to General Sir Bernard Paget, Commander-in-Chief of the Home Forces, Sikorski outlined the principles which would govern the employment of Polish forces in allied operations on the Continent.[89] He stated emphatically that he was setting out these principles for co-operation in order that:

(a) they secure for the coming offensive on the Continent the participation of Polish operational formations

(b) it renders possible the expansion of the Polish Army on the Continent
using the existing reserve of officers

(c) support for an insurrection in Poland is secured.[90]

Sikorski also wanted British military planners to treat military action by the Home Army as being part of the great allied offensive. However, plans for the invasion of Europe were not advanced to such a degree of detail. In any case the SOE had been established to co-ordinate such actions. As a result of Polish insistence the Joint Planning Committee agreed in July 1942 to look at Polish proposals for co-ordinating the Home Army's actions with allied military plans.[91] Only in October 1943 did the Chiefs of Staff Committee return to the Polish initiative and then only to defer it.[92]

The reorganization of Polish formations in the Middle East coin-
cided with a major revision of British military thinking concerning that region. In September Auchinleck was replaced by General Alexander and General Maitland Wilson became responsible for the Persia–Iraq front. In July Auchinleck had presented a project for the reorgani-
zation of the Polish forces in the Middle East. Sikorski disagreed with its detail and as a result the proposal was temporarily shelved.[93] Events nevertheless overtook Sikorski. During his visit to Moscow and the Middle East Churchill discussed the manpower issue with his generals. Although he was out-manoeuvred by Anders, Sikorski tried at least to ensure that the reorganization of the Polish army in the Middle East fitted in with his ideas for the future action by the troops on the Balkan front. These and disciplinary problems led him to send his Chief of Staff to the Middle East in September.

General Klimecki left Britain on 20 September. Sikorski's written instructions to him were left intentionally vague. The most important directives were not written down.[94] Klimecki's report reveals the extent of his mission. In the first place he was to discuss the reorganization of Polish units in the Middle East. Sikorski wanted the establishment of a framework for the development of a full Polish army in the east. Auchinleck's earlier proposal for the creation of an army corps consisting of two divisions and a tank brigade was rejected on grounds that it did not utilize fully the available officer corps.[95] Instead Sikorski had proposed an army of two corps each made up of two divisions. He based his plans on a confident assumption that the Polish army in the Middle East would continue to be replenished by men evacuated from recruiting centres in the Soviet Union. The two proposals were discussed at a War Office meeting on 5 August. Because of irreconcilable differences the whole project was temporarily shelved.[96] While Klimecki was to discuss the proposals with the British Command in the Middle East he was also supposed to prevent Anders from negotiating on behalf of the government in London. At stake was not merely the question of a reorganization of the military units. There were vital political discussions around these decisions and they were disputed by various factions within the Polish community.

The creation of an army in the Middle East was being promoted in anticipation of a Balkan front. Kopański has admitted that the training schedule in the summer of 1942 was aimed at preparing soldiers for action in the mountainous regions of the Balkans, the Caucasus, in Turkey and in Italy.[97] In November Sikorski submitted to Brooke and Churchill an extensive and detailed proposal for the future use of the Polish army. In it Sikorski made the suggestion that the Balkan area was the obvious and most promising operational zone for the Poles.[98] Sikorski's reorganization plan assumed that the British would invest in rearming the Polish army and would provide it with tanks and mechanized equipment.

On his arrival in Cairo Klimecki had several meetings with high-ranking British military commanders. On 24 August he had a preliminary interview with Brigadier Elringham in the course of which he became acutely aware of the possibility that Anders had already agreed key issues with the British Middle East Command.[99] This meeting was followed by an interview with General Wilson. Klimecki's suspicion that Anders and the British had already concluded agreements for the reorganization of the Polish units was confirmed. He was told that Anders had given Brooke a copy of his own proposal. Anders' project for the restructuring of Polish units was found to be more acceptable than Sikorski's because the former coincided with the British plans. Anticipating the imminent collapse of the Soviet defences in the Caucasus, Anders wanted the reorganization of Polish units in the Middle East to be as simple as possible in order that they go into action with British units there.[100] The document containing Anders' plan had been taken to London by Churchill who intended to put pressure on Sikorski to accept it.[101] Klimecki sent a radio message to Sikorski imploring him to reject the proposal put forward by Brooke and Churchill. He explained to Sikorski that Anders' aim was to make Polish troops available to the British as soon as possible. The objective of Auchinleck and Brooke, according to Klimecki, was to prepare three front line Polish divisions for action. This, he suspected, was being presented as a plan for a future army, whereas in reality it would mean no more than the provision of cannon fodder for enemy tanks, since the three divisions would be without adequate tank and artillery back up and thus would be incapable of offensive action.[102]

Anders' determination to facilitate British plans and Churchill's pressure caused Sikorski to abandon his own suggested reorganization. On 12 September Sikorski accepted Anders' proposal and approved the formation of a Polish army in the east commanded by Anders. From its inception the new army was short of men and was no more than an army corps. Although it was assumed that recruitment would continue and that manpower would be available from the Soviet Union, Anders wanted it to be available for action within the shortest possible time. Its creation meant that the Poles were staking a claim to action in the Caucasus and the Mediterranean.[103]

Klimecki's other task was to establish Sikorski's authority among the officers of the units which had left the Soviet Union. Sikorski's intentions in relation to Anders merit some consideration. It appears that at this stage he did not want to remove Anders from his extremely influential position even though Anders was at times using it to challenge Sikorski's policies. He seemed to want merely to bring Anders to heel, rather than have him removed from the Middle East. This emerges from letters which Sikorski wrote to Kot in August.[104] Discouraging Kot from trying to protect Anders from his anger, Sikorski explained that he felt that Anders had to be reminded that he was Sikorski's subordinate. In a statement which, in the circumstances, was probably as critical of the British as it was of the Soviet Union, he wrote about Anders: 'He'd better not play into the hands of foreign elements which do not intend to stand by promises made to Poland'.[105] Two days later Sikorski informed Kot of Klimecki's mission.[106] In it he explained once more that he had previously trusted Anders. This trust had been eroded, if only slightly. Nevertheless Klimecki's mission was to re-establish trust between the two men. In view of Anders' duplicity, Klimecki's trip had an unexpected result. Sikorski nominated Anders to the post of Commander of the Polish Army in the East. Reorganization and training commenced on 5 September. The majority of Polish units were concentrated in Iraq under the Persia–Iraq Command of General Maitland Wilson.

The middle of 1942 was the high point of British military involvement in Iraq. The possibility of a German breakthrough in the Caucasus region made the defence of Iraq a matter of vital importance. Control of that area meant that Britain could plan the movement of troops from India to Egypt without having to think of the possibility of the Suez Canal being blocked. In addition, oil obtained from the Iraqi oilfields was used to supply the British Mediterranean fleet.[107] The importance of maintaining Iraq's commitment to the British war effort was forcefully made clear in May 1941 when Britain facilitated the overthrow of the anti-British government of Rashid Ali and its replacement by the compliant and pro-British rule of the regent Prince Abd al-Ilah.[108] The British and Soviet occupation of Iran in August 1941 added to anxieties over that region. In order to retain a hold over Iran, Iraq had to be secure. Supplies to the Soviet Union were moved along the Trans-Iranian Rail route. But its capacity was limited and from May 1942 a supplementary route through Iraq was used from Basra to northern Iran and the Soviet Union.[109]

Iraq was also seen as a supply route to Turkey. These supplies were becoming the most important bargaining counter against Turkish submission to Germany. Although Turkey remained committed to neutrality, in the summer of 1942 the Turkish government introduced a nuance into their interpretation of the word 'neutrality'. It spoke of 'active neutrality', which in effect meant courting both Germany and Britain and willingly receiving their economic assistance.[110] In August the British Ambassador in Ankara reported that Turkey might be moving towards Germany as a result of a pragmatic Turkish judgment that Britain was unable to secure a victory.[111] Not until 1943 did the German threat to the south-eastern regions of Russia diminish, although in early October 1942 the Soviet High Command believed that it had halted the German momentum.[112] It is important to note that Churchill too perceived that the German failure to capture Stalingrad then marked the beginning of Germany's defeat.[113] But short of allied military achievements there was little that Britain could do to impress the Turkish government of the advantages of remaining neutral.[114]

For the British, the autumn of 1942 was a time of military success. On 8 November operation 'Torch', the invasion of North Africa, was launched. The initial stages of the American landing in North Africa in the wake of operation 'Supercharge' aimed at defeating Rommel's units seemed to have been successful. By 6 November the victory of that operation was a foregone conclusion.[115] With allied control of the Mediterranean coast of North Africa being virtually assured, even if not yet achieved, both Churchill and Roosevelt considered their next move with greater confidence than hitherto. Churchill returned to the subject of the German threat to the Caucasus. He and Roosevelt considered it likely that Turkey could now be induced to come in on the allied side.[116]

In these circumstances it was not surprising that the Poles tried to plan their military strategy on the basis of that being widely discussed by the British and the American leadership. But the Polish leaders had to adjust to a new situation, which had not been considered in earlier plans. The bulk of the Polish fighting capacity was now concentrated in Iraq. The dilemma of finding the most direct route to Poland, one that did not entail dependence on the Soviet war effort, had to be faced once more with the added quandary of how to make Polish troops indispensable to the British without ending up fighting for British imperial interests alone. The likelihood of Polish troops assuming a direct role in the defeat of Germany and the liberation of Poland appeared smaller than at any time since the beginning of the war.

Nevertheless at the end of 1942 Polish military leaders thought that the dispersal of Polish soldiers to faraway places was a situation which could be turned to their advantage in pursuit of their ultimate objective of marching back to liberate Poland. This very point was made in an exposé of the Minister for National Defence dated 11 December 1942.[117] General Kukiel reported to the Military Commission of the National Council that 'it is an advantageous circumstance that we have our forces so distributed, that they can place themselves in any of the two hypothetical directions of allied offensive in the continent'.

Sikorski wrote to Churchill on 17 November[118] and to General Brooke on 18 November,[119] in both cases enclosing the same extensive memorandum which explained Polish plans for the future war and stating where and how the Polish military effort could assist the allied grand strategy, while aiming at the liberation of Poland.[120] Polish military estimates for the winter and spring of 1943 were based on the assumption that the defeat of Rommel in North Africa was a foregone conclusion and that Germany was unlikely to be successful in any future actions against the Soviet Union. It was believed by the Poles that the Soviet Union would be unable to mount a counter-offensive until the spring of 1943 while the Germans were unlikely to capture Stalingrad, occupy the Caucasus, or make progress in north-east Russia. According to the Polish military analysts, German initiative would therefore go in the direction of consolidating already occupied regions and preventing the Allies from capturing strategic areas. Sikorski therefore felt that the Allies should watch carefully German actions in the Iberian peninsula and in the Balkans since, having reached stalemate elsewhere, these were the only two areas in which the Germans were likely to launch military offensives.[121] He felt that it would be undesirable to allow the Germans to move crack troops from the east to the west or the south-east. Sikorski concluded this section of the memorandum with a recommendation that the Allies immediately and resolutely assume the initiative.

Sikorski's key recommendation was that the Allies should attempt to divide the two German areas of troop concentration, in the east and in the west respectively. 'To enter between them, to separate them and to defeat them separately, appears to be the correct central idea', wrote Sikorski. This separation of the German defences could be done by military action from the north into the heartland of Germany and by eliminating the main defence lines on the Rhine and the Siegfried Line. An attack from the south through Italy was considered inadvisable because of geographical difficulties. Therefore, according to Sikorski, the Balkan front offered the best opportunity for the Allies to break the stalemate and defeat German troops before they could regroup.[122] This plan was developed further:

> Operations organized here [in the Balkans], and provided with well-developed bases in the Middle East, will bring the Allies to the Romanian oil fields, which are vital to the German interests, and the capture of which would deprive the Germans of one of their main assets in their arguments concerning their alleged invincibility. Even comparatively small forces used in this route, which would pass through Allied countries such as Greece, and Yugoslavia, or through countries quarrelling with each other such as Bulgaria, Romania or Hungary, might penetrate fairly easily. An attack from the Balkans coinciding with an armed rising in Poland, and subsequently supported by Czechoslovakia, would completely separate the German forces and cut them off from German armies fighting in Russia.[123]

The Poles rejected the suggestion that the defeat of Germany should be viewed as a long, drawn-out effort, in which the Allies could count on exhausting Germany's resources and will to fight. Aerial action aimed at breaking down the morale of the enemy was likely to lead only to a partial victory. Nor should the war effort against Japan be allowed to distract the Allies from the main task of defeating the key enemy, Germany.

While assuring the Poles of the possibility of liberating Poland, Sikorski's plan encompassed most of the deeply cherished political hopes of the Polish military leadership. Poland would make a major military contribution to the war effort and with it Poland's political importance would be recognized. Military action in the Balkans would establish Polish primacy in areas which were considered a Polish sphere of influence. Finally the Red Army would not be given an opportunity to venture outside Russian territories since the Soviet military role was to be limited to holding the Caucasus and the Eastern front, and the Soviet political role was to be reduced to placating Turkey. Sikorski recommended that the Soviet Union should be allowed to 'play the most important part ... by guaranteeing Turkey's territorial integrity and giving up her claims to the Straits'.[124] Even the withdrawal of the German army from Russia was not to be the result of a Soviet counter-offensive. The secret army in occupied Poland would, in co-operation with Britain, render German lines of communication inoperative and the Germans would withdraw from the Eastern front from fear of being cut off from the Reich.

In the letter to Churchill, which accompanied the above memorandum, Sikorski outlined the role envisaged for Polish troops in the forthcoming allied offensive.[125] He emphasized that, 'In the expectation of decisive action on the continent in 1943, I would like to make it clear that all the existing Polish Fighting Forces desire to take part in them'. The Polish air force and the Parachute Brigade were to be reserved for action in Poland. The use of units presently being trained in Scotland could not be predicted but the army corps in the Middle East, according to Sikorski, 'ought to be present wherever decisive action will be undertaken'.[126] In the report Sikorski had already stated that he considered the defence of the Iran–Iraq front to be of key importance, since he believed that the Soviet army was unlikely to be able to contribute anything there, other than to continue holding the Caucasus, which was where Sikorski wanted them to stay. Sikorski proposed to assume command over the Polish army if and when it went into battle, his understanding being that such a battle would be not merely decisive but most probably also final, and would lead to the defeat of Germany.

The Chiefs of Staff were directed to consider Sikorski's memorandum. On 8 December General Leslie Hollis, Minister of Defence, duly reported to Churchill that in the view of his colleagues, 'it was as yet too early to enter into any firm commitment for the employment of the Polish First Army Corps, but that we should bear in mind General Sikorski's wishes when the appropriate time comes'.[127] A letter from Brooke to Sikorski made this very point but also cautioned against raising hopes regarding the deployment of the Parachute Brigade in the liberation of Poland.[128] Shortages of suitable aircraft and the great distances involved were given as reasons. It is interesting to note the relative scale of Sikorski's request. In accordance with Polish plans, the Parachute Brigade was to number 2,300 men. When Brooke wrote his letter to Sikorski in effect refusing to make any commitment to British assistance in the liberation of Poland, the Poles had already placed at British disposal, in addition to the 75,000 men in the Middle East, approximately 9,700 air crew, 22,750 infantry men in Scotland and 2,400 in the navy. The British military leaders therefore had under their direct command and in training approximately 112,000 Polish men.

At this stage it was still not possible to forecast developments in Eastern Europe. Even though it increasingly seemed likely that Poland was going to be liberated by Soviet troops it was still impossible to predict the Soviet Union's economic and military situation at the end of the war. Brooke's letter to Sikorski suggested that, notwithstanding the increasing Polish contribution to the war, British military leaders had no plans for action in that region. To assume any military initiative in Central and Eastern Europe would have meant a major readjustment in British troop disposition. More importantly it would have meant either closer co-operation with Soviet troops or, at worst, a confrontation with the Soviet Union, whose belief that the region was its sphere of interest had been articulated from the onset of British–Soviet co-operation. British military leaders clearly thought in the same way as the political leaders, namely that the fate of that part of Europe was not a matter of immediate concern to the British empire. Attempts by the Polish government-in-exile to nudge British military planners in the direction of direct involvement in plans for the liberation of Polish territories were therefore always bound to be unsuccessful.

In November 1942 Sikorski set out for another trip to the United

States. The officially stated reason for the visit was to liaise with American Chiefs of Staff on matters of future strategy. There is no doubt though that this was no more than a pretext. It had become vital for Sikorski to obtain United States support in his dealings with the Soviet Union in particular since British support was not forthcoming.[129] The other objective of the trip was to mobilize the Polish community in America, the importance of which Sikorski had not fully appreciated during his earlier visits. The Polish government in London had come round to the view that Polish–American support could prove vital in persuading Roosevelt's administration to take a keener interest in Polish affairs.[130] Arriving in Washington on 2 December, Sikorski was greeted by Roosevelt with apparent warmth and concern for the difficulties experienced by the Poles in their dealings with the Soviet leaders.[131] In reality the visit was a waste of time. Ciechanowski perceived no possibility of the State Department allowing itself to be diverted from pursuing its chosen course of diplomatic relations with the Soviet Union.[132] Roosevelt too was unwilling to go beyond generalizations. He encouraged Sikorski to visit Stalin again but was only prevailed upon to support the Polish cause to the extent of giving Sikorski a letter stating his support for Poland in vague platitudes.[133] Sikorski knew that he had failed to obtain any real guarantees from the United States. On 10 January he told Ciechanowski about Roosevelt, 'and yet he has not discussed with me the subjects he intends to raise at his pending meeting with Churchill and possibly with Soviet representatives'.[134]

Attempts to obtain the support of the Polish community in America were unsuccessful because Sikorski did not show sufficient sensitivity to divisions within that community. His contacts were confined to talks with the Polish Council whereas the more influential and better organized Committee of Americans of Polish Extraction was ignored.[135] Not only were Sikorski and his policies towards the Soviet Union attacked in the American press, but, more importantly, the Polish community was not united in putting pressure on Roosevelt to support the Polish cause in talks with the Russians.

Back in London Mitkiewicz brutally damned Sikorski's attempts to drum up support in America by describing them as the travels of Don Quixote, 'gathering the fruits of cheap press references, and even inspired articles'.[136] Some tangible commitment from Roosevelt would have given Sikorski a diplomatic success with which to fend off criticism of his policies from within his own government and the National Council. The failure of his trip unleashed further attacks on his style of governing and on his foreign policy.[137]

For the Poles 1942 had been a year during which gradually but conclusively most illusions had been destroyed. They had started the year in hope that Poland's position as one of the major wartime Allies would be enhanced rather than diminished. With its end came the realization that what were now the Three Big Allies were not willing to accord Poland a position of influence. Poland's bitterness in relation to the Allies was to increase precisely because it came at a time of maximum Polish effort to become militarily involved in the war. Indeed, the sad irony of the government-in-exile's situation was that it was allowed few illusions concerning its minor role at the very time when the Polish military effort was encouraged, and became associated directly and more than ever before with the British war effort. Internal conflicts, most notably between Sikorski and Anders, contributed to the collapse of Poland's political position at a time when her military contribution was channelled in directions perceived vital to the British empire but clearly away from areas of consequence to the liberation of Poland. To withhold that military contribution was inconceivable to most Poles, notwithstanding differences of opinion about the relative importance of co-operation with the Soviet Union and Britain.

In contrast to the Poles, by the end of 1942 most British political and military leaders could realistically plan for the final military offensive. This meant that Britain's relations with the Soviet Union, never characterized by clarity of vision, could at least be more assertive. The first stages of Britain's Grand Strategy, the liberation of North Africa and the securing of the Mediterranean, appeared to be within reach. Plans for the invasion of Europe could now be considered in detail. But precisely because of this the need for Soviet co-operation increased rather than diminished: hence the collapse of Poland's negotiating position. The Poles and the policies of the Polish government-in-exile elicited strong reactions at times. But major policy decisions were based neither on romantic and heroic adulation of the Poles nor on latent antipathies for the pettiness of the old regime. On the contrary, the disdain so frequently expressed by Foreign Office officials as much as the callousness displayed by the military leaders was allowed to prevail only because neither the restoration of Poland nor the establishment of a pro-British regime there could be a central plank of Britain's European policy.

7   1943, the end of Polish–Soviet co-operation

In 1943, for the first time since the beginning of the war, the military initiative seemed to have passed from Germany to Britain and the Soviet Union. In the European theatres of war plans were developed for the major thrust against the enemy. As a result post-war territorial settlements became less matters of testing the Allies' goodwill towards each other and more questions of the post-war European balance of power. Irrespective of plans developed in Washington and London, military realities were increasingly likely to define territorial and political changes. When it appeared that neither British nor American troops were likely to set foot on the Continent, the entry of Soviet troops into Central and South-eastern Europe was likely to be the overriding reality. The negotiating power of all small allied governments would be diminished unless agreements were reached with the liberating armies and their governments.

For the Polish government-in-exile these developments were particularly unpropitious. Since it aimed to return in advance of, or at least at the same time as allied troops reached Poland, in 1943 it faced only a few policy choices and those only confirmed its weakening position. The stark reality of the exile government's position was that it had ended up in the wrong place and had committed all its resources to the wrong ally. It is doubtful whether in 1940, when the key decisions were made, or even subsequently anyone in the politically active Polish circles in exile could have foreseen what would happen. Unexpected events in the first half of 1943 only confirmed the Polish government's inability to control developments in their country.

The withdrawal of Polish troops from the Soviet Union marked the end of Polish military and political co-operation with that country. The Katyń revelations led to a formal break in diplomatic relations between the two governments. These developments had momentous long-term implications for both sides, but most notably for the Poles. As far as the

British were concerned, the ending of Polish–Soviet relations did little to alter their already established attitude towards Poland. By the beginning of 1943 Polish–British relations had settled into an irreversible pattern. The two signal features of British relations with the exile government became heavy use of Polish manpower resources and a bland acceptance that Britain would not be able to repay the moral debt by supporting the Poles in their dealings with the Soviet Union. In that respect 1943 saw few surprises in relations between the British and Polish government. Neither the Katyń revelations, nor preparations for the liberation of Italy in which the Polish forces were to take part, altered the already established British attitude towards Poland. Sikorski's death on 3 July 1943 merely added the inconvenience of having once more to establish control over the fractious Polish leaders. While it was appreciated within British political and military spheres that a valuable allied leader had been lost, this did little to alter British policy towards the Polish question.

The breakdown of Polish–Soviet relations in the first half of 1943 led to an estrangement which was never resolved. This situation was to be more damaging to Polish interests than those of the other Allies. The Polish government's determination to end diplomatic relations with the Soviet Union coincided with the Soviet leadership's decision to create and back a new Polish authority in the Soviet Union, the Union of Polish Patriots. This measure signalled a break with previous Soviet initiatives. The Polish government-in-exile had heard rumours of the creation of Red Polish units, a Polish-speaking radio station had been broadcasting in the Soviet Union since 1942 and in December 1941 an Initiative Group had been parachuted into Poland by the Comintern and had sought to gain backing for a broad programme of national unity and political reform. The Soviet authorities' decisions in the spring of 1943 could not be seen only as a means of putting pressure on the London Poles or other Allies. They all had the appearance of a major shift which came in the wake of a dramatic deterioration in relations between the Polish government-in-exile and the Soviet government.

On 28 April 1943, Wanda Wasilewska broadcast a statement that decisions relating to Poland were to be made in Poland and not in London and would depend upon the Poles' own contribution to the defeat of the Nazis. Her broadcast was on Soviet radio, rather than the Polish language service, presumably to give it world-wide exposure.[1] On 6 May the formation of a Polish Division in Russia, headed by General Zygmunt Berling, was announced. The political implications of the decision could not be overlooked. In March the Polish government-in-exile had discussed the possibility that the Soviet authorities would make such an announcement and issued a directive aimed at preventing the Soviet authorities from being able to claim that this was a Polish initiative. The directive firmly stated that the formation of Polish units in the Soviet Union without prior political agreements with the Polish government constituted a provocation and could not be approved by that government.[2] An air of unreality hung over the deliberations of the exile government. Sikorski felt that the Soviet winter offensive was slowing down and that, having briefly secured a strong negotiating position, in the spring the Soviet government's military and hence also political position would be challenged by the other Allies.[3]

The exile government's ability and willingness to negotiate with the Russians diminished in the first months of 1943. The Soviet authorities refused to allow any more Poles to leave and stopped all recruitment by the Polish government in London. Talks on the eastern borders had reached a stalemate. There was an evident unwillingness on the part of the Soviet government to pursue discussions concerning Poland. The British government felt that the Poles were being unrealistic and that the Russians were being intransigent.[4] German radio broadcasts on 12 April announcing the discovery of mass graves of Polish officers converted what might still conceivably have been a temporary impasse into a permanent breach. On 17 April, without prior consultation with the British and acting on the recommendation of its Council of Ministers, the Polish government requested the International Red Cross to investigate the matter. On 25 April the Soviet authorities responded by breaking off diplomatic relations with the Polish government-in-exile. At a crucial time in allied negotiations on the future conduct of the war, Poland had no diplomatic contact with the Soviet Union. The Polish–Soviet estrangement alienated Britain further from Poland. Churchill was now even less willing to see the Polish issue intrude upon the course of British–Soviet relations. These were going through a particularly difficult stage, in which Churchill increasingly sought to reassure the Soviet leadership of Britain's commitment to the war.

During Churchill's visit to the United States in May 1943 the future conduct of the war was discussed.[5] The result of combined British and American Staff talks was agreement that the Mediterranean was to be the next theatre of operation. The cross-Channel landing was to be postponed until 1 May 1944.[6] While never entirely discounting the need for Mediterranean action, Stalin apparently harboured appre-

hensions about its consequences for the Eastern front in the spring of
1943.[7] The suspension of the Arctic convoys, the failure of the
American daylight raids to halt or disrupt military production in
Germany, combined with a whole variety of smaller but significant
issues raised doubts about allied understanding of the Soviet war
effort. Although plans had been mooted for a possible meeting of the
leaders of the three major Allies they did little to remove these real
sources of distrust.

In July Stalin showed his displeasure with allied actions and plans
by recalling to Moscow the Soviet Ambassador in London, Ivan
Maisky. According to the latter the decision to postpone the cross-
Channel landing and the manner in which it had been reached,
without prior consultation with the Soviet leader, caused extreme
irritation in Moscow.[8] Only in September was he officially replaced by
Feodor Gusev, a man of evidently less standing.[9]

A reappraisal in Stalin's policy appeared to be taking place not only
in relation to the Polish question. The dissolution of the Comintern,
the creation of a new Polish authority and army in the Soviet Union,
the recognition of the Free French authorities, the formation of the
National Committee for a Free Germany in July 1943 and the establishment of constructive relations with Beneš all indicate that the
Soviet authorities were exploring new options. It has been suggested
that Stalin had hoped for an agreement with Hitler at the beginning of
1943 and, only when the Nazis appeared unwilling to enter into
negotiations, did he seek to strengthen his contacts with Britain and
the United States.[10] This implies that the failure to establish closer and
therefore constructive contacts between the Allies should be blamed
entirely on the Soviet Union. The creation of the Free Germany
Committee in May 1943 and the League of German Officers in September, conspicuously neither comprising Communists, is seen as an
attempt by Stalin to cultivate an alternative, this time internal, source
of opposition to Hitler.[11] Soviet determination to pursue closer contacts with the western Allies in September is attributed to the failure of
their German policy.[12] There is another explanation for these diplomatic initiatives. According to the military historian John Erickson,
'these events and *démarches* did not suggest that Stalin was embarking
on any new major policy initiatives, but he was certainly establishing
bridgeheads, enlisting lesser Allies within the alliance and clearing the
ground for action against a number of eventualities'.[13]

At the root of Stalin's apprehensions in the first half of 1943 lay the
belief that the Germans were preparing a new counter-offensive

against the Soviet Union. This indeed was launched on 5 July. By October 1943 Stalin was sufficiently confident of ultimate victory over German forces to be able to plan for the liberation of the Ukrainian and Byelorussian region. He went further and, at a Foreign Ministers meeting in Moscow at the end of October, he signalled his willingness to assist the Allies in the defeat of Japan.[14] Plans for future military action would no longer be confined to the liberation of Soviet territory, but would broadly address the issue of the European war and the Pacific theatre. Thus the dominant position of the Soviet Union in all debates concerning the future of Central and South-eastern Europe was dramatically asserted by the autumn of 1943. The division of Europe into spheres of influence was clearly going to take effect because the Soviet army was increasingly likely to defeat Germany in Eastern and South-eastern Europe. Furthermore these military victories were likely to be achieved without any major military action being taken in Western Europe. Even more importantly, the Soviet thrust west was neither accompanied nor preceded by political agreements concerning spheres of influence or operational zones.

This does not adequately explain the lack of any tangible diplomatic initiative on the part of Britain and the United States. At the beginning of 1943 no long-term planning in relation to Central and South-eastern Europe was attempted by both states either individually or jointly. In the autumn when the Soviet army was poised to establish control over the whole of Central Europe, neither Britain nor the United States had developed plans for the future of Europe. Nor had they discussed policies for the economic and military reconstruction of a Europe which would obviously be in need of some assistance and aid, while coping with the inevitable problems which would stem from the redrawing of frontiers that were no longer viable. Thus an additional factor, permitting the establishment of Soviet primacy over decisions concerning the future of Central and South-eastern Europe, was the deliberate British and American decision to concentrate on consolidating their own still slender victories. In effect the western Allies had established no avenues for influencing Soviet policies in liberated territories, irrespective of public statements to the contrary and official messages to the Soviet authorities that they should not think of retaining territories acquired in September 1939 and subsequently. It may be that these issues went unexplored by the British and United States authorities because of their preoccupation with the more pressing matter of securing a victory against the enemy. While this point is a valid one, it remains a puzzling feature of British and American discussions in 1943 that so little attention was paid to the implications of the establishment by the Soviet Union of a dominant political position in Central and South-eastern Europe in the wake of military action.

The standing of the western Allies with the Soviet leadership was reduced not just by the postponement of the second front, but also by the equally controversial question of supplies to the Soviet Union. Because of the heavy losses incurred by the Arctic convoys the British Cabinet decided in March 1943 to cancel them for the time being.[15] But the decision had also been motivated by the British desire to concentrate all resources on planning the invasion of Sicily.[16] After the Anglo-American conference in Casablanca in January 1943, both British and American leaders appear to have agreed that supplies to the Soviet Union should be a priority in case the Soviet ally took the opportunity to negotiate with Germany. But even if a decision to continue supplies to the Soviet Union was made on the highest level, the realities of the complex undertaking destroyed any political credit that might have been obtained from it. Aid was increased as a result of the Third Protocol, signed by representatives of the Soviet Union, Britain and the United States in October 1943. But the British aid was of the wrong kind.[17] Throughout 1943 the clear contrast between, on the one hand, official statements concerning aid to Russia and, on the other, the logistical difficulties of delivering it, diminished the political value of the exercise, even if the aid given was increased and invariably was at the expense of British needs. Conflicts between Soviet and British personnel cast long shadows over all dealings. At the Moscow Conference of Foreign Ministers in October 1943 it was agreed to establish committees and bodies to discuss post-war matters. These eventually settled the issues of planning for post-war Europe raised by the Soviet Union.[18]

By the end of 1943, it has been said,

> The British ceased to think that they could extract any political benefits from their relations with Poland, and, instead, those relations were increasingly seen as exclusively ones of moral obligation to an ally, though that factor had obviously been present since the earliest days of the alliance.[19]

An uneasy feeling of owing a moral debt to Poland did indeed hang over all Cabinet deliberations concerning Poland. To some extent the British leadership knew that it had a real duty towards the Poles. But contacts between the Polish and British governments had not been based entirely on sentiments and vague feelings of obligation. Since the Poles sought desperately and by all military means to assert their worth as fighting Allies, their appeal to the British to side with them in their difficulties with the Soviet Union invoked not the British sense of fair play, but the understanding that a debt of gratitude had been earned and was to be discharged. But the link between the Polish military contribution and British political support was not one which the British wanted to acknowledge and the Poles, because of their own keenness to fight, were never able to exploit it.

At the beginning of 1943 the British, like the Soviet authorities but for entirely different reasons, found themselves negotiating with two separate Polish authorities. Anders, now in the Middle East, entered with relish into political discussions, in particular those relating to the Soviet war effort and the policies of the Sikorski government. The already strongly pronounced anti-Soviet feelings among the Polish soldiers in the Middle East were swelled by Soviet unwillingness to allow the families of Polish soldiers to leave the Soviet Union, and news of changes in Soviet nationality laws obliging Poles from the eastern territories to assume Soviet nationality. Anders' open hostility to any policy of co-operation with the Russians was very popular with the soldiers who saw him as their protector.

Sikorski, after his return from the United States, faced once more the well-rehearsed criticism of his dictatorial style of governing. The hostility of the Polish President towards him continued to be a problem.[20] Raczkiewicz and Sosnkowski officially supported Sikorski against his critics but at the same time associated themselves with calls for broadening the government and reducing the powers of the Prime Minister.[21] Reports from the Middle East caused the British and Sikorski sufficient anxiety for both sides to appreciate that it was essential for the Polish Prime Minister to travel there in person. The government-in-exile's response to rumours of insubordination among the troops in the Middle East and anti-government agitation among Poles based there was to make several key appointments, most notably a Government Delegate, to re-establish London's authority among the soldiers and the refugees.[22]

The quarrels among the Poles in London and the Middle East were of direct interest to the British authorities. There was an understandable concern about the morale of the troops, but the political consequences were also serious. Anders appeared to be posing a challenge to Sikorski's position and that created preconditions for further instability within the Polish community and moreover could affect British–Soviet relations. Since plans had not yet been drawn up for the use of Polish troops, British anxiety about Anders' actions reflected apprehensions about the political implications of his statements and actions. On 1 February the Minister of State in Cairo reported that, during a dinner he had with Anders, the latter called for the launching of a 'propaganda effort throughout the world to persuade people how bad the Russians really are'.[23] Open criticism of Sikorski was also expressed on this and other occasions. The British authorities were keen to know what was happening and an enquiry was instigated. On 6 February it was reported from Cairo that a group headed by Anders' aide-de-camp, apparently without Anders' explicit approval but possibly with his knowledge, hoped to 'set up General Anders in opposition to General Sikorski, as the head of state largely on German lines, with a totalitarian youth movement to ensure a strong Poland after the war'.[24] From Cairo came the suggestion that Sikorski should visit the troops as soon as possible.

Anders was trying to achieve precisely what Sikorski had tried to do earlier, namely to link political demands with the willingness and ability of the Polish troops to fight the allied cause. Having destroyed the basis of Sikorski's negotiating position in the Soviet Union, Anders independently pursued a policy of trying to obtain British support for his own version of Polish demands. On 2 April the Minister of State in Cairo reported that Anders, while extolling the fighting capacity of the Poles, was also insinuating that their morale was being affected by their lack of confidence in their government in London.[25] The content of the report suggests that Anders was hoping that the British government would in some way get rid of Sikorski and replace him with someone whose policies would be less damaging to the fighting capacity of the Polish army under British command.

The matter was sufficiently important for Churchill to take an interest in it and for it to be presented at the next Cabinet meeting.[26] In a personal minute to Cadogan dated 3 April Churchill instructed that all assistance should be given to Sikorski in his planned visit to the Middle East.[27] It was not considered wise or opportune for the British to take up the Polish cause with the Soviet Union. Candidly Churchill noted, 'my influence is not supported by a sufficient military contribution to the common cause to make my representations effective'. But at the same time Churchill wanted the Polish troops and warned:

> The troops should be made aware that any failure on their part of discipline and of readiness to act against the common foe in a coherent manner will relieve the Allies, and particularly Great Britain, of the obligation they have to secure the existence of a strong Poland after the war.[28]

Churchill's high-handed warning bore little relation to the realities of diplomatic exchanges between the British and the Polish authorities during the past year. Nevertheless henceforth Anders was kept on a very short leash. In particular the Katyń revelations and the acrimonious exchanges taking place between the Polish and Soviet authorities required, from the British point of view, firm handling so as not to disrupt training in the Middle East. The British authorities wished to side-step the problem and its ensuing ramifications and in order to do so orders were given to Anders 'that there was to be no criticism of Russia or any objectionable publicity or provocative action'.[29]

In order to forestall any further intrigues within Middle East-based Polish units the British authorities had already decided that Sikorski's visit there was vital. The possibility of bringing Anders to London was also considered. Clearly some sort of reconciliation between Anders and Sikorski was advisable.[30] On 24 May, prior to his departure for the Middle East, Sikorski had an interview with Eden. Eden's minute makes depressing reading. It was clear that Sikorski had seen the end of all his political hopes. If Katyń marked the end of a hope for a future *rapprochement* with the Soviet Union, it also signalled Sikorski's failure to rally the other Allies in support of the Polish cause. The hallmark of Sikorski's previous exchanges with allied leaders was his determination to allow no one to forget that he represented a fighting ally, not a supplicant minor state. From the very beginning Sikorski sought to maintain the clear connection between the political objectives to be achieved through military co-operation and the need to plan for the liberation of Poland by Polish forces. On 24 May, according to Eden, Sikorski 'did not know what our plans were and he did not ask'. Instead he 'begged most earnestly' that Polish troops should have the opportunity of going into battle.[31]

It seems that Sikorski did not believe that the Katyń affair and its diplomatic consequences would result in a total and irreversible breach in Polish–Soviet relations. Mitkiewicz reported that at the beginning of May 1943 within Polish government circles the crisis was viewed as a likely long-term problem, but not a terminal one. He himself thought that the most damaging aspect of the breach in relations between the London government and the Soviet Union was the fact that henceforth the Poles would be entirely dependent on Britain and the United States arguing their case with the Soviet authorities.[32] Sikorski still hoped to be able to go back to the idea of creating new Polish units in the Soviet Union, a point which he put to Eden on 24 May. This suggests that, in spite of all his pessimism, he had not abandoned the hope that negotiations with the Soviet Union would ultimately be resumed. Eden noted that Sikorski tried unconvincingly to present Berling's initiative as a continuation of the previous policy. Sikorski went even further in trying to identify issues which would make it more difficult to re-establish relations with the Soviet Union in the future. He considered the creation of new Polish military units to be a particularly difficult issue. As he told Eden:

> One division might be endured but if further troops were to be raised this was bound to create complications for Polish Government both now and later when relations with Russia were restored. If it were possible for the Polish and Soviet Governments to reach agreement on other matters he could accept this one division as being part of Polish forces and leave it in Russia.

Eden made no comment.[33] From the British embassy in Moscow came a despairing note, 'It shows he has a long road to go before he understands the present situation'.[34] To Sikorski's credit, it was remarked that he was not prepared to go along with Anders' calls for the execution of Berling who would, like Anders, have to be evacuated from the Soviet Union before this could be done.

Sokolnicki's memoirs offer further proof that Sikorski still hoped that Polish–Soviet relations could be re-established. During his last trip to the Middle East, Sikorski briefly stopped in Beirut where he met Polish diplomatic representatives from the area. In the course of several conferences and meetings he frequently expressed his conviction that Britain would assume the initiative in reconciling the Soviet and Polish governments.[35] When explaining to Sokolnicki the manner in which the breach between the Polish government-in-exile and the Soviet Union took place, Sikorski gave the impression that he was still expecting further developments, in particular that British mediation would solve all difficulties.[36]

When Sikorski arrived in Cairo on 26 May the British Minister of State was able to report that he and the British government were successful in forestalling a confrontation between Sikorski and Anders, and keeping the latter muzzled. Prior to Sikorski's arrival the Minister rehearsed with Anders 'lines of conversation ... that would probably take place with Sikorski'.[37] British interests required Sikorski in London and Anders, provided he kept his mouth shut, in command of the Polish forces in the Middle East. This seemed to have been achieved. On 29 May Cairo once more reported that meetings between Sikorski and Anders appeared to have gone well. Anders kept to his lines and Sikorski accepted his apparent contrition. That at least was what the British observers believed.[38]

Sokolnicki, who had daily meetings with Sikorski in Beirut between 20 and 29 June, has left a relatively detailed account of the issues which preoccupied Sikorski in his last days. While discussing the extremely delicate matter of Turkey's entry into the war, Sikorski warned Sokolnicki that he had been told that there would not be a post-war conference at which decisions concerning the new order would be made.[39] Instead 'conditions of peace would be decided by those who had conducted the war'.[40] This was a point to which Sikorski returned on several occasions. It suggests that he increasingly doubted the validity and durability of any commitments made by the Allies, fearing that unless Polish or British troops were physically in Poland at the time of its liberation from German occupation, then Soviet troops would make their own decisions.

Sikorski discussed widely with Sokolnicki whether it was still possible to trust in British support for the Polish cause. Again this subject was touched upon in the context of Polish–Turkish relations. Sokolnicki, who had come to know Turkish political life well, resented British interference in his efforts to establish close Polish–Turkish relations. At stake was not only the question of Turkish willingness to facilitate Polish plans for a Balkan front but also Turkey's relations with the Soviet Union.[41] Sikorski accepted Sokolnicki's arguments and the gist of his complaints was taken up by Cazalet who accompanied Sikorski. Still Sikorski insisted that, in spite of difficulties and pronounced differences of opinion on the subject of the Soviet Union, the Poles should stick with the British.[42]

Soviet influence and Soviet objections to long-term Polish aspirations in Central and South-eastern Europe were not subjects which Sikorski could easily put out of his mind. He was deeply wounded by what he considered to be Beneš' recent defection to the Soviet side and he was anxious that a Balkan campaign, planned by the Poles, could be affected by Soviet disapproval. Sikorski told Sokolnicki that he had received information from a British liaison officer in the Soviet Union that the Soviet authorities did not approve of the Polish army proceeding through the Balkans on its way from Egypt to Poland, 'since it was felt that contact between the Polish army and the nations of that region was very undesirable'.[43]

At the beginning of 1943 the British Foreign Office had tried to continue the previous policy of distancing itself from the course of Polish–Soviet relations. This proved difficult since both sides repeatedly appealed to the British for support. In any case such distance was difficult to maintain since the Soviet authorities, for once, refused to believe that the British government was disinterested. Concern about issues which could affect the fighting capacity of the Polish soldiers drew British military leaders, political representatives and Churchill into the continuing Polish–Soviet difficulties.

On 25 February Sir Owen O'Malley, the British Ambassador to the Polish government-in-exile, reported to the Foreign Office Polish anxieties about the possibility of the Soviet authorities creating a Polish Red Army.[44] Frank Roberts' minute revealed that, were this possibility to be realized, it would be considered by him 'the result of the growing Soviet strength'. On 13 March the British Chargé d'affaires in Moscow, Lacy Baggallay, reported from Kuibyshev that the publication of the newspaper *Wolna Polska* signalled the creation of a new Polish authority in the Soviet Union.[45] It was still not certain whether this meant that a new Polish government was being set up but, as Baggallay noted, this 'would apart from anything else, greatly complicate Soviet relations with Great Britain and the United States'.

The Foreign Office maintained its sang-froid and its distance, as it did when enquiries were made by the British embassy in Moscow about whether to get involved in internal intrigues within the Polish embassy there. Apparently some members of the Polish legation believed that Stalin was seeking to continue discussions on the subject of Polish frontiers. Since the Polish Ambassador, following instructions from his government, refused to enter into any dialogue on the subject, these Poles asked the British Ambassador to intercede with the Polish Ambassador.[46] Not surprisingly the Foreign Office advised against involvement in the intrigue and British determination to remain aloof was reaffirmed. It was stressed:

> We have hitherto taken the line that the frontier question is one that must be settled in the first place between the Polish and Soviet Governments . . . I doubt whether the present is a favourable moment to embark on them [i.e. negotiations about the borders] and should certainly not wish to advise the Polish Government to do so against their better judgment.[47]

In any case the Polish Ambassador resolutely refused to be drawn on the subject, in spite of the evident friendliness of Molotov who, during a meeting which took place on 13 March, suggested that the Soviet government might make some concessions in defining the frontiers.[48]

The Soviet Ambassador to the Polish government in London, Alexander Bogomolov also tried to involve the British in Polish–Soviet difficulties. In an interview with Eden on 10 March he reiterated that the Soviet government sought to maintain good relations with the future Polish government, although he stressed that the London government, with the exception of Sikorski and Raczyński, were considered unacceptable. He further stated that, 'as far as the Eastern frontier of Poland was concerned, something in the nature of the Curzon Line would be agreeable to the Russians'.[49]

A further request for British support came in an interview that Raczyński had with Cadogan on 26 March. Raczyński officially asked the British government to intervene with the Soviet government but only to discuss matters relating to the welfare of Poles still in the Soviet Union.[50] More importantly, the Poles did not want the Soviet authorities to know that the British were doing this at the request of the Poles. They preferred the British to pretend that their intervention was their own initiative. The Foreign Office recognized that the Soviet Union would not enter into discussions on the subject of Poland with the British authorities without including in those discussions the future of Poland's eastern frontiers. The Poles on the other hand refused to enter into a dialogue on that very subject. The Foreign Office preferred to direct a British enquiry on the subject of the Poles in Russia personally to Stalin and Churchill's view on the matter was sought.[51]

It was unlikely that the British would assume any initiative on the subject of post-war territorial settlements without taking the United States into account. While there were signs that the Foreign Office believed the matter could not be entirely avoided, attempts to draw the Americans on the subject were not very successful. In fact Roosevelt's recent pronouncement on the subject of Poland to Eden on 16 March caused a certain consternation in the Foreign Office. Eden had reported that in answer to his enquiries on the subject of Soviet territorial demands Roosevelt bluntly stated:

> if Poland had East Prussia and perhaps some concessions in Silesia she would gain rather than lose by agreeing to the Curzon Line. In any event we, the United States and Russia should decide at the appropriate moment what was a just and reasonable solution, and if we were agreed Poland would have to accept.[52]

Strang minuted anxiously, 'What was behind the President's thoughts?' Although he remained unsure he and Roberts both recognized that in the present circumstances Britain could not afford to 'risk our future relations with the Soviet Government simply because the Poles dream imperialistic dreams and threaten to commit suicide if they do not come true'.[53]

On 13 April German radio broadcast information about the discovery of graves containing the bodies of Polish officers. From the beginning it was obvious that the British government would seek to minimize the impact of these revelations, and the ensuing crisis, upon their relations with the Soviet Union. At best it could be said that Churchill and Eden hoped that the problem would go away. They would have preferred to concentrate on the war and not to dwell on the past.[54] Therefore their efforts went towards conciliating both sides and in particular into pacifying the Poles.

On 28 April Churchill saw Sikorski and Raczyński and presented to them the draft of a message which he wanted them to send to Stalin. Raczyński believed that only then, after the Poles had already broken off relations with the Soviet Union, did the British leader decide to assume an active role in the affair.[55] Churchill's letter to Stalin, which was sent at the same time as the Polish communiqué announcing the breach in diplomatic relations with the Soviet Union was released, must have left very little doubt in Stalin's mind as to the British attitude towards the impending breach.[56] Churchill made himself responsible for disciplining the Poles and confirmed Britain's and the Poles' commitment to the common struggle. In return he asked Stalin to allow the departure from the Soviet Union of Polish children and women, relatives of men serving with British forces. Churchill would have dearly wanted the matter to end there. An optimistic note was injected by him when he wrote to the Foreign Office on 10 May: 'I trust you will be successful in inducing Sikorski to reconstruct his Government'.[57] He had learned from Stalin's letter, recently conveyed to him by Maisky, that Stalin hoped to see the composition of the Polish government changed, with the active assistance of the three allied governments.[58]

From London to Moscow went messages assuring Stalin that Britain had not had a hand in the Polish response to the Katyń revelations.[59] From Moscow came assurances that, in spite of the recent public announcement that the Union of Polish Patriots had been formed to take care of Polish citizens in Russia, it was not claiming to represent Polish interests as a whole and therefore did not constitute a direct challenge to the London Poles.[60] Likewise assurances were given by Molotov that the proposed Kościuszko Division would be formed from 'people formerly living in the Western Ukraine and Western White Russia who, though Polish by nationality, were in fact Soviet citizens'.[61] This was a lie, since no such restriction was ever mentioned to Berling. Because neither the British nor the Russians sought a confrontation, the Poles who did were marginalized. Sikorski's departure for the Middle East with the explicit objective of building up the morale of the Polish troops and disciplining those opposed to his policies went ahead. On his way back Sikorski and his entire entourage, including Victor Cazalet, died in an accident off Gibraltar on 4 July 1943.

Sikorski's policies during the last month of his life differed little from those pursued in 1942. In reality there was no scope for the Poles to assume any major initiatives. The apparent British indifference to Polish requests for support in negotiations with the Soviet Union was compounded by a lack of response to Polish attempts to discuss future military action on the Continent. Sikorski also had to contend with increasing attacks upon his policies from within the Polish community in Britain. Another Polish government crisis, of the sort that tended to confirm worst British prejudices about the instability of Polish politics, led to the removal of Stanisław Stroński of the right-wing National Democracy Party from the post of Minister of Information. His replacement by Professor Kot meant that intrigues and quarrels continued, and were only slightly altered in character.

While having to contend with attacks on his foreign policy and his style of governing from within the Polish community in Britain and the troops, Sikorski tried to secure for Poland a new political base. This would have enabled him to refute his opponents' suggestions that he had betrayed Poland and had unduly trusted Britain. At the end of 1942 Sikorski had hoped that by courting American support the Poles would be able to assume a higher profile in political and military discussions, in particular in relation to the Soviet Union. These hopes had not been realized in spite of Roosevelt's apparent sympathy for the Poles. Briefly at the beginning of 1943 it was thought that some new opportunity of entering into the hallowed circle of decision-making bodies had been opened to them. Leon Mitkiewicz, who in 1940 had the distinction of being appointed the Polish representative to the Executive War Council, was now appointed as Polish delegate to the Combined Chiefs of Staff (CCS), which was co-ordinating allied military strategy in the west.[62] In February 1943 Mitkiewicz had several preparatory meetings with Sikorski and other military leaders. Since they believed that the CCS would make decisions in relation to military as well as political and territorial issues, Mitkiewicz was instructed to act as custodian of Poland's interests in the broadest meaning of the term. Following his most recent visit to the United States, Sikorski appeared to be under the impression that American politicians might still support Poland. American backing for Poland, Sikorski reasoned, could still reverse the tendency in London to pay what he regarded as too much attention to Soviet susceptibilities.[63]

The Poles knew that plans for the liberation of Europe were being formulated by British and American Chiefs of Staff, even if the Poles were not invited to submit their own proposals. Sikorski had already tried to open up discussions on the subject of the Balkan front and the contribution which the Polish Home Army could make to the allied campaign against Germany. The exclusion of Polish representatives from what they regarded as their rightfully earned places on military planning committees was considered to be an insulting denial of the contribution which Britain's first wartime ally was making to the allied effort. Equally distressing was their failure to obtain further information on plans which they suspected were being formalized. Since the earlier Polish initiative in support of a Balkan campaign had failed to elicit a response there was a renewed determination to force the Allies to consult, take the Polish government into their confidence and assume responsibility for the liberation of Poland. The Polish Chiefs of Staff wanted the allied offensive co-ordinated with action by the Home Army in Poland.[64] A continental offensive by the Allies from the north, rather than the Balkans, was considered particularly unhelpful to the Poles, since it would mean that the Polish front would be a peripheral one.[65] But the deployment of the Home Army and the co-ordination of its activities was not merely a matter of military planning. According to Mitkiewicz it came to symbolize Polish co-operation with Britain and the United States. The subject of Polish participation in allied fighting had always been a political issue. Therefore in the summer of 1943, when the Poles once more insisted that Poland be included in talks on future military plans, they were not merely hoping to become privy to military debates. They were also testing allied goodwill towards the Polish question.

At the end of May 1943 Mitkiewicz analysed the matter in the new context of the collapse of Polish–Soviet relations. The Soviet announcement of the creation of the Union of Polish Patriots and the new Polish units in the Soviet Union was accompanied by revelations that pro-Soviet partisan units were being particularly active in the Lublin area.[66] As Mitkiewicz put it, if British and American statements that they would continue to recognize the London Polish government were to be believed, both should have been willing to enter into military talks concerning the use of the Home Army.[67] Instructions to Mitkiewicz, ostensibly to find out what the CCS in Washington had in mind when discussing future continental action, were in reality instructing him to test the allied political commitment to Poland.

Mitkiewicz left for Washington on 10 March. His last message to Sikorski in Cairo in June contained a report on the first inconclusive meetings with British and American military representatives to the CCS. He wrote to Sikorski that having conducted extensive talks with General Albert Wedemeyer, American Chiefs of Staff Army Planner, and Sir John Dill, the Head of the British delegation to the CCS, he had concluded that 'the British did not wish to see a military uprising staged by the Home Army in Poland, they fear that Poles back home will militarily rise against the Soviet troops'. In his view American military leaders would most likely give way to the demands of the politicians and Roosevelt would probably defer to Churchill's policies.[68] Allied failure to include the Home Army in their military plans and estimates was seen by the insecure exile government, desperate for reassurance, as a sign of dissociation from Poland.

On 30 June Grot-Rowecki, Commander of the Home Army, was arrested by the Nazis in Warsaw.[69] In January he had tried to persuade Sikorski that the moment of Soviet entry on to Polish territory would be the most appropriate time to start the rising.[70] But allied military co-operation was a critical factor in all these plans. The leadership of the Home Army and the Polish Chiefs of Staff in London hoped that the uprising would be assisted by the arrival of the Parachute Brigade being trained in Britain. Grot-Rowecki also wanted the uprising to be part of the allied continental offensive. It was never intended to be a localized or limited military operation.[71] None of these matters were clarified in the spring of 1943. Grot-Rowecki's arrest and Sikorski's death, as well as the inconclusive attempts to draw the Allies into plans for the liberation of Poland, meant that the Allies made no military plans for a Polish campaign. Those which had been developed by the Polish government and Home Army were inconsistent because they had not been co-ordinated in any way with the Allies. They therefore failed to resolve the major problem of securing active allied assistance in the face of the Soviet thrust westward.

Mitkiewicz's efforts in Washington were seriously disrupted in the first place by Sikorski's death and in the second by the internal discord and the lack of direction which seemed to overwhelm the new exile government. Mitkiewicz's main objective continued to be to co-ordinate the planned national uprising by the Polish Home Army with the CCS's plans for the liberation of Europe. His first contacts with General G. N. MacReady, the British representative to the CCS, revealed that it was generally assumed that the matter rested with the SOE.[72] By the middle of September, after extensive enquiries, Mitkiewicz was able to ascertain that the CCS was unwilling to make any decisions concerning the Polish Home Army, and had refused to make any commitments to supply it, because of what was described to Mitkiewicz as Poland's undefined diplomatic situation in relation to the Soviet Union. He was warned that neither the British nor American Chiefs of Staff would be willing to proceed with discussion on the Polish proposals until Polish–Soviet relations were clarified.[73] On 22 September Mitkiewicz was informed that the issue of the future allied use of the Polish Home Army had been postponed until the forthcoming allied conference with Stalin.[74]

In spite of setbacks in opening talks on the subject of future allied plans at the end of 1942, the potential offered by the Balkan front continued to spur Polish efforts. During his last visit to the Middle East Sikorski tried to clarify the question of Turkish participation in the war. Sokolnicki, who was strongly committed to the idea of Turkey as a counterbalance against the growth of Soviet strength, pointed out that there were no advantages in Turkey joining the Allies.[75] In fact he believed that Turkish neutrality offered the Poles the possibility of obtaining from Turkey assistance in a future confrontation with the Soviet Union. Sikorski on the other hand sought to ascertain the possibility of Turkey abandoning her neutral stance and joining the Allies during the war. It was clear that he wanted Turkey involved in order that the Balkan front become a priority.[76] Even though the continental invasion had been put off until 1944 the Mediterranean continued to be viewed as a future area of British military operations. Sikorski believed that Churchill was not disinclined to use the Balkans as a means of putting pressure on Italy and Germany.[77] The Polish Chiefs of Staff thought in terms of a landing in Turkey, followed by a move through Thrace to Bulgaria and Greece.[78]

However, Sikorski's view was based on Churchill's misplaced confidence in the result of his recent visit to Turkey. During the Adana conference which opened on 30 January 1943 Churchill had tried, in his view successfully, to persuade the Turks to abandon neutrality. For their part the Turks believed that they had successfully fended off British pressures to commit them to the war.[79] In reality Turkey continued dodging British pressure to abandon neutrality. The fiasco of the British landing on the island of Rhodes in September and the disastrous attempt to capture the neighbouring islands of Kos and Leros, which were all intended to impress the Turks with the need to make a swift commitment to the British side, sealed Turkish determination to stay out of the war.[80] Until the Turks could be persuaded to change their policy the Balkan front could not be considered.

Sikorski's death marked the end of active British–Polish co-operation. The relationship between the two governments had been enhanced by personal contacts between Sikorski and a number of British politicians. His successors were not men of the same calibre. In any case in 1943 there were fewer reasons for British politicians to consider Poland as a useful ally, as they had to some extent been prepared to do in 1940. Contacts between British politicians and the Poles became formal and infrequent. Stanisław Mikołajczyk, Sikorski's successor, did not enjoy the sort of filial relationship with Churchill which Sikorski had at times.

On the surface, at least, Sikorski's death was a source of grief to the politicians of the exile government. Sikorski's leadership was able to rally disparate groups and loyalties. His demise removed all constraints among Polish politicians and freed officers from their remaining moral apprehensions over taking direct action against their own government. Within hours of hearing of Sikorski's death Anders sent a message to the President, pledging his and his army's loyalty to Raczkiewicz. Ominously, he informed: 'I report that, until you, the President, decide otherwise, I will only carry out your exclusive orders'.[81] Presuming to speak on behalf of his men, he also demanded that the political and military leadership be, at last, separated. The quarrels and political disunity which had been the constant feature of Polish life in exile surfaced within days of the tragedy. The appointment of General Sosnkowski as Commander-in-Chief of the Polish forces was generally considered to have been internationally the most damaging outcome of these conflicts. At the time of his death Sikorski was Prime Minister and Commander-in-Chief of the Armed Forces. This duplication of authority had given his opponents an excuse to attack him for his supposed dictatorial tendencies. After the Polish government crisis in the summer of 1941, Sikorski gave an assurance that political and military powers would be separated. But he never relinquished either. With Stanisław Mikołajczyk, leader of the Peasant Party, in charge of the government and Sosnkowski controlling the army, a major change had now been introduced. This was to exacerbate disunity and lack of co-ordination between the civilian and military authorities. This could only have been detrimental to Polish interests as a whole, since the government's claim to political authority and international recognition was based on its military contribution.

Again Anders epitomized everything in the Polish community that was so difficult for the British to understand. On 7 July, he wrote to General Sosnkowski demanding a purge of all the ministers who had been in Sikorski's government.[82] The army's direct involvement in political matters was justified by calls for national unity.

Sikorski's successors still had to face the most intractable strategic problem which Sikorski had failed to resolve, namely the contribution which the Polish forces in the west would make to the liberation of Poland. During Sikorski's visit to the Middle East, he had suggested to General Kopański that he accept the post of Chief of Staff in London. Sosnkowski confirmed this appointment and on 5 August Kopański arrived in London to assume his new position. In that capacity he submitted to Sosnkowski an unusual memorandum dealing with the deeply emotive and complex question of the role of the Polish army-in-exile.[83] Kopański's submission was unorthodox in that it questioned most of the assumptions on which Sikorski had based his foreign policy and military strategy. He asserted that Poland's contribution to the allied war effort up to then had been insignificant. Kopański believed that in view of inevitably high casualties in the near future and without access to reinforcements this contribution could only decrease. He suggested that Poland's military forces should be consolidated, since the political gains would in any case be purely nominal and at best would only result in moral credit accruing to Poland. According to Kopański Polish forces should not be used as a whole in any campaign. Departing radically from hitherto accepted theories that Poland should be represented in as many joint allied military ventures as possible, he suggested that even his proposed consolidated Polish military participation could only have a symbolic character, and that this should be its stated aim. It would be impossible, if not outright inadvisable, to seek an independent area of operation for such a force. He cast doubts upon the idea of a Balkan front, suggesting that for climatic and political reasons that region could prove to be the longest route back to Poland. Finally Kopański pointed out that the Poles would never be able to ascertain, in advance, the strategic and political objectives of the big Allies, in order to co-ordinate their plans.[84] This striking dose of realism appears to have made no impression on Sosnkowski. It was undoubtedly a voice in the wilderness.

Sosnkowski had previously disagreed with Sikorski over the question of the government's re-establishment of relations with the Soviet Union. He had opposed this because of Soviet unwillingness to make a commitment to the restoration of the pre-September 1939 borders.

Nevertheless, he continued military policies which were not dissimilar to those pursued by Sikorski. In October and November 1943 Sosnkowski undertook a trip to the Mediterranean region to inspect Polish troops. Once there he attempted to extend Polish military contacts and thereby increase his government's authority in matters military and political. On 19 November Ralph Stevenson, the British Ambassador to the Yugoslav government, which was then based in Cairo, reported that Sosnkowski wanted an increase in the number of Polish soldiers who were fighting with Mihailiović's Chetnik forces.[85] The Foreign Office anxiously enquired of Stevenson whether there was a possibility of the Poles and the Chetniks collaborating against the Soviet Union. Stevenson was able to reassure London that there seemed to be no signs of such an outcome.[86]

While in Italy Sosnkowski approached the British and American military authorities with the aim of establishing a base for airborne supplies to Poland. Major-General Gubbins refused to be drawn since the matter clearly was not just a military issue but primarily a question of political priorities.[87] General Eisenhower too refused to discuss supplies to Poland, explaining that these decisions 'went beyond his competence. These were directed from London'.[88] Eisenhower also refused Sosnkowski's request for a Polish officer to be attached to his headquarters. For the Poles the failure of Sosnkowski's initiatives confirmed the decisive importance which they attributed to Soviet influence in British and American involvement in Polish matters. Until the Polish–Soviet relations were resolved, decisions to aid the Poles would not be made in London or in Washington.

Sosnkowski ostensibly busied himself with military matters, while Mikołajczyk took charge of political issues. In reality they acted independently, failing to co-ordinate their initiatives. According to Kopański, Sosnkowski and Mikołajczyk distrusted each other, and with time their dislike of each other increased. From September 1943 until Sosnkowski resigned in September 1944, they apparently met no more than ten times.[89] At the same time contacts between Sosnkowski and British military leaders and between Kopański and his British counterparts were minimal.[90] Both sides knew that major decisions concerning the future continental invasion, the Italian campaign and eventual territorial arrangements were being considered. For the Poles, an added source of deep anxiety was the inevitable approach of Soviet troops towards Polish territories. To their horror the Poles realized that neither the British nor the Americans envisaged participating in the administration of liberated territories east of Germany.

Allied Military Governments (AMGOTs) were not going to be set up on sovereign liberated territories, only in ex-enemy areas.[91] Now it was the Poles' turn to seek desperately to re-establish diplomatic relations with the Soviet Union.

The British now stepped in to indicate to the Soviet authorities that Britain favoured a Polish–Soviet frontier on the basis of the old Curzon Line. This decision was made without Polish approval. In fact any attempt to draw in the Poles in planning for the October Moscow Foreign Ministers' conference had been totally unsuccessful.[92] On 5 October the War Cabinet approved Eden's suggestion that the Curzon Line, with possibly Lvov, should form Poland's eastern border, while Silesia and East Prussia should be added to Poland from German territory.[93] The next day Eden had lunch with Mikołajczyk during which he noted: 'The Poles were not ready to discuss the frontier line and I would accordingly have to go as a mediator with a very weak hand to the 3–Power meeting'.[94]

The Polish position had been extensively presented in memoranda submitted respectively to the American and British governments on 5 October 1943.[95] In a desperate attempt to make a virtue of its impending irrelevance, in the wake of entry on to Polish territory of Soviet forces, the government-in-exile put forward the idea that Soviet willingness to resume diplomatic relations with Poland should in some way constitute proof of Soviet long-term objectives in relation to Poland.[96] The Polish communication stated:

> The real intentions of Soviet Russia can best be tested by ... demanding that the relations between the Soviet Government and the Polish Government in London should be resumed forthwith – without entering into any discussion on frontier differences between the two countries.

According to the Poles, Soviet incursion into Polish territory in pursuit of German forces, without prior Soviet–Polish agreements and without accepting limits on their powers while there, would mean that a puppet Communist authority would be established and that in turn would cause an uprising in Poland. The Polish memorandum went on to point out that this would have incalculable implications for the allied nations.[97]

The Poles still hoped to obtain from their British and American Allies assistance in their dealings with the Soviet Union, but also extensive recognition of their military investment into the allied war effort. They wanted the Allies to grant Poland the sole right to occupy and administer eastern German territories and participation in the Mediterranean

Commission. The latter was justified by the envisaged Polish action in the liberation of Italy, the presence there of Polish prisoners of war and potential recruits, and an interest in the Holy See. Finally the Poles wanted to see the establishment of 'a special inter-Allied general staff for planning strategy in Europe'. In the latter, Polish rights were to be commensurate with their extensive contribution to the war effort.

This communication was aimed at forestalling allied agreements at the expense of the Poles. It should be seen as a pathetic sign of the extent to which the Poles failed to understand the implications of the swiftly emerging Soviet military superiority in Eastern Europe. In effect the Mikołajczyk government was telling the Allies that the choice which they were facing, ostensibly relating to the Polish question, had much wider implications. The Allies could choose to side with the Soviet Union and face chaos in Europe, caused by an uprising in Poland. Or they could support the Poles, commit themselves to controlling Soviet entry into Poland, and station troops there and possibly in other parts of Southern and Central Europe. Support for the Poles would also mean granting them extensive influence over allied plans and proposals for military action and post-war administration in potentially all European theatres of war. It is easy to see why the British had no difficulty in continuing with their previous inclinations and decided not to seek a confrontation with the Soviet Union over Poland's eastern frontier. The Foreign Office knew that the Soviet government would not enter into any dialogue with the Poles, especially one in which any discussions on the subject of the eastern frontier were excluded. Nor would the Soviet government be indifferent to the Home Army's proposed action and Polish aspirations to determine security arrangements in Central Europe.[98]

The indirect Polish attempt to resume diplomatic relations with the Soviet Union was a desperate move motivated not only by a desire to forestall Soviet entry on to Polish territory without prior agreement from London. There was also a belated realization that the western Allies were inclined to proceed with their own strategy without reference to Poland. While it could be argued that this tendency had always been apparent in the actions of the British government, the Polish government-in-exile still did not fully appreciate the implications of this. On 25 October a meeting took place between the Polish President, the Commander-in-Chief, the Minister for Foreign Affairs and the Minister for National Defence.[99] During their discussion it was admitted that Poland's position was weak and would remain so as long as there were no diplomatic relations with the Soviet Union. Even allied military supplies and air drops to Poland could not take place as long as this situation remained. That there was still no commitment to provide these supplies was not noted by the participants of the meeting. According to the exile government, at stake was not just the old question of the liberation of Polish territories, which required the co-operation of the Home Army with Polish units in the west, but also, and more importantly now, the whole issue of Poland's international standing. The failure to re-establish diplomatic relations with the Soviet Union could adversely affect the west's willingness to co-operate with the Poles.

Events nevertheless overtook the Poles. Poland was referred to only on the margin of the Moscow conference. According to Eden this was because the Poles requested that all frontier issues should be avoided.[100] But Britain too no longer wished to champion the Polish cause and, in any event, the Soviet negotiators made it quite clear now that they would not tolerate back in Warsaw the present Polish government in London.[101] In his conversation with Eden and Cordell Hull, Molotov brushed aside Eden's tentative request that the Soviet authorities should grant Britain and the United States permission to fly arms and material to the Polish resistance. Eden's timorously presented point that the Polish troops would soon go into action in Italy made no difference to Molotov, who pointed out that Sosnkowski's control of military matters cast doubt upon the main objectives of that government.

When the autumn campaign drew to a close Soviet troops had regained the initiative on all fronts. In the south Dnepropetrovsk had been recaptured on 25 October and Kiev, the capital of the Ukraine, on 5 November. Continuing progress in the south-east became Stalin's main objective for the winter.[102] If successful, Soviet troops would not only recapture the Ukraine but would also be strategically placed to enter into Romania and/or Poland.[103] Unlike the Czechs, whose First Independent Brigade fought with the Red Army and distinguished itself in the recapture of Kiev, the Polish government had made and would make no contribution to the Soviet war effort.

By November nothing could redeem the Poles in the eyes of the Soviet ally. They did not need the Poles in the west, even if Mikołajczyk put all his efforts into persuading the British that he and his government emphatically did want to talk to the Soviet leadership before their troops entered Poland. The Poles' permission was not sought by the Soviet military commanders. Since continuing Soviet victories against Germany allowed the postponement of the North

European invasion until 1944, neither Britain nor America would henceforth expend much effort on championing the Polish cause. As to the political consequences of Poland's contribution to the allied war, Churchill's comment in July 1943 explains how little it was appreciated. Planning for the invasion of Italy he minuted 'The Polish troops in Persia should be brought to Egypt for this task. These Poles wished to fight ... and once engaged will worry less about their own affairs, which are tragic.'[104]

Conclusion

At the Tehran conference Churchill was anxious to place the Polish issue into the context of agreements made with the Soviet ally. The Soviet Union, which hitherto had sought to clarify the issue of Poland's eastern border, and used it as a test of British and American goodwill, now merely responded to British initiatives.

During Churchill's meeting with Stalin on 28 November 1943 both sides accepted that the Soviet Union would not return the territories annexed in September 1939 and Poland would be compensated for this loss in the west.[1] As Churchill summarized, 'Nothing was more important than the security of the Russian Western frontier'. British obligations to Poland were subsidiary to this consideration. Both leaders accepted that the redrawing of Poland's borders would take place without Polish participation. Churchill later described the way in which the future map of Poland was agreed: 'this was all informally between themselves and they could go to the Poles later'.[2] Even if Churchill had not meant this to imply that Polish agreement was irrelevant, this is how Stalin understood the above statement. On 1 December during discussions between the three leaders Stalin was visibly irritated by Roosevelt's suggestion that the Polish government's acceptance of the decisions made by the Big Three would be desirable. Stalin interrupted Churchill to say that when he had previously discussed the matter with Churchill he understood this to be 'the question of prescribing something to the Poles'.[3] The re-establishment of diplomatic relations with the Polish government-in-exile was not viewed by him as necessary nor could it form a precondition for settling the Polish issue. As he frankly stated, 'he separated Poland from the Polish government-in-exile'. During that meeting the three agreed on the Curzon Line becoming Poland's eastern border with the towns of Lvov and Vilna going to the Soviet Union and the Oder Line becoming the Polish western border. Neither Roosevelt nor Churchill objected to Stalin's suggestion that the London government's aims could not be seen as representing Polish interests. This spelled the end of that government's tenuous influence and *raison d'être*.

It could be argued that during 1943 the Polish government in London had become increasingly irrelevant in British and United States politics, in spite of its increased military contribution to the war. Its ability to convince the British and American Allies that it represented the interests of the bulk of Poles in Poland decreased with the establishment, at the initiative of the Soviet Union, of a new Polish authority. The Polish government-in-exile's control over its manpower was weakened by internal disagreements and its own eagerness to co-operate militarily with the British. Soviet entry on to Polish territory would complete the picture by formalizing the separation between the London Poles, who controlled their government but had no way back to their country, and those supported by the Soviet Union, who would return to their country with a government set up under Soviet auspices.

The implications of the Moscow and Tehran conferences were extensively analysed by the Poles. But it was difficult to arrive at a clear interpretation because, at the very time when Churchill suggested to Stalin that Britain would accept Soviet claims on Poland, the British military authorities in the Middle East finalized their plans for the Polish units in the Middle East. During 21 and 22 July Anders was informed that the Polish Corps was to be moved from Iran and Iraq to Palestine in preparation for action in Italy.[4] General Wilson announced that Polish units, after completing their training, would be ready for action after January 1944.[5] During his inspection of Polish troops in the Middle East, General Sosnkowski approved further reorganization and agreed that the Polish Corps would operate as part of the British Eighth Army.[6] The whole Polish Corps, numbering approximately 70,000 men, would be deployed in Italy. The first units were moved towards the Italian front in the middle of December 1943.

The organization of Polish units in Britain was limited by shortages of men. In 1942 there were approximately 15,000 Polish officers and soldiers in Britain. Subsequently the reorganization of units in the Middle East became a priority and therefore plans to send to Britain men leaving the Soviet Union had to be abandoned. At the end of 1943 further plans for building up these units remained unclear.[7] The only plans were made in relation to the Parachute Brigade since the Poles assumed that the Brigade would be in the vanguard of Polish troops entering Poland.

The assignment of a clear role in future military operations to the Polish units in the Middle East had an important effect upon the exile government's evaluation of its position in Britain. It allowed the major misunderstandings between Britain and the Polish government-in-exile to continue. On 27 December 1943 the government issued to Polish army commanders a communiqué about the political situation. The government's basic claim was that the two inter-allied conferences had not determined anything conclusively, although Poland's position could have been temporarily weakened.[8] In addition to invoking well-known arguments about Poland being Britain's staunch ally throughout the war, stress was laid on the imminent commitment to battle of Polish units. Finally it was emphasized:

> In relation to the English our soldiers' most effective propaganda is to manifest the will to fight, battle readiness, stressing our unity and the solidarity of all sections, the President's institutions, the country, the government, the Commander-in-Chief and the Fighting Forces.[9]

Three years after the outbreak of the war, the Polish government-in-exile apparently still failed to appreciate either the strength and durability of the Soviet Union, or the finer points of the diplomacy.

The purpose of this study has been to ascertain why the Polish wartime politicians failed to obtain from Britain a commitment to the reconstruction of Poland in her pre-war boundaries. It was necessary to enquire why Britain did not support the Polish government-in-exile in its dealings with the Soviet Union. This study therefore concentrated on investigating the course of Polish–British relations with special reference to their attitude towards the Soviet Union. To British politicians the exile Polish authority was one of a few which had sought sanctuary in Britain during the war. The Poles' military contribution was always appreciated but a key question is why this gratitude was never translated into actual political commitments.

The Polish government-in-exile did not have an easy relationship with its British hosts. It was nevertheless notable for its determination to contribute to the common objective of fighting the enemy. Indeed, the eagerness of the Poles to fight was continuously noted by the western Allies, even though this was not so apparent to the Soviet leadership. In their evaluation of the strategic developments and in their understanding of the need to participate in the liberation of Polish territory the Polish politicians at times displayed much realism. On other occasions they succumbed to false expectations and unreal hopes. Circumstances and Polish attitudes seem also to have played a part. From the onset of its exile, the Polish government was trapped by its perception of how it could exercise influence on the strategy of its Allies during the course of the war. Romantic traditions played a part in their conviction that the war was a common effort in which all that would count was the ability to fight, no matter where. But there were moments when both Sikorski and his opponents formulated realistic and credible military plans for the return of the Polish army to fight for the liberation of Poland. Nevertheless, Britain's choice of North Africa and the Mediterranean as preferred theatres of war prior to the invasion of the European continent was not advantageous to the Poles. The British decision not to develop a Balkan offensive and repeated postponement of the continental offensive in the long run removed Polish fighting units further and further away from militarily practical and politically advantageous access to Polish territory. This caused the Polish government-in-exile to commit itself to the common effort in distant areas, which were of no interest to Poland. Plans for the liberation of Poland by Polish units in the west had to be postponed. By the beginning of 1943 Polish units in the Middle East were being prepared to assist a British war effort that brought them no closer to liberating Polish territory. In matters relating to the general conduct of the war, Polish politicians and military leaders had no say. By 1943 they knew that they would not be consulted even though their military contribution would be increased.

The choice of wartime Allies had been deliberately made by the Poles. It was always understood that victories on the West European front would lead to the ultimate defeat of Germany and thus to the liberation of Polish territory. Initially therefore the Poles in exile thought in terms of co-operating with France. In the end, although Sikorski was willing to negotiate with and take into account the Soviet Union, even he was not able to envisage the possibility of that country being Poland's major ally. Thus, after the fall of France, Britain became Poland's obvious host and ally. From the onset of the war it was unlikely that a common European policy would evolve between the two. But none of the Polish politicians who made their way to Britain could follow a different policy, since co-operation with the Soviet Union was not naturally favoured by them. The difference between Sikorski and his more anti-Russian opponents in the Polish government lay in the degree of pragmatism displayed by him in his evaluation of the need, for diplomatic and military reasons, to enter into agreements with the Soviet Union.

These two dogmas of the exile government's thinking, its commitment to gaining credibility by being a fighting partner, and co-operation with the western Allies, became ideological constraints on their actions. This proved to be so limiting that the Polish government-in-exile could not think its way through to an active diplomatic and military strategy. Total military commitment to the war on the side of the western Allies, it was thought, would give Poland a say in post-war plans. When Poland's diplomatic influence was not established, in spite of its military contribution to the war, and it realized that under-takings to support the Polish cause were not forthcoming, the exile government merely stepped up its recruitment drive and reiterated demands to participate in military action against the enemy. The possibility that the fate of Poland would be decided as a result of Soviet troops entering that country was never realistically considered by the exile politicians until the end of 1943, by which time the London government could not assume any initiatives in relation to the Soviet Union. They notably failed to take into account the durability of the Soviet Union and hence the possibility that the Red Army would liberate Polish territory. This was probably the single most important failure of the Polish government-in-exile's evaluation of the military, and consequently the political, course of the war. The second mistake compounded that failure. They hoped that by being brave and selfless they would gain British respect, support or at least gratitude. They achieved none of this. The only lingering positive impression created by the Poles was of reckless heroism.

British policy towards Poland, however callous it might appear with hindsight, was not premeditated. To British politicians the Polish government-in-exile at best represented a defeated ally; at the worst it was occasionally an obstacle to the exercise of Britain's foreign policy. The latter aspect surfaced most strongly in Britain's relations with the Soviet Union, but was also apparent in the British government's dealings with other European governments and representatives in exile of defeated nations.

The Poles demanded and expected, in return for their war contri-bution, long-term commitments against the Soviet Union. In relation to the Soviet Union Britain pursued a policy characterized by hesi-tancy and inconsistency. Inevitably therefore the Polish government-in-exile appeared to British politicians to be pushing them to support the Polish case irrespective of British priorities. They saw the Poles as forcing them to make decisions at a time when they felt unable and unwilling to face the issues of the post-war balance of power. In 1943 the British government was forced at last to address itself to long-term

questions of the future of Germany and post-war territorial adjustments. The commitments made earlier by the Foreign Office and
British politicians to stave off Polish demands for support of their
long-term objectives, in 1943 appeared to be obstacles in British–Soviet
relations. This explains why Churchill appears to have had no qualms
in responding to Stalin's demands at the Tehran conference. Poland
was an area which did not lie within the British sphere of influence.
Notwithstanding the complex association which had been established
between the British government and the Polish exile government, the
defence of Poland and of her territorial aspirations could not assume a
major role in British foreign policy.

The fact that Britain did make full use of the Polish manpower which
was offered to them with few restrictions by the Polish government had
not been an obstacle in Britain's negotiations with the Soviet Union.
Had the government-in-exile not raised an army abroad, the absence of
a military contribution to the allied war effort would not have altered
the British government's response to the Polish issue. The Polish military contribution was accepted in the spirit in which it was offered,
namely as part of the joint effort to defeat the aggressors. From the
outset it was apparent that unless the future of Poland directly affected
Britain's post-war situation, the British would not become involved in
the defence of that region. On the other hand if there were a threat of
the Polish issue becoming a difficulty in British–Soviet relations, British
politicians and Foreign Office advisors were pragmatically and deliberately prepared to distance themselves from Poland. The early years of
the war offered few moments when Polish and British aims would coincide on issues other than the obvious one of the defeat of Germany. In
1943, when it became apparent that Britain would have to choose
between humouring the Poles in London and accepting Stalin's territorial demands, they chose the latter. At the Tehran conference
Churchill did not merely accept Stalin's demands that Poland's border
be based on the territorial adjustments of September 1939 and Poland
be recompensed for this at Germany's expense. More notably he undertook to compel the Polish government to accept this decision. The
Tehran conference reversed the previous inconsistent and inconclusive
Polish badgering of Britain to put pressure on the Soviet government
on Poland's behalf. Britain now assumed full responsibility for making
sure that the Poles accepted Soviet demands.

It was another two years before the Polish government-in-exile was
consigned to history. In October 1944 Mikołajczyk accompanied

Churchill to Moscow. The London Poles' negotiating strength had been whittled down to nothing. The Warsaw uprising in August 1944 exposed the Home Army's inability to prevent the Red Army from assuming total control over liberated Polish territories. In October the Soviet Union recognized the Communist-dominated Polish Committee for National Liberation (PKWN) as the provisional authority in Poland. Churchill's determination to force Mikołajczyk to accept the Soviet decision meant that the Polish Prime Minister had no freedom to manoeuvre.

Mikołajczyk was reduced to fighting for the provisional authority in Poland to be broadened by the inclusion of the London Poles. In that task he faced the hostility of his government. As a result he resigned from the exile government and joined the provisional government in Poland. In July 1945 Britain and the United States withdrew recognition from the government-in-exile.

The break with wartime entanglements was not to be easy or clear cut. This was primarily because Polish–British relations had not been confined just to contacts between the exile government and the British host. By 1944 military co-operation was extensive and the opening of the North European front meant that Polish units fought with the British on all European fronts. The transfer of recognition from the London Poles to the Soviet-backed authority in Poland appeared to resolve political matters but the military entanglements were more complex. The British government remained responsible for the servicemen who had enlisted in the Polish forces during the course of the war. They were now a source of political difficulties with the new Polish authority and the Soviet Union. The Polish servicemen were also seen as a potential drain on British resources even though Anders attempted to persuade the British Prime Minister and Chiefs of Staff that they should allow the continuing expansion of the Polish armies based in Italy and Holland. His efforts were doomed to failure. The London Poles' assumption that sooner or later the western Allies would need an army to fight the Soviet Union met with little understanding in the spring of 1945. Churchill briefly considered the possibility of the Polish troops being converted into a Foreign Legion in order to do policing duties in the British zone of occupation in Germany. This proposal was abandoned when the full implications of such plans were considered. Polish actions in Italy suggested that the Polish army was totally unsuited for such action. Polish soldiers were unlikely to set aside wartime grievances and transform themselves into obedient instruments of the British.

Thus at the beginning of 1945, even before the end of hostilities and the withdrawal of recognition from the Polish government-in-exile, the British government sought to find out whether it would be possible to return the Poles to their own country. The new Polish authorities let it be known that those who had fought with the British forces would be welcomed back. Indeed they would be appreciated all the more since the Warsaw authority assumed that the Soviet officers who had formed the bulk of the officer corps within their Polish army, which was fighting with the Red Army, were due to return to the Soviet Union.

As it turned out, most Poles who had fought in the west opted not to return to their own country. The commanders of units conducted extensive campaigns against this proposal. Anti-Soviet feelings remained very strong within the Polish units in the west. The few who decided to go back experienced intimidation and violence from their comrades in Britain. The processing of soldiers who wanted to return to Poland was done by the British authorities and no effort was spared to give their return journey the appearance of an honourable return home. Only approximately 20,000 men returned to Poland, very few of them officers. Over the next three years, with the establishment of Communism in Poland, all those who returned suffered in some way. Their contribution to the war effort was questioned. At the height of the cold war they were accused of collaboration with the 'Imperial Powers' and most experienced spells in prison. Only after the fall of the Communist regime was the contribution of Polish soldiers to the defeat of Germany in the west fully honoured.

Those who stayed in Britain and the Commonwealth also faced difficulties in adjusting to the fact that they were unlikely to return to Poland within the near future. In addition, with the end of the war they were no longer viewed as Allies, but as people who were expected to leave Britain. Only by the spring of 1946 were plans formulated by the British government for the resettlement of approximately 160,000 Poles who had become the responsibility of the British government.

The leaders of the Polish community in Britain persisted in their belief that they represented the legitimate government of the Republic of Poland. Since this fact, in itself, did not prevent any of the ex-allied governments from establishing diplomatic relations with the new Communist regime in Poland, it remained a source of comfort to the Poles in exile, but one of no broader significance.

Notes

1 The formation of the Polish government-in-exile

1 Starzeński, *Trzy Lata z Beckiem*, pp. 148–151; Szembek, *Diariusz*, pp. 26–27
2 Skrzypek (ed.), *Wrzesień 1939*, p. 74
3 Ibid. pp. 82–83
4 Starzeński, *Trzy Lata z Beckiem*, p. 148
5 Ibid. p. 205
6 Szembek, *Diariusz*, p. 37
7 Ibid. p. 55
8 Lungu, *Romania and the Great Powers*, pp. 196–197
9 Ibid. pp. 200–201
10 Ibid. p. 199
11 Szembek, *Diariusz*, pp. 71–72. Szembek quotes a conversation he had with August Zaleski while travelling from Romania to France on 23 September. Zaleski had been Minister for Foreign Affairs until he was replaced by Colonel Józef Beck in 1932. Zaleski took now the opportunity to attack the government and its foreign policy. When Sikorski formed his first government on 30 September Zaleski was appointed Minister for Foreign Affairs.
12 Jędrzejewicz (ed.), *Diplomat in Paris*, pp. xviii–xx
13 Szembek, *Diariusz*, pp. 80–81
14 Ibid. p. 41
15 For an outline of the way in which this transfer of power was done see Jędrzejewicz (ed.), *Diplomat in Paris*, pp. 338–372
16 Szembek, *Diariusz*, pp. 80–81
17 Alexander, *The Republic in Danger*, pp. 303–304
18 Terlecki, *Generał Sikorski*, p. 141
19 Pestkowska, *Uchodźcze Pasje*, pp. 27–29
20 Witold Biegański, *Wojsko Polskie we Francji*, pp. 176–177
21 Ibid. p. 96
22 Ibid. p. 178
23 Klimkowski, *Byłem Adiutantem Generała Andersa*, p. 72
24 Duraczyński, *Rząd Polski na uchodźstwie*, pp. 66–67
25 Witold Biegański, *Wojsko Polskie we Francji*, pp. 162–163

26 Beauvois, *Stosunki polsko-francuskie*, pp. 16–17
27 Alexander, *The Republic in Danger*, pp. 343–348; Witold Biegański, *Wojsko Polskie we Francji*, pp. 40–41
28 Witold Biegański, *Wojsko Polskie we Francji*, pp. 42–43
29 Klimkowski, *Byłem Adiutantem Generała Andersa*, p. 72
30 Polish Institute and Sikorski Museum, London (henceforth PISM) AID 1/1 January 1940
31 Witold Biegański, *Wojsko Polskie we Francji*, p. 29; Pestkowska, *Uchodźcze Pasje*, pp. 27–34
32 Witold Biegański, *Wojsko Polskie we Francji*, p. 32
33 Duraczyński, *Rząd Polski na uchodźstwie*, pp. 53–54
34 Ibid. pp. 55–56
35 Public Records Office, London (henceforth PRO) FO 371 23159 C16373/16049/55 12 October 1939
36 PISM PRM 3/14 November 1939
37 Archiwum Akt Nowych, Warsaw (henceforth AAN) Paderewski Archives, 3087, 30 December 1939
38 Duraczyński, *Rząd Polski na uchodźstwie*, pp. 61–62
39 PISM AID 1/1 21 February 1940
40 Nevakivi, *The Appeal that was Never Made*, pp. 179–180
41 PISM ALII 46/2 7 February 1940
42 PRO CAB 99/3 SWC39/40 23 April 1940
43 PRO CAB 99/3 SWC39/40 27 April 1940
44 PISM PRM K 102/22 26 April 1940
45 Duraczyński, *Rząd Polski na uchodźstwie*, pp. 64–65
46 Mitkiewicz, *Z Generałem Sikorskim na Obczyźnie*, pp. 26–27
47 Ibid. p. 34
48 Prażmowska, *Britain, Poland and the Eastern Front*, p. 186
49 Duraczyński, *Rząd Polski na uchodźstwie*, p. 48
50 Archives of the Zjednoczone Stronnictwo Ludowe, Warsaw, archives of Stanisław Kot, 119, 28 February 1940
51 PISM PRM 13/30 15 April 1940
52 Ibid.
53 Beauvois, *Stosunki polsko-francuskie*, p. 70
54 PISM AID 1/1 26 April 1940
55 PISM PRM 13/18 26 April 1940
56 Ibid.
57 Beauvois, *Stosunki polsko-francuskie*, p. 70
58 Klimkowski, *Byłem Adiutantem Generała Andersa*, p. 73
59 Sokolnicki, *Dziennik Ankarski 1939–1943*, pp. 60–61
60 Witold Biegański, *Wojsko Polskie we Francji*, pp. 221–222
61 Gates, *The End of the Affair*, pp. 58–59
62 Ibid. pp. 59–63
63 Ibid. p. 82
64 Ibid. p. 77
65 *Polskie Siły Zbrojne*, Vol. II, part 1, pp. 129–130
66 PRO FO 371 244468 C73006/3/55 19 June 1940

67 Smoleński, 2 *Dywizja Strzelców Pieszych*, pp. 73–74

2 Britain and German expansion in Eastern and South-eastern Europe

1 Gates, *The End of the Affair*, p. 27
2 Ibid. p. 27
3 Alexander, *The Republic in Danger*, pp. 351–352
4 Ibid. pp. 314–315
5 Newman, *March 1939*, pp. 46–53. The author suggests that the result of Foreign Office pressure on the government and Treasury was an agreement that economic means should be used to counteract the growth of German political influence in South-eastern Europe. He nevertheless concedes that the slow and limited implementation of this policy raises doubts about the effectiveness of these gestures.
6 Prażmowska, *Britain, Poland and the Eastern Front*, pp. 38–44
7 Prażmowska, 'Polish Foreign Policy', pp. 867–871; Lungu, *Romania and the Great Powers*, pp. 174–175
8 Lungu, *Romania and the Great Powers*, pp. 175–178
9 Prażmowska, 'Polish Foreign Policy', pp. 865–867
10 Prażmowska, 'The Eastern Front', pp. 192–196; Lungu, *Romania and the Great Powers*, pp. 179–181
11 Prażmowska, 'The Eastern Front', pp. 205–206
12 Howard, *The Continental Commitment*, p. 129
13 Peden, *British Rearmament and the Treasury*, pp. 92–93
14 Douglas, *The Advent of War*, pp. 59–60
15 Prażmowska, *Britain, Poland and the Eastern Front*, pp. 83–86
16 PRO CAB 65/1 War Cabinet 8(39) 8 September 1939
17 PRO CAB 65/1 War Cabinet 9(39) 9 September 1939
18 PRO FO 371 22882 C14383/13545/49 20 September 1939
19 Prażmowska, *Britain, Poland and the Eastern Front*, p. 187
20 PRO CAB 82/1 COS (39)5 Mtg 15 September 1939
21 Ibid.
22 PRO CAB 65/1 War Cabinet 10(39) 10 September 1939
23 PRO CAB 65/1 War Cabinet 11(39) 11 September 1939
24 Skrzypek (ed.), *Wrzesień 1939*, p. 113
25 PRO FO 371 23092 C13253/12590/18 8 September 1939
26 PRO CAB 65/1 War Cabinet 8(39) 8 September 1939
27 PRO CAB 66/1 WM 39/38 20 September 1939
28 Neville Chamberlain private papers (henceforth NC), NC 187/1/1121 17 September 1939
29 PRO CAB 65/1 War Cabinet 9(39) 9 September 1939
30 Parliamentary Debates, Commons 1938–1939, Vol. 351 August 24–October 5, 648 13 September and 749–750 14 September 1939
31 PRO CAB 65/1 War Cabinet 9(39) 6 September 1939
32 PRO FO 371 23147 C13082/110/55 7 September 1939
33 PRO T.160 F16073/3 1 September 1939
34 PRO FO 371 23151 C14059/8526/55 16 September 1939

35 Ibid.
36 Lungu, *Romania and the Great Powers*, pp. 197–198
37 PRO FO 371 23151 C14339/8526/55 19 September 1939
38 Lungu, *Romania and the Great Powers*, pp. 199–200
39 Ibid. pp. 204–207
40 Coutouvidis and Reynolds, *Poland 1939–1947*, pp. 25–26
41 PRO FO 371 23152 C15148/8526/55 27 September 1939
42 Ibid.
43 Raczyński, *W Sojuszniczym Londynie*, p. 53
44 Sir Peter Wilkinson, 'Sikorski's Journey to England June 1940', in Sword (ed.), *Sikorski, Soldier and Statesman*, pp. 159–160
45 PRO CAB 65/1 War Cabinet 22(39) 21 September 1939
46 PRO ADM 1 9963 25 August 1939
47 PRO ADM 1 100520 11 September 1939
48 PRO AIR 2 4211 13 September 1939
49 PRO CAB 65/1 WM 17(39) 16 September 1939
50 PRO FO 371 C14432/8526/55 20 September 1939
51 PRO AIR 2 4211 24 September 1939
52 Prażmowska, *Britain, Poland and the Eastern Front*, p. 146
53 Ibid. pp. 147–148
54 Starzeński, *Trzy Lata z Beckiem*, p. 158. Szembek, *Diariusz*, pp. 56–57
55 PRO FO 371 23103 C14090/13953/18 18 September 1939
56 PRO CAB 65/1 War Cabinet 19(39) 18 September 1939
57 Ibid.
58 Kitchen, *British Policy Towards the Soviet Union*, pp. 1–2
59 Douglas, *The Advent of War*, pp. 76–77
60 PRO FO 371 23104 C15948/13953/18 5 October 1939
61 Ibid.
62 Kacewicz, *Great Britain, the Soviet Union and the Polish Government in Exile*, p. 75
63 PRO FO 371 22946 C14930/13669/62 26 September 1939
64 Kitchen, *British Policy Towards the Soviet Union*, pp. 3–4
65 Gorodetsky, *Stafford Cripps' Mission to Moscow*, pp. 10–11
66 Miner, *Between Churchill and Stalin*, p. 6
67 Kitchen, *British Policy Towards the Soviet Union*, pp. 5–6
68 Barker, *British Policy in South-East Europe*, pp. 20–21
69 Deringil, *Turkish Foreign Policy*, pp. 85–86
70 Ibid. p. 88
71 Barker, *British Policy in South-East Europe*, pp. 28–29
72 PRO CAB 66/1 WP (39)3 6 September 1939
73 PRO CAB 65/3 WM 19(39) 18 September 1939
74 PRO FO 371 23852 R8126/1716/37 28 September 1939
75 PRO FO 371 23852 R8957/1716/37 17 October 1939
76 PRO FO 371 23848 R7436/529/37 11 September 1939
77 PRO WO 104/30 Registered File 12 September 1939
78 PRO FO 371 23849 R10177/529/37 13 November 1939
79 Ibid. p. 5

80 Munch-Petersen, *The Strategy of Phoney War*, p. 72
81 Ibid. p. 47
82 Howard, *The Mediterranean Strategy*, p. 9
83 Deringil, *Turkish Foreign Policy*, pp. 82–88
84 Butler, *Grand Strategy*, pp. 64–65
85 Miller, *Bulgaria During the Second World War*, pp. 13–14
86 Deringil, *Turkish Foreign Policy*, pp. 88–89
87 PRO CAB 99/3 SWC 39/40 2nd Mtg 22 September 1939
88 PRO CAB 99/3 SWC 39/40 4th Mtg 19 December 1939
89 Ibid.

3 Britain's only fighting ally

1 Salmon, 'Great Britain, the Soviet Union and Finland', pp. 104–107
2 Ibid. pp. 115–117
3 Gates, *The End of the Affair*, p. 38
4 Douglas, *The Advent of War*, pp. 84–87
5 Butler, *Grand Strategy*, pp. 156–157
6 Ibid. p. 166
7 Ibid. p. 170
8 Gates, *The End of the Affair*, pp. 58–59
9 Ibid. pp. 124–125
10 Ibid. p. 381
11 Thomas, *Britain and Vichy*, pp. 41–42
12 Ibid. p. 82
13 Ross (ed.), *The Foreign Office and the Kremlin*, p. 6
14 Kitchen, *British Policy Towards the Soviet Union*, pp. 20–21
15 Ibid. pp. 22–23
16 Ibid. p. 21
17 Ibid. pp. 24–26
18 The authors whose works meticulously cover this period in British–Soviet relations are Gorodetsky, *Stafford Cripps' Mission to Moscow*; Kitchen, *British Policy Towards the Soviet Union*; Hanak, 'Sir Stafford Cripps as British Ambassador in Moscow'; Ross (ed.), *The Foreign Office and the Kremlin*
19 Hanak, 'Sir Stafford Cripps as British Ambassador in Moscow', pp. 53–55
20 Kitchen, *British Policy Towards the Soviet Union*, pp. 26–27
21 Gorodetsky, *Stafford Cripps' Mission to Moscow*, pp. 36–37
22 Hanak, 'Sir Stafford Cripps as British Ambassador in Moscow', p. 56
23 Gorodetsky, *Stafford Cripps' Mission to Moscow*, pp. 38–39
24 Ibid. pp. 44–47
25 Ross (ed.), *The Foreign Office and the Kremlin*, p. 7
26 Gorodetsky, *Stafford Cripps' Mission to Moscow*, p. 78
27 Carlton, *Anthony Eden*, p. 171
28 Ibid. p. 181
29 Gilbert, *Finest Hour*, pp. 1050–1055
30 Ibid. p. 1056
31 Rhodes James, *Victor Cazalet*, p. 226

32 Ibid. p. 235
33 PRO FO 371 24468 C7933/3/55 9 July 1940
34 Raczyński, W Sojuszniczym Londynie, pp. 66–67
35 Ibid. p. 71
36 Ibid. p. 43
37 Żaroń, Kierunek wschodni, p. 25
38 Pestkowska, Uchodźcze Pasje, pp. 61–63
39 Ibid. p. 62
40 Ibid. pp. 76–77
41 Ibid. p. 78
42 PRO FO 371 24482 C788/7177/55 19 June 1940
43 Ibid.
44 Preamble to the Polish–British Military Agreement 5 August 1940. *Polskie Siły Zbrojne*, Vol. II, part 1, p. 226
45 Polonsky, *The Great Powers and the Polish Question*, p. 77
46 PRO FO 371 24482 C12485/7177/55 18 November 1940
47 PRO FO 371 26419 C14/14/62 21 November 1940
48 PRO FO 371 26419 C741/14/62 Memorandum by Anthony Eden 25 January 1941
49 PRO FO 371 26419 C741/14/62 22 January 1941
50 Mitkiewicz, *Z Generałem Sikorskim na Obczyźnie*, pp. 68–69
51 Ibid. pp. 363–365
52 Ibid. p. 69
53 Pragier, *Czas Przeszły Dokonany*, p. 610
54 PISM KGA 2 July 1940
55 Ibid.
56 PRO FO 371 26722 C188/188/55 1 January 1941
57 PRO FO 371 28447 Z495/495/17 22 January 1941
58 Ibid.
59 PISM AXII 1/27 30 August 1940
60 PRO FO 371 24464 C2181/3/55 30 January 1940
61 PRO FO 371 24464 C2184/3/55 10 February 1940
62 PRO FO 371 24465 C4197/3/55 18 March 1940 and C4197/3/55 23 March 1940
63 Kacewicz, *Great Britain, the Soviet Union and the Polish Government in Exile*, pp. 64–65
64 PRO FO 371 24368 C11017/1419/62 7 October 1940
65 Gates, *The End of the Affair*, pp. 127–129
66 Butler, *Grand Strategy*, p. 252
67 Kacewicz, *Great Britain, the Soviet Union and the Polish Government in Exile*, pp. 58–59
68 Coutouvidis and Reynolds, *Poland 1939–1947*, p. 41
69 PRO FO 371 24468 C73006/3/55 19 June 1940
70 *Polskie Siły Zbrojne*, Vol. II, part 1, p. 226
71 Ibid. p. 300
72 Ibid. p. 181
73 Ibid. pp. 187–188
74 Ibid. p. 188

75 Kacewicz, *Great Britain, the Soviet Union and the Polish Government in Exile*, pp. 56–57
76 PRO AIR 2 4213 March 1940
77 PRO AIR 2 7196 4 May 1940
78 PRO AIR 2 7196 24 May 1940 Report by Wing Commander C. Perri, 'Polish Air Force Contingent in England'
79 PRO AIR 2 4184 14 July 1940
80 *Polskie Siły Zbrojne*, Vol. II, part 1, pp. 330–331
81 Kopański, *Wspomnienia Wojenne*, pp. 113–114
82 *Polskie Siły Zbrojne*, Vol. II, part 1, pp. 252–253
83 Ibid. pp. 261–263
84 Ibid. p. 264
85 Kopański, *Wspomnienia Wojenne*, p. 149
86 PRO PREM 3 357 7 January 1941 and 24 January 1941
87 Instytut Piłsudskiego, London (henceforth IP), General Sosnkowski's archives KOL 19/15 21 February 1941
88 PRO PREM 3 357/2 16 February 1941
89 PRO PREM 3 357 14 March 1941
90 PRO FO 371 26751 3977/2784/55 Sikorski to Churchill 24 March 1941 and Churchill to Sikorski 15 April 1941
91 Kopański, *Wspomnienia Wojenne*, p. 177
92 Ibid. p. 132
93 PRO FO 371 24482 C7964/7570/55 7 August 1940
94 Butler, *Grand Strategy*, p. 377
95 Ibid. p. 377
96 PRO FO 371 26751 C2784/2784/55 17 March 1941

4   Britain, Poland and the Soviet Union

1   Duraczyński (ed.), *Układ Sikorski–Majski*, pp. 173–174
2   Gorodetsky, 'The Origins of the Cold War', p. 155
3   Woodward, *History of the Second World War*, pp. 13–14
4   Kitchen, *British Policy Towards the Soviet Union*, pp. 58–59
5   Ibid. pp. 64–65
6   Ibid. p. 65
7   Ibid. pp. 65–66
8   Ibid.
9   Hanak, 'Sir Stafford Cripps as Ambassador in Moscow', p. 332
10 Duraczyński (ed.), *Układ Sikorski–Majski*, p. 82
11 Ibid. p. 9
12 Raczyński, *W Sojuszniczym Londynie*, p. 119
13 Dilks (ed.), *The Diaries of Sir Alexander Cadogan*, p. 391
14 Rhodes James, *Victor Cazalet*, p. 262
15 Mitkiewicz, *Z Generałem Sikorskim na Obczyźnie*, p. 164
16 Sokolnicki, *Dziennik Ankarski 1939–1943*, p. 292
17 Ibid. p. 299
18 Mitkiewicz, *Z Generałem Sikorskim na Obczyźnie*, p. 161

19 PRO F0 371 26755 C7590/3226/55 8 July 1941
20 *Polskie Siły Zbrojne*, Vol. II, part 2, pp. 40–42
21 Ibid. p. 42
22 PRO FO 371 26733 C8173/395/55 3 July 1941
23 Bennett, *Franklin D. Roosevelt and the Search for Victory*, p. 27
24 Lash, *Roosevelt and Churchill*, pp. 369–370
25 Bennett, *Franklin D. Roosevelt and the Search for Victory*, p. 27
26 Ibid. p. 28
27 PRO FO 371 26756 C8498/3226/55 29 July 1941
28 Ciechanowski, *Defeat in Victory*, pp. 39–41
29 Ibid. pp. 40–42
30 PRO FO 371 26756 C8567/3226/55 31 July 1941
31 Kacewicz, *Great Britain, the Soviet Union and the Polish Government in Exile*, pp. 100–101
32 PRO FO 371 26756 C8375/3226/55 26 July 1941
33 PRO FO 371 26756 C8529/3226/55 29 July 1941
34 *Documents on Polish–Soviet Relation* (henceforth DPSR) No. 107 p. 142
35 Harvey (ed.), *The War Diaries of Oliver Harvey*, p. 19
36 Ibid. p. 21
37 Ibid. p. 55
38 Dilks (ed.), *The Diaries of Sir Alexander Cadogan*, p. 394
39 Grenville, *The Major International Treaties*, pp. 198–199
40 PISM PRM 55/12 Bureau for Political, Economic and Legal Affairs, August 1941
41 PRO FO 371 26758 C9279/3226/55 18 August 1941
42 PRO FO 371 26424 C10382/14/62 25 August 1941
43 Gilbert, *Finest Hour*, pp. 1162–1163
44 Lash, *Roosevelt and Churchill*, pp. 400–401
45 Gilbert, *Finest Hour*, p. 1162
46 PISM PRM 55/12 August 1941
47 Terry, *Poland's Place in Europe*, pp. 88–92
48 PRO FO 371 26758 C9279/3226/55 18 August 1941 and C10382/14/62 25 August 1941
49 PRO FO 371 26424 C10382/14/62 25 August 1941
50 PRO FO 371 26775 C9563/5996/55 26 August 1941
51 DPSR No. 112, 14 August 1941, pp. 147–148
52 Kot, *Conversations with the Kremlin*, p. xiii
53 Ibid.
54 Raczyński, *W Sojuszniczym Londynie*, p. 141
55 DSPR No. 120, 1 September 1941, pp. 161–165
56 PISM AII/49/Sow/8 28 August 1941
57 Klimkowski, *Byłem Adiutantem Generała Andersa*, pp. 128–129
58 The Diaries of Stafford Cripps, 3 September 1941, courtesy Professor Gabriel Gorodetsky
59 Kopański, *Wspomnienia Wojenne*, p. 260
60 PISM AXII 1/4 1 September 1941
61 Ibid.

62 Ibid.
63 Ibid.
64 PRO PREM 3 351/8 11 September 1941
65 PRO FO 371 26760 C10394/3226/55 15 September 1941
66 PRO FO 954 1913 386 24 September 1941
67 Ibid.
68 Seaton, *The Russo-German War*, pp. 142–144
69 Ibid. p. 151
70 Erickson, *The Road to Stalingrad*, p. 214
71 Ibid. pp. 220–221
72 Ibid. pp. 256–257
73 Deringil, *Turkish Foreign Policy*, pp. 126–127
74 Ibid. pp. 130–131
75 PISM KGA 18a 2 October 1941
76 PRO CAB 79/13 COS (41)283 Mtg 11 August 1941
77 PRO CAB 85/20 AFO (41)10 Mtg 15 August 1941
78 Ibid.
79 PRO CAB 79/14 COS (41)327 Mtg 18 September 1941
80 PRO WO 193 661 18 September 1941
81 PRO CAB 79/14 COS (41)340 Mtg 2 October 1941
82 Ibid.
83 PRO CAB 79/14 COS (41)333 Mtg 25 September 1941
84 PISM KGA 18a 4/5 October 1941
85 Klimkowski, *Byłem Adiutantem Generała Andersa*, p. 147
86 Ibid.
87 Ibid. p. 148
88 Ibid. pp. 154–155
89 Ibid.
90 Kopański, *Wspomnienia Wojenne*, pp. 164–169
91 Ibid.
92 Langer, 'The Harriman–Beaverbrook Mission', pp. 463–465
93 Ibid. pp. 466–467
94 Taylor, *Beaverbrook*, p. 488
95 Bennett, *Franklin D. Roosevelt and the Search for Victory*, pp. 32–33
96 Ibid. p. 33
97 Gilbert, *Finest Hour*, p. 1198
98 Ross (ed.), *The Foreign Office and the Kremlin*, p. 14
99 Lord Beaverbrook Papers, House of Lords Records Office BBK D/94–96 8
   October 1941
100 Taylor, *Beaverbrook*, p. 560
101 Ross (ed.), *The Foreign Office and the Kremlin*, p. 15
102 Gilbert, *Finest Hour*, pp. 1172–1173
103 Gorodetsky, *Stafford Cripps' Mission to Moscow*, pp. 209–215
104 Gilbert, *Finest Hour*, p. 1196
105 Gwyer, *Grand Strategy*, p. 207
106 Ibid. p. 208
107 Ibid. p. 210

108 Gwyer, *Grand Strategy*, p. 214; Gilbert, *Finest Hour*, p. 1217
109 DPSR No. 132, pp. 182–184, 24 October 1941
110 Ibid.
111 Ibid.
112 Day, *The Great Betrayal*, pp. 172–173
113 Gilbert, *Finest Hour*, pp. 1190–1192
114 PISM AII/49/Sow/5 25 October 1941
115 PISM AII/49/Sow/5 undated
116 Ibid.
117 PRO FO 371 26761 C12286/3226/55 6 November 1941. The content of the letter was communicated to Churchill by Roosevelt prior to its despatch, but according to Ciechanowski, the Polish Ambassador in Washington, he did not see it but was merely told of its content by Harriman on 14 November. See Ciechanowski, *Defeat in Victory*, p. 72
118 Kot, *Conversations with the Kremlin*, pp. 109–110
119 PRO CAB 79/15 COS (41)381 Mtg 10 November 1941
120 PRO WO 193/1 19 November 1941
121 PRO WO 32/10114 5 December 1941
122 Pestkowska, *Uchodźcze Pasje*, pp. 123–126
123 Kot, *Conversations with the Kremlin*, p. 148
124 Ibid. pp. 151–153
125 Ibid. p. 150
126 PISM PRM 44/1/20 7 December 1941
127 Sokolnicki, *Dziennik Ankarski 1939–1943*, pp. 300–301
128 Victor Cazalet's diary, 29 October 1941
129 Anders, *Bez Ostatniego Rozdziału*, p. 104
130 Klimkowski, *Byłem Adiutantem Generała Andersa*, p. 181
131 Kopański, *Wspomnienia Wojenne*, p. 179
132 Sokolnicki, *Dziennik Ankarski 1939–1943*, p. 299
133 Ibid.
134 PRO FO 371 26761 C3728/3226/55 December 1941
135 Ibid. 10 December 1941

5 1942, year of disappointments

1 Woodward, *History of the Second World War*, pp. 244–251
2 Kitchen, *British Policy Towards the Soviet Union*, p. 106
3 Woodward, *History of the Second World War*, p. 220
4 Ibid. p. 221
5 Beaumont, *Comrades in Arms*, pp. 80–85
6 Woodward, *History of the Second World War*, p. 232
7 Ibid. p. 234
8 Ibid. pp. 117–118
9 PRO FO 371 32875 WP(42)48 28 January 1942
10 Ibid.
11 Ibid. Annex
12 Ibid.

13 Ross (ed.), *The Foreign Office and the Kremlin*, p. 20
14 Ibid. p. 21
15 Carlton, *Anthony Eden*, p. 194
16 Bell, *John Bull and the Bear*, p. 77
17 Ibid. pp. 78–79
18 Gilbert, *Road to Victory*, pp. 72–73
19 Woodward, *History of the Second World War*, pp. 244–245
20 Ibid. p. 274
21 Carlton, *Anthony Eden*, pp. 198–199
22 Bennett, *Franklin D. Roosevelt and the Search for Victory*, pp. 39–41
23 Ibid. p. 45
24 Ibid. p. 46
25 Ibid. p. 47
26 Ibid. p. 49
27 King, *The New Internationalism*, p. 31
28 Kitchen, *British Policy Towards the Soviet Union*, pp. 117–118
29 Ibid. p. 118
30 Rhodes James, *Anthony Eden*, p. 264
31 Gilbert, *Road to Victory*, p. 75
32 Ibid. p. 76
33 Liddell Hart Centre for Military Archives, King's College, London, Alanbrooke Papers 5/5 Diary entry 3 December 1941
34 Gwyer, *Grand Strategy*, pp. 214–216
35 PRO FO 371 31077 C495/19/55 20 January 1942
36 PRO FO 371 31077 C794/19/55 19 January 1942
37 Ibid.
38 Ibid.
39 Ibid.
40 Raczyński, *W Sojuszniczym Londynie*, p. 129
41 Ibid. p. 134
42 Pastusiak, *Roosevelt a sprawa polska*, pp. 55–57
43 Ibid. p. 57
44 Ibid. p. 60
45 Ibid. pp. 57–60
46 Ciechanowski, *Defeat in Victory*, pp. 110–114
47 Mitkiewicz, *Z Generałem Sikorskim na Obczyźnie*, pp. 240–241
48 PRO FO 31077 C347/19/55 9 January 1942
49 PRO FO 31077 C1071/19/55 26 January 1942
50 PRO FO 371 31091 C2188/464/55 6 February 1942
51 PRO FO 371 31079 C2982/19/55 Eden to Dormer 27 March 1942
52 PRO FO 371 31081 C3438/19/55 27 March 1942
53 PRO FO 371 33018 N3220/3059/38 16 April 1942
54 Ciechanowski, 'Armia polska w Rosji', pp. 93–96
55 Ibid. p. 96
56 Ibid. p. 96
57 PISM KGA 9a 7 February 1942
58 Anders, *Bez Ostatniego Rozdziału*, p. 132

59 PISM PRM 73/1/9 10 February 1942
60 PISM KGA 7e 22 February 1942 and KOL 138/156 Dtwo PSZ w ZSRR 23 February 1942
61 PISM KGA 76 9 March 1942
62 Anders, *Bez Ostatniego Rozdziału*, pp. 134–145
63 Ibid. p. 137
64 Ibid. p. 142
65 Kot, *Conversations with the Kremlin*, p. 222
66 Garlicki (ed.), 'Wspomnienia: Zygmunt Berling'
67 'Wspomnienia Wandy Wasilewskiej', p. 378
68 Ibid. p. 386
69 Rutkiewicz, *Granica Istnienia*, pp. 34–41
70 PISM AXII 22/31–E 19 March 1942
71 PRO FO 371 31081 C3437/19/55 22 March 1942
72 PISM AXII 30/19 29 March 1942, also PRO FO 371 31082 C3643/19/55 29 March 1942
73 PISM AXII 1 April 1942, also PRO FO 371 31082 C3643/19/55 1 April 1942
74 Ibid.
75 PRO FO 371 31082 C3643/19/55 1 April 1942
76 Harvey (ed.), *The War Diaries of Oliver Harvey*, p. 116
77 PISM AXII 22/31–H 27 March 1942
78 PISM KGA 9a 27 March 1942
79 Kot, *Conversations with the Kremlin*, p. 226
80 Ibid. pp. 229–230
81 Klimkowski, *Byłem Adiutantem Generała Andersa*, pp. 218–219
82 Kopański, *Wspomnienia Wojenne*, pp. 245–247
83 Klimkowski, *Byłem Adiutantem Generała Andersa*, pp. 239–241
84 Ibid. p. 239
85 PRO WO 32 10675 8 April 1942
86 PRO WO 32 10117 22 April 1942
87 PRO CAB 79/20 COS (42)128 Mtg 23 April 1942
88 Ibid.
89 PRO CAB 79/20 COS (42)134 Mtg 29 April 1942
90 Klimkowski, *Byłem Adiutantem Generała Andersa*, p. 244
91 Mitkiewicz, *Z Generałem Sikorskim na Obczyźnie*, p. 269
92 PISM KGA 7i 23 April 1942
93 Mitkiewicz, *Z Generałem Sikorskim na Obczyźnie*, pp. 278–279
94 PISM KGA 7i 23 April 1942
95 PISM KGA 7e 24 April 1942
96 Ibid.
97 PISM AXII 24 April 1942
98 Anders, *Bez Ostatniego Rozdziału*, p. 131
99 Klimkowski, *Byłem Adiutantem Generała Andersa*, p. 244
100 PRO CAB 79/20 COS (42)134 Mtg 29 April 1942
101 Gilbert, *Road to Victory*, pp. 93–94
102 Ibid. p. 114
103 Ibid. p. 115

104 Pestkowska, *Uchodźcze Pasje*, p. 133
105 Pragier, *Czas Przeszły Dokonany*, p. 629
106 Pestkowska, *Uchodźcze Pasje*, pp. 163–164
107 Mackiewicz (Cat), *Cała Prawda*
108 PISM PRM 90 April 1942
109 Klimkowski, *Katastrofa w Gibraltarze*, p. 19
110 Mackiewicz (Cat), *Cała Prawda*, p. 13
111 Mackiewicz, *Cel Najdalszy*, pp. 6–7

6 **The illusion of an alliance ends**

1 Erickson, *The Road to Stalingrad*, pp. 360–361
2 Ibid. p. 363
3 Ibid. p. 376
4 Ibid. p. 380
5 Gilbert, *Road to Victory*, pp. 142–143
6 Ibid. p. 143
7 Ibid. pp. 150–151
8 Bennett, *Franklin D. Roosevelt and the Search for Victory*, p. 57
9 PRO FO 371 33133 R584/43/67 22 January 1942
10 Ibid.
11 PRO FO 371 32087 13 May 1942
12 PRO FO 371 31108 C11885/6436/55 29 November 1942
13 PRO FO 371 31108 C1223/6436/55 4 December 1942
14 Kolenda, 'Działalność Mieszanego Komitetu', pp. 207–208
15 Wandycz, *Czechoslovak–Polish Confederation and the Great Powers*, pp. 36–37
16 Ibid. pp. 61–63
17 Kolenda, 'Działalność Mieszanego Komitetu', p. 211
18 PISM PRM 86/7 1942
19 PRO FO 371 30871 C1544/1443/62 9 February 1942
20 Wandycz, *Czechoslovak–Polish Confederation and the Great Powers*, p. 60
21 PRO FO 371 32918 N727/50/38 7 February 1942
22 Raczyński, *W Sojuszniczym Londynie*, p. 154
23 PRO FO 371 30871 C10396/1543/62 27 October 1942 and Raczyński, *W Sojuszniczym Londynie*, p. 154
24 PRO FO 371 31535 U1742/1742/70 23 October 1942
25 PRO FO 371 30871 C1544/1543/62 9 February 1942
26 PRO FO 371 30871 C2230/1543/62 23 March 1942
27 PRO FO 371 31535 U1742/1742/70 23 October 1942
28 PRO FO 371 31535 U1742/1742/70 23 October 1942
29 Ibid.
30 PISM PRM 79/1/21 1 May 1942
31 Ibid.
32 Ibid.
33 PISM KGA 76 4 May 1942
34 Klimkowski, *Katastrofa w Gibraltarze*, p. 37 and *Byłem Adiutantem Generała Andersa*, p. 244

35 PISM AXII 22/31–G 26 May 1942
36 PISM AXII 30/19–E 22 June 1942
37 PISM AXII June 1942
38 Ibid.
39 PISM PRM 73/1/30 7 June 1942
40 Ibid.
41 PISM PRM 73/1/30 11 June 1942
42 PRO WO 193 41 30 June 1942
43 PRO WO 193 41 30 June 1942 and, *Polskie Siły Zbrojne*, Vol. II, part 2, p. 67
44 Ciechanowski, 'Armia polska w Rosji', pp. 106–107
45 Ibid. p. 105
46 PRO FO 371 31084 C6746/19/55 4 July 1942
47 Ibid.
48 PRO FO 371 31084 C6912/19/55 10 July 1942
49 PRO FO 371 31085 C7213/19/55 15 July 1942
50 *Polskie Siły Zbrojne*, Vol. II, part 2, pp. 69–70
51 *Polskie Siły Zbrojne*, Vol. II, part 2, p. 295
52 Anders, *Bez Ostatniego Rozdziału*, p. 181
53 Ibid. p. 182: Anders dates his communication to Sikorski as 18 December
    1942. In, *Polskie Siły Zbrojne*, Vol. II, part 2, this letter is referred to as being
    of 18 February 1943
54 Anders, *Bez Ostatniego Rozdziału*, pp. 183–184
55 Klimkowski, *Byłem Adiutantem Generała Andersa*, p. 300. This view is
    further elaborated upon in his book *Katastrofa w Gibraltarze*, pp. 38–41
56 *Polskie Siły Zbrojne*, Vol. II, part 2, pp. 75–78
57 Pestkowska, *Uchodźcze Pasje*, pp. 146–147
58 Ibid. p. 160
59 Ibid. p. 161
60 Ross, 'Operation Bracelet', pp. 105–106
61 Gilbert, *Road to Victory*, pp. 164–165
62 Ibid. pp. 205–206
63 Ibid. pp. 173–208; Kitchen, *British Policy Towards the Soviet Union*, pp. 124–140
64 Ross, 'Operation Bracelet', p. 117
65 PRO FO 800 42/29
66 PISM PRM 73/4/148 17 August 1942
67 Ibid.
68 Ibid.
69 Ibid.
70 Ibid.
71 PISM KOL 1/37 17 August 1942
72 Pestkowska, *Uchodźcze Pasje*, pp. 164–165
73 PISM PRM 73/2/15 21 August 1942
74 Ibid.
75 PISM PRM 73/1/37 22 August 1942
76 PISM KGA 7e 22 August 1942
77 Ibid.

78 Ibid.
79 PISM KOL 1/37 30 August 1942
80 Ibid.
81 Ibid. p. 137
82 Ciechanowski, *The Warsaw Rising of 1944*, p. 133
83 Stafford, *Britain and the European Resistance*, pp. 80–81
84 Ibid. p. 83
85 Ibid. pp. 82–83
86 Ibid. p. 85
87 Ibid. p. 85
88 Ibid. pp. 87–90
89 PISM AXII 42/33 26 August 1942
90 Ibid.
91 PRO CAB 84/4 JP (42)137 Mtg 31 July 1942
92 PRO CAB 79/66 COS (43)255 Mtg(O) 20 October 1943
93 *Polskie Siły Zbrojne*, Vol. II, part 2, pp. 307–308
94 PISM KOL 1/37 Sikorski to Klimecki 20 August 1942
95 *Polskie Siły Zbrojne*, Vol. II, part 2, p. 309
96 Ibid. p. 310
97 Kopański, *Wspomnienia Wojenne*, p. 212
98 See below, pp. 160–163
99 PISM KOL 1/37 Report by Klimecki 20 August–30 September 1942
100 Ibid.
101 Ibid.
102 Ibid.
103 *Polskie Siły Zbrojne*, Vol. II, part 2, pp. 312–313
104 PISM PRM 73/1/37 22 August 1942
105 Ibid.
106 PISM PRM 73/1/38 24 August 1942
107 Silverfarb, *Twilight of British Ascendancy in the Middle East*, p. 12
108 Ibid. p. 15
109 Ibid. p. 12
110 Deringil, *Turkish Foreign Policy*, p. 136
111 Ibid. p. 139
112 Erickson, *The Road to Stalingrad*, pp. 452–453
113 Gilbert, *Road to Victory*, p. 239
114 Ibid. pp. 140–141
115 Ibid. pp. 249–251
116 Ibid. p. 259
117 PISM AXII 3/80 11 December 1942
118 PRO PREM 3 351/11 17 November 1942
119 Alanbrooke papers 14/57 004/65A 18 November 1942
120 The memorandum, in addition to being attached to the letters sent to Alan
     Brooke and Churchill, is available in the Sikorski archives at PISM AXII
     4/80 17 November 1942
121 Ibid.

122 Ibid.
123 PRO PREM 3 35/11 17 November 1942
124 Ibid.
125 PRO PREM 3 351/11 17 November 1942
126 Ibid.
127 PRO PREM 3 351/11 8 December 1942
128 PRO WO 32 10139 15 December 1942
129 Mitkiewicz, *Z Generałem Sikorskim na Obczyźnie*, pp. 302–303 and Ciechanowski, *Defeat in Victory*, pp. 136–138
130 Pestkowska, *Uchodźcze Pasje*, p. 165
131 Ciechanowski, *Defeat in Victory*, pp. 135–136
132 Ibid. p. 138
133 Ibid. p. 144
134 Ibid. p. 147
135 Pestkowska, *Uchodźcze Pasje*, pp. 168–172
136 Mitkiewicz, *Z Generałem Sikorskim na Obczyźnie*, p. 307
137 Ibid. pp. 176–177

7 1943, the end of Polish–Soviet co-operation

1 'Wspomnienia Wandy Wasilewskiej' pp. 381–382
2 PISM PRM 102/1/7 2 March 1943
3 PISM PRM 105/21 24 March 1943
4 Kitchen, *British Policy Towards the Soviet Union*, pp. 152–153
5 Gilbert, *Road to Victory*, pp. 410–414
6 Ibid. p. 410
7 Erickson, *The Road to Berlin*, pp. 89–90
8 Maisky, *Memoirs of a Soviet Ambassador*, pp. 364–365
9 Kitchen, *British Policy Towards the Soviet Union*, pp. 160–161.
10 Mastny, *Russia's Road to the Cold War*, pp. 76–77
11 Ibid. pp. 80–83
12 Ibid. p. 83
13 Erickson, *The Road to Berlin*, p. 92
14 Ibid. p. 132
15 Beaumont, *Comrades in Arms*, p. 137
16 Ibid. p. 137
17 Ibid. pp. 149–154
18 Ibid. pp. 164–165
19 Rothwell, *Britain and the Cold War*, p. 160
20 Pestkowska, *Uchodźcze Pasje*, pp. 180–183
21 Ibid. p. 182
22 Ibid. p. 184
23 PRO FO 921 53 1 February 1943
24 PRO FO 371 34591 C1424/259/G55 6 February 1943
25 PRO FO 371 34593 C3623/335/G55 2 April 1943
26 PRO CAB 65/34 WM 52(53)
27 PRO FO 371 34593 C3742/335/G55 3 April 1943

28 Ibid.
29 PRO FO 371 34570 C4743/258/55 29 April 1943
30 PRO FO 624/234 810 6 May 1943
31 PRO FO 371 34600 C5972/598/G55 24 May 1943
32 Mitkiewicz, *Z Generałem Sikorskim na Obczyźnie*, pp. 347–348
33 PRO FO 371 34600 C5972/598/G55 24 May 1943
34 PRO FO 371 34577 C611/258/G55 28 May 1943
35 Sokolnicki, *Dziennik Ankarski 1939–1943*, p. 534
36 Ibid. p. 540
37 PRO FO 371 34614A C5992/5889/G55 28 May 1943
38 PRO FO 624/34 810 29 May 1943
39 Sokolnicki, *Dziennik Ankarski 1939–1943*, pp. 537–538
40 Ibid. p. 538
41 Ibid. pp. 529–530
42 Ibid. p. 543
43 Ibid. p. 534
44 PRO FO 371 34565 C2482/258/55 25 February 1943
45 PRO FO 371 34568 C4130/258/55 13 March 1943
46 PRO FO 371 3465 C2463/258/G55 3 March 1943
47 Ibid. 19 March 1943
48 PRO FO 371 34566 C2836/258/G55 13 March 1943
49 PRO FO 371 36991 N1605/499/G39 10 March 1943
50 PRO FO 371 34567 C3386/258/G55 29 March 1943
51 Ibid.
52 PRO FO 371 34589 C4133/258/G55 15 April 1943
53 Ibid.
54 PRO CAB 65/34 WM 59(43) 27 April 1943
55 Raczyński, *W Sojuszniczym Londynie*, pp. 173–174
56 Gilbert, *Road to Victory*, pp. 389–392
57 PRO PREM 3 354/9 10 May 1943
58 PRO FO 371 34574 C5138/258/G55 6 May 1943
59 PRO PREM 3 354/9 12 May 1943
60 PRO FO 371 34576 C5652/258/G55 19 May 1943
61 Ibid.
62 Mitkiewicz, *Z Generałem Sikorskim na Obczyźnie*, pp. 313–314
63 Ibid. pp. 326–327
64 Ibid. p. 330
65 Ibid. p. 331
66 Ibid. p. 348
67 Ibid. pp. 348–349
68 Ibid. pp. 353–354
69 Ciechanowski, *The Warsaw Rising of 1944*, p. 139
70 Ibid. p. 139
71 Mitkiewicz, *Z Generałem Sikorskim na Obczyźnie*, pp. 330–334
72 Mitkiewicz, *W Najwyższym Sztabie Zachodnich Aliantòw*, pp. 28–31
73 Ibid. p. 76
74 Ibid. p. 77

75 Sokolnicki, *Dziennik Ankarski 1939–1943*, p. 537
76 Ibid. pp. 537–538
77 Ibid. p. 538
78 Mitkiewicz, *Z Generałem Sikorskim na Obczyźnie*, p. 330
79 Deringil, *Turkish Foreign Policy*, p. 146
80 Ibid. pp. 150–151
81 PISM AXII 3/82 5 July 1943
82 General Sosnkowski papers. KOL 19/13 7 July 1943
83 Kopański, *Wspomnienia Wojenne*, pp. 240–241
84 Ibid. pp. 241–243
85 PRO FO 371 34594 C14145/335/G55 19 November 1939
86 PRO FO 371 39460 28 December 1943
87 PISM C.24/VI–A 12 November 1943
88 PISM C.24/VI–A 6 November 1943
89 Kopański, *Wspomnienia Wojenne*, p. 245
90 Ibid. p. 301
91 PRO FO 371 34561 C10483/23/G55 9 September 1943 and PISM T. Romer collection (henceforth TR), KOL 5, Film 5, 1 October 1943
92 PRO FO 371 34561 C10409/23/G55 9 September 1943
93 Sharp, 'The Origins of the "Teheran Formula" on Polish Frontiers', p. 390
94 PRO FO 371 34587 C11782/258/G55 6 October 1943
95 PRO FO 371 34562 C11657/1265/G 7 October 1943 and PISM A12 52/8 5 October 1943
96 Ibid.
97 Ibid.
98 PRO FO 371 34562 C11657/23/G55 October 1943
99 PISM TR KOL 5, Film 5, File General No. 3, 25 October 1943
100 PRO FO 371 34562 C13543/23/G55 12 November 1943
101 PRO FO 371 34588 C13335/258/G55 November 1943
102 Erickson, *The Road to Berlin*, p. 148
103 Ibid. pp. 148–149
104 Quoted in Gilbert, *Road to Victory*, p. 442

Conclusion

1 PRO PREM 3 136/8 28 November 1943
2 Ibid.
3 PRO PREM 3 136/8 1 December 1943
4 *Polskie Siły Zbrojne*, Vol. II, part 2, p. 331
5 Ibid.
6 Ibid. p. 337
7 Ibid. pp. 132–133
8 PISM AXII 2/82 27 December 1943
9 Ibid.

Bibliography

Unpublished documents

Public Records Office, London

FO 181 Embassy and Consular Archives, Russia
FO 371 Foreign Office Correspondence
FO 624 Minister of State Baghdad
FO 921 Minister of State Cairo
FO 954 Eden papers
PREM 3 Prime Minister's Office
CAB 65 War Cabinet minutes
CAB 66 War Cabinet memoranda
CAB 67 War Cabinet memoranda
CAB 68 War Cabinet memoranda
CAB 69 Defence Committee (Operations)
CAB 70 Defence Committee (Supply)
CAB 79 Chiefs of Staff minutes
CAB 80 Chiefs of Staff memoranda
CAB 82 Deputy Chiefs of Staff Sub Committee
CAB 83 Military Co-ordination Committee
CAB 84 Joint Policy Committee
CAB 85 Allied Forces (Official) Committee
CAB 92 Polish Forces (Official) Committee
CAB 99 Supreme War Council
CAB 122 British Joint Staff Mission, Washington
ADM 1 Admiralty and Secretariat papers
AIR 2 Air Ministry Correspondence
AIR 8 Air Ministry, Chief of Air Staff
AIR 14 Air Ministry, Bomber Command
WO 32 War Office, registered papers
WO 104 War Office, registered file
WO 106 War Office, Directorate of Military Operations and Intelligence
WO 193 War Office, Directorate of Military Operations

Private papers

Alanbrooke papers – Liddell Hart Centre for Military Archives, King's College London
Neville Chamberlain – University of Birmingham
Lord Beaverbrook – House of Lords Record Office
Victor Cazalet – courtesy Sir Edward Cazalet

Polish Institute and Sikorski Museum, London (PISM)

The Prime Minister's Office
The Polish High Command, General Staff, Ministry of National Defence, military attachés with Yugoslav government, the Free French and in the Middle East
The Ministry for Foreign Affairs
General Anders collection
General Sosnkowski collection
Stanisław Kot collection
Tadeusz Romer collection, microfilm Polish Embassy in London
Polish Embassy in Kuibyshev

Archiwum Akt Nowych, Warsaw

Polish Embassy in Ankara
Polish Consulate in Berne
Polish Consulate in Tehran
Polish Consulate in Athens
Paderewski collection

Archiwum Ruchu Ludowego, Warsaw

Stanisław Kot collection
Correspondence from the country to Stanisław Kot and Alexander Ładoś

Instytut im. Ossolińskich, Wrocław

General Sosnkowski collection

Published sources

Alexander, Martin S., *The Republic in Danger. General Maurice Gamelin and the Politics of French Defence, 1933–1940* (Cambridge: Cambridge University Press, 1992)
Anders, Władysław, *Bez Ostatniego Rozdziału. Wspomnienia z Lat 1939–1946* (Newtown: Montgomeryshire Printing Co. Ltd, 1949)
Barker, Elizabeth, *British Policy in South-East Europe in the Second World War* (London: Macmillan, 1976)

Beaumont, Joan, *Comrades in Arms, British Aid to Russia 1941–1945* (London: Davis-Poynter, 1980)

Beauvois, Yves, *Stosunki polsko-francuskie w czasie dziwnej wojny* (Cracow: Oficyna Literacka, 1991)

Bell, P. M. H., *John Bull and the Bear. British Public Opinion, Foreign Policy and the Soviet Union 1941–1945* (London: Edward Arnold, 1990)

Bennet, Edward M., *Franklin D. Roosevelt and the Search for Victory. American–Soviet Relations 1939–1945* (Wilmington, Delaware: A Scholarly Resources Inc. Imprint, 1990)

Berling, Zygmunt, *Wspomnienia. Z łagrów do Andersa* (Warsaw: Polski Dom Wydawniczy Sp.z o.o., 1900)

Wspomnienia. Przeciw 17 Republice (Warsaw: Polski Dom Wydawniczy Sp. z o.o., 1991)

Berthaud, Sir Eric, *An Unexpected Life* (London: Anchor Press Ltd, 1980)

Biegański, Stanisław, 'Plany wojenne związane z polskim wysiłkiem zbrojnym w basenie Morza Śródziemnego', *Niepodległość*, Vol. 1, 1948

Biegański, Witold, *Wojsko Polskie we Francji 1939–1940* (Warsaw: Wydawnictwo Ministerstwa Obrony Narodowej, 1967)

Butler, J. R. M., *Grand Strategy, Vol. II, September 1939–June 1941* (London: Her Majesty's Stationery Office, 1957)

Carlton, David, *Anthony Eden. A Biography* (London: Allen Lane, 1981)

Ciechanowski, Jan, *Defeat in Victory* (London: Victor Gollancz Ltd, 1948)

Ciechanowski, Jan, 'Armia polska w Rosji w swietle dziennika szefa sztabu z 1942 roku', *Zeszyty Historyczne*, 1981

The Warsaw Rising of 1944 (Cambridge: Cambridge University Press, 1974)

Coutouvidis, J. and Reynolds, Jaime, *Poland 1939–1947* (Leicester: Leicester University Press, 1986)

Day, David, *The Great Betrayal: Britain, Australia and the Onset of the Pacific War 1939–1942* (London: Angus & Robertson Publishers, 1988)

Deringil, Selim, *Turkish Foreign Policy During the Second World War* (Cambridge: Cambridge University Press, 1989)

Dilks, David, *The Diaries of Sir Alexander Cadogan 1938–1945* (London: Cassell, 1971)

Documents on Polish–Soviet Relations 1939–1945, Vol. 1, General Sikorski Instytut (London: Heinemann, 1961)

Douglas, Roy, *The Advent of War 1939–1940* (London: Macmillan, 1978)

Duraczyński, Eugeniusz, *Rząd polski na uchodźstwie 1939–1945* (Warsaw: Książka i Wiedza, 1993)

Duraczyński, Eugeniusz (ed.), *Układ Sikorski–Majski. Wybór dokumentów* (Warsaw: Państwowy Instytut Wydawniczy, 1990)

Erickson, John, *The Road to Stalingrad. Stalin's War with Germany* Vol. 1 (London: Weidenfeld & Nicolson, 1983)

The Road to Berlin. Stalin's War with Germany Vol. 2 (London: Weidenfeld & Nicolson, 1983)

Feis, Herbert, *Churchill, Roosevelt, Stalin. The War they Waged and the Peace they Sought* (Princeton: Princeton University Press, 1957)

Garlicki, Andrzej, 'Wspomnienia: Zygmunt Berling', *Kultura*, No. 16, 16 April 1967 and *Kultura*, No. 18, 30 April 1967

Gates, Eleanor M., *The End of the Affair, the Collapse of the Anglo-French Alliance, 1939–1940* (London: George Allen & Unwin, 1981)

Gilbert, Martin, *Finest Hour. Winston S. Churchill 1939–1941* (London: Heinemann, 1983)

Road to Victory. Winston S. Churchill 1941–1945 (London: Heinemann, 1986)

Gorodetsky, Gabriel, 'The *Hess* affair and Anglo-Soviet Relations on the Eve of "Barbarossa"', *English Historical Review*, Vol. 101, 1986

'The Origins of the Cold War: Stalin, Churchill and the Formation of the Grand Alliance', *The Russian Review*, Vol. 47, 1988

Stafford Cripps' Mission to Moscow 1940–1942 (Cambridge: Cambridge University Press, 1984)

Grenville, J. A. S., *The Major International Treaties 1914–1973. A History and Guide with Texts* (London: Methuen & Co., 1974)

Gwyer, J. M. A., *Grand Strategy, Vol. III, June 1941–August 1942* (London: Her Majesty's Stationery Office, 1964)

Hanak, Henry, 'Sir Stafford Cripps as Ambassador in Moscow, June 1941–January 1942', *English Historical Review*, Vol. 97, 1982

'Sir Stafford Cripps as British Ambassador in Moscow, May 1940 to June 1941', *English Historical Review*, Vol. 94, 1979

Harriman, W. Averell and Abel, Elie, *Special Envoy to Churchill and Stalin 1941–1946* (London: Hutchinson, 1976)

Harvey, John (ed.), *The War Diaries of Oliver Harvey* (London: William Collins, Sons and Co. Ltd, 1978)

Howard, Michael, *The Continental Commitment. The Dilemma of British Defence Policy in the Era of Two World Wars* (London: Penguin Books Ltd, 1974)

The Mediterranean Strategy in the Second World War (London: Greenhill Books, 1993)

Jędrzejewicz, Wacław (ed.), *Diplomat in Paris 1936–1939. Memoirs of Juliusz Łukasiewicz Ambassador of Poland* (New York: Columbia University Press, 1970)

Kacewicz, George, *Great Britain, the Soviet Union and the Polish government in Exile (1939–1945)* (The Hague: Martinus Nijhoff, 1979)

Kettenacker, Lothar, 'The Anglo-Soviet Alliance and the Problem of Germany, 1941–1945', *Journal of Contemporary History*, Vol. 17, 1982

King, F. P., *The New Internationalism. Allied Policy and the European Peace, 1939–1945* (London: David & Charles Archon Books, 1973)

Kitchen, Martin, *British Policy Towards the Soviet Union During the Second World War* (London: Macmillan, 1986)

Klimkowski, Jerzy, *Byłem Adiutantem Generała Andersa* (Warsaw: Wydawnictwo Ministerstwa Obrony Narodowej, 1959)

Katastrofa w Gibraltarze (Bielsko Biała: Wydawnictwo 'Śląsk', 1965)

Kolenda, Ireneusz, 'Działalność Mieszanego Komitetu Koordynacyjnego Polsko-Czechosłowackiego w Londynie (1941–1943)', *Dzieje Najnowsze*, Vol. 14, No. 1–2, 1983

Kopański, Stanisław, *Wspomnienia Wojenne 1939–1946* (London: Veritas, 1961)

Kot, Stanisław, *Conversations with the Kremlin and Dispatches from Russia* (London: Oxford University Press, 1963)

Kuropieska, Józef, *Misja w Londynie* (Warsaw: Czytelnik, 1981)
Kwapiński, Jan, *1939–1945, Kartki a pamiętnika* (London: Wydawnictwo Światowego Zwiąku Polakow z zagranicy, 1947)
Langer, J. D., 'The Harriman-Beaverbrook Mission and the Debate over Unconditional Aid for the Soviet Union, 1941', *Journal of Contemporary History*, Vol. 14, 1979
Lash, Joseph P., *Roosevelt and Churchill 1939–1941* (Durham: Duke University Press, 1989)
Lungu, Dov, *Romania and the Great Powers 1933–1940* (Durham: Duke University Press, 1989)
Mackiewicz, Stanisław, (Cat), *Cała Prawda* (London: M. I. Kolin (Publishers) Ltd, 1942)
Cel Najdalszy (London: published by author, 1942)
Macleod, Col. R. and Kelly, Denis (eds.), *The Ironside Diaries 1937–1940* (London: Constable and Co. Ltd, 1962)
Maisky, Ivan, *Memoirs of a Soviet Ambassador. The War 1939–1943* (London: Hutchinson, 1967)
Mastny, Vojtech, *Russia's Road to the Cold War* (New York: Columbia University Press, 1979)
Miller, Marshall Lee, *Bulgaria During the Second World War* (Stanford: Stanford University Press, 1975)
Miner, Steven Merritt, *Between Churchill and Stalin. The Soviet Union, Great Britain and the Origins of the Grand Alliance* (North Carolina: The North Carolina Press, 1988)
Mitkiewicz, Leon, *Z Generałem Sikorskim na Obczyźnie (Fragmenty Wspomnień)* (Paris: Instytut Literacki, 1968)
W Najwyższym Sztabie Zachodnich Aliantòw 1943–1945 (London: Veritas, 1971)
Munch-Petersen, Thomas, *The Strategy of Phoney War. Britain, Sweden and the Iron Ore Question, 1939–1940* (Stockholm: Militarhistoriska Forlager, 1981)
Nevakivi, Jukka, *The Appeal that was Never Made. The Allies, Scandinavia and the Finnish Winter War 1939–1940* (London: C. Hurst and Co., 1976)
'Sprawa udziału polskich Sił Zbrojnych w wojnie fińskiej (1939–1940)', *Studia Historyczne* RXXXI 1988, No. 4
Newman, Simon, *March 1939: the British Guarantee to Poland* (Oxford: Oxford University Press, 1976)
Nisbet, Robert, *Roosevelt and Stalin. The Failed Courtship* (London: Simon & Schuster, 1988)
Pastusiak, Longin, *Roosevelt a sprawa polska, 1939–1945* (Warsaw: Książka i Wiedza, 1981)
Peden, George C., *British Rearmament and the Treasury 1932–1939* (Edinburgh: Scottish Academic Press, 1979)
Pestkowska, Maria, *Uchodźcze Pasje* (Paris: Editions Dembinski, 1991)
Polonsky, Anthony, *The Great Powers and the Polish Question, 1941–1945. A Documentary Study in Cold War Origins* (London: London School of Economics, 1976)
'Stalin and the Poles 1941–7', *European History Quarterly*, Vol. 17, 1987

Polskie Siły Zbrojne w Drugiej Wojnie Światowej, Komisja Historyczna Polskiego Sztabu Głównego w Londynie (London: Instytut Historyczny im. Gen. Sikorskiego, 1959)

Pomian, John (ed.), *Joseph Retinger, Memoirs of an Eminence Grise* (Sussex: Sussex University Press, 1972)

Pragier, Adam, *Czas Przeszły Dokonany* (London: B. Świderski, 1966)

Prażmowska, Anita J., *Britain, Poland and the Eastern Front, 1939* (Cambridge: Cambridge University Press, 1987)

'The Eastern Front and the British Guarantee to Poland, March 1939', *European History Quarterly*, Vol. 14, 1984

'Polish Foreign Policy, September 1938–September 1939', *The Historical Journal*, Vol. 29, No. 4, 1986

Przygoński, Antoni, *Alfred Lampe* (Warsaw: Iskry, 1969)

Putrament, Jerzy, *Pòł wieku. Wojna* (Warsaw: Czytelnik, 1969)

Raczyński, Edward, *W Sojuszniczym Londynie. Dziennik ambasadora Edwards Raczyńskiego 1939–1945* (London: Orbis, 1960)

Rhodes James, Robert, *Anthony Eden* (London: Weidenfeld & Nicolson, 1986)

Victor Cazalet: a Portrait (London: Hamish Hamilton, 1976)

Ross, Graham, 'Operation Bracelet: Churchill in Moscow 1942', in David Dilks (ed.), *Retreat from Power. Studies in British Foreign Policy in the Twentieth Century*, Vol. I (London: Macmillan, 1981)

Ross, Graham (ed.), *The Foreign Office and the Kremlin. British Documents on Anglo-Soviet Relations, 1941–1945* (Cambridge: Cambridge University Press, 1984)

Rothwell, Victor, *Britain and the Cold War 1941–1947* (London: Jonathan Cape, 1982)

Rutkiewicz, Maria, *Granica Istnienia* (Warsaw: Czytelnik, 1980)

Salmon, Patrick, 'Great Britain, the Soviet Union and Finland', in John Hiden and Thomas Lane (eds.), *The Baltic and the Outbreak of the Second World War* (Cambridge: Cambridge University Press, 1992)

Seaton, Albert, *The Russo-German War 1941–1945* (London: Arthur Barker Ltd, 1971)

Sharp, Tony, 'The Origins of the "Tehran Formula" on Polish Frontiers', *Journal of Contemporary History*, Vol. 12, 1977

Silverfarb, Daniel, *The Twilight of British Ascendancy in the Middle East. A Case Study of Iraq 1941–1950* (New York: St Martin's Press, 1994)

Skrzypek, Andrzej (ed.), *Wrzesień 1939 w relacjach dyplomatów* (Warsaw: Państwowe Wydawnictwo Naukowe, 1989)

Smoleński, Józef, *2 Dywizja Strzelców Pieszych* (Warsaw: 1992)

Sokolnicki, Michał, *Dziennik Ankarski 1939–1943* (London: Gryf Publications Ltd, 1956)

Dziennik Ankarski 1943–1946 (London: Veritas, 1974)

Starzeński, Paweł, *Trzy Lata z Beckiem* (Warsaw: Instytut Wydawniczy Pax, 1991)

Strumph Wojtkiewicz, Stanisław, *Gwiazda Władysława Sikorskiego* (Warsaw: Czytelnik, 1946)

Sword, Keith (ed.), *Sikorski, Soldier and Statesman. A Collection of Essays* (London: Orbis Books Ltd, 1990)

Syzdyk, Eleonora, *Działalność Wandy Wasilewskiej w latach drugiej wojny światorej* (Warsaw: Wydawnictwo Ministerstwa Obrony Narodowej, 1981)

Szembek, Jan, *Diariusz, Wrzesień – Grudzień 1939* (Warsaw: Instytut Wydawniczy Pax, 1989)

Taylor, A. J. P., *Beaverbrook* (London: Hamish Hamilton, 1972)

Terlecki, Olgierd, *Generał Sikorski* (Cracow: Wydawnictwo Literackie, 1981)

Terry, Sarah Meiklejohn, *Poland's Place in Europe. General Sikorski and the Origin of the Oder–Neisse Line, 1939–1943* (Princeton: Princeton University Press, 1983)

Thomas, R. T., *Britain and Vichy. The Dilemma of Anglo-French Relations 1940–1942* (New York: St Martin's Press, 1979)

Torańska, Teresa, *Oni, Stalin's Polish Puppets* (London: Collins, 1987)

Turlej, Stefan, *Koncepcje ustrojowe obozu londyńskiego* (Warsaw: Książka i Wiedza, 1978)

Volkogonov, Dmitri, *Stalin. Triumph and Tragedy* (London: Weidenfeld & Nicolson, 1991)

Wandycz, Piotr S., *Czechoslovak–Polish Confederation and the Great Powers 1940–1943* (Westport, Connecticut: Greenwood Press Publishers, 1979)

Woodward, Sir Llewellyn, *History of the Second World War. British Foreign Policy in the Second World War*, Vol. II (London: Her Majesty's Stationery Office, 1971)

'Wspomnienia Wandy Wasilewskiej', in Feliks Tych (ed.), *Archiwum Ruchu Robotniczego*, Vol. VII (Warsaw: Książka i Wiedza for Centralne Archiwum KC PZPR, 1982)

Zabiełło, Stanisław, *Na posterunku we Francji* (Warsaw: Instytut Wydawniczy Pax, 1967)

Żaroń, Piotr, *Kierunek wschodni w strategii wojskowo-politycznej gen. Władysława Sikorskiego 1940–1943* (Warsaw: Państwowe Wydawnictwo Naukowe, 1988)

Index

Series list (continued)

Printed in the United States
22690LVS00005B/23

9 780521 483858